Library of
Davidson College

Collaborative Research and Social Change

Applied Anthropology
in Action

About the Book and Editors

Community case studies are basic to anthropology, yet there are relatively few examples in which the promotion of social change has been the explicit goal of the research. The case studies included here are all "natural experiments" that involve long-term community-based research, close collaboration between researchers and representatives of the host community, and the application of research methods and findings to social-change goals within the community. The cases are also unusual because they report on long-term projects that span several years—in some cases, decades.

Donald D. Stull is associate professor of anthropology and research associate in the Institute for Public Policy and Business Research at the University of Kansas. **Jean J. Schensul** is executive director of the Community Council of the Capitol Region, Hartford, Connecticut, and associate professor of anthropology at the University of Connecticut.

Collaborative Research and Social Change

Applied Anthropology in Action

edited by
Donald D. Stull
and Jean J. Schensul

Westview Press / Boulder and London

Westview Special Studies in Applied Anthropology

This Westview softcover edition is printed on acid-free paper and bound in softcovers that carry the highest rating of the National Association of State Textbook Administrators, in consultation with the Association of American Publishers and the Book Manufacturers' Institute.

All rights reserved. No part of this publication may be reproduced or transmitted in any form or by any means, electronic or mechanical, including photocopy, recording, or any information storage and retrieval system, without permission in writing from the publisher.

Copyright © 1987 by Westview Press, Inc.

Published in 1987 in the United States of America by Westview Press, Inc.; Frederick A. Praeger, Publisher; 5500 Central Avenue, Boulder, Colorado 80301

Library of Congress Cataloging-in-Publication Data
Collaborative research and social change.
  (Westview special studies in applied anthropology)
  Includes index.
  1. Applied anthropology. 2. Social change. I. Stull, Donald D. II. Schensul, Jean J. III. Series.
GN27.C646 1987   303.4   86-10973
ISBN 0-8133-7221-6

Composition for this book was provided by the editors.
This book was produced without formal editing by the publisher.

Printed and bound in the United States of America

∞ The paper used in this publication meets the requirements of the American National Standard for Permanence of Paper for Printed Library Materials Z39.48-1984.

6 5 4 3 2 1

The normal role of human beings in and with the world is not a passive one. Because they are not limited to the natural (biological) sphere but participate in the creative dimension as well, men can intervene in reality in order to change it. Inheriting acquired experience, creating and re-creating, integrating themselves into their context, responding to its challenges, objectifying themselves, discerning, transcending, men enter into the domain which is theirs exclusively--that of History and of Culture.

Paulo Freire
Education for Critical Consciousness, 1973

If we have the knowledge and the skill which makes us capable of applying anthropology, then we cannot divest ourselves of the responsibility that goes with that knowledge.

Margaret Mead
"The Evolving Ethics of Applied Anthropology," 1978

They have, in fact, joined themselves with native or exotic peoples on an assumed common basis of involvement in this troubled world of bright and terrible progress. They have acted, to do what they thought was right, although they know, beyond their declaration of supreme values, that they have helped to bring about or to affect a course of change the end of which they cannot see.

Robert Redfield
"Values in Action: A Comment," 1958

Contents

LIST OF FIGURES AND TABLES xi
ACKNOWLEDGMENTS. xiii

INTRODUCTION
    Jean J. Schensul and Donald D. Stull.   1

PART 1
COLLABORATIVE RESEARCH IN THE UNITED STATES

1   URBAN COMADRONAS: Maternal and Child
    Health Research and Policy Formulation
    in a Puerto Rican Community
    Jean J. Schensul, Donna Denelli-Hess,
    Maria G. Borrero, and Ma Prem Bhavati   9

2   IN THE PEOPLE'S SERVICE: The Kansas Kickapoo
    Technical Assistance Project
    Donald D. Stull, Jerry A. Schultz,
    and Ken Cadue, Sr.. 33

3   COMMUNITY ACTION AND SOCIAL ADAPTATION:
    The Farmworker Movement in the Midwest
    W. K. Barger and Ernesto Reza 55

4   LINGUISTICS IN ACTION: The Hualapai
    Bilingual/Bicultural Education Program
    Lucille J. Watahomigie and Akira Y.
    Yamamoto. 77

5   COLLABORATIVE EDUCATIONAL ETHNOGRAPHY:
    Problems and Profits
    Margaret A. Gibson. 99

PART 2
COLLABORATIVE RESEARCH IN THE THIRD WORLD

6   AGAINST THE ODDS: Collaboration and Development at Vicos
Paul L. Doughty 129

7   THE MEXICAN URBAN HOUSING PROJECT: A Collaboration Between *la Área Técnica y la Área Social*
Arthur D. Murphy, Ignacio Cabrera Fernández, Henry A. Selby, and Ignacio Ruiz Love 159

8   SAVING THE CITY: University Research, Political Action, and the Squatter Problem in Davao City, Philippines
Robert A. Hackenberg and Beverly H. Hackenberg. 179

PART 3
CONCLUDING COMMENTS

9   PERSPECTIVES ON COLLABORATIVE RESEARCH
Stephen L. Schensul 211

BIBLIOGRAPHY 221

CONTRIBUTORS 245

INDEX. 251

Figures and Tables

FIGURES

1.1 Alternative models for research and intervention to improve maternal and child health. 14

6.1 The Callejón de Huaylas (map) 136

TABLES

4.1 Comprehensive Test of Basic Skills scores of students at the Peach Springs School compared with the national average, 1975-1978 92

4.2 California Achievement Test scores for Peach Springs School, grades 2-8, 1982-1984. 93

5.1 Competency test results: students whose first scores were above passing, by ethnic group, with national comparison 101

Acknowledgments

As in any long-term collaboration, this book could not have been completed without the efforts of many people. The editors wish to thank the contributors for their insightful discussions of collaborative research and for their patience and encouragement over "the long haul." We also wish to thank the American Anthropological Association for permission to publish Margaret Gibson's chapter.

Gwen Stern was instrumental in the inception of this volume and provided valuable critiques on early drafts of many of the chapters. Bernard A. Hirsch provided much needed editorial advice. We also appreciate the initial enthusiasm and continued patience of Barbara Ellington and Bruce Kellison of Westview Press.

We are especially grateful to the Institute for Public Policy and Business Research of the University of Kansas for providing Don Stull with the time to carry out his editorial responsibilities and the support services necessary to produce the volume. Special recognition is due Jan Beecham for her tireless typing and retyping of the manuscripts and final copy, Judy Schrick for patient coordination of staff efforts on our behalf, and Laura Kriegstrom Poracsky for production of the map and figure.

Donald D. Stull
Jean J. Schensul

Introduction

Jean J. Schensul and Donald D. Stull

Anthropology began with a commitment to utilize research in the solution of human problems. The work of the Aboriginal Protection Society in London (see Schensul and Schensul 1976) and the Women's Anthropological Society of Washington (Helm 1966) in the 19th century initiated a series of dialogues on the proper role of the social sciences in problem solving and social change. The dialogue still continues as anthropologists work with colleagues in other fields on problems of health, education, development, self-determination, global peace, in fact, all aspects of the human condition.

In our search for solutions to human problems, we have found that definitions of these problems, identification of their causes, and their potential solutions are *complex*. Indeed, if there is a core element that distinguishes applied social researchers from policy makers and politicians, it is our continual cry for recognition of the complexity of social phenomena. Early on, we concluded that no individual, no single theoretical framework, no single disciplinary or sectoral approach is able to address effectively the serious issues of survival and well-being facing our world.

For this reason, much contemporary social science is carried out collaboratively, that is, investigators act in an *interdisciplinary partnership* to address common conceptual problems. Sometimes this interdisciplinary partnership is further enhanced by the inclusion of multiple "sectors." For example, nutritional research may include representatives from agriculture, housing, or employment sectors whose perspectives are useful in defining complex research models and providing contexts for the use of the information. Intersectoral research of this type is generally *applied research*, since the term "sector" usually refers to an institution or network of institutions with the ability to make and carry out policy decisions.

"Sector" may also refer to populations that are the target of research. We may speak about the rural agricultural sector, the female sector, or the student sector. Not infrequently, research may encompass two or more population sectors that may not have worked together or may have contradictory perspectives on a problem.

Notable in the work of anthropologists is concern with those sectors that have pressing needs and receive the least attention in national systems. This focus is apparent in the papers included in this volume. We believe that social and cultural factors have a significant influence on "dependent variables"--the arenas we wish to influence--but we generally have less understanding of these arenas than do the major actors in them (e.g., community activists, physicians, teachers, politicians, etc.). For this reason we seek expertise in these areas from our intersectoral collaborators and depend on them to take an active stance in the quest for equity.

The case materials in this volume clearly show that social problems cannot be effectively addressed without political intervention. Such intervention may be sought through various means, including policy changes, redistribution of economic or other scarce resources, and new legislation. Solutions to social problems involve factors beyond the scope of research and thus call for intersectoral and nonresearch collaboration. Anthropologists and other social researchers are not usually primary actors in these situations and need to work with people who are. Indeed, any anthropologist seriously interested in influencing social change *must* work with nonresearch collaborators.

But why should these collaborators want to work with applied social scientists? The answer is to be found in the utility of the tools of social science research: the degree to which social science can help outline theoretical frameworks or approaches to a problem that might otherwise go unnoticed, or whether it can point to contradictions in an argument or rationale for intervention or policy change. Data, if collected and presented properly, can tell collaborators much about their constituencies. The process of formulating a research design and gathering information provides tools that can be adapted for use in future work. We must not forget that information is power. Controversial though it may be at times, data can provide an important argument for supporting a particular policy, development, or mobilization strategy.

But can social science research fulfill expectations? Our research may not be readily usable for social change purposes, hidden as it is in reports and couched in too many words. More often than not, the data may not tell a clear story or the results may be contradictory. Data may be old, untimely, or too complicated. Generally, data tell a complex, multifaceted story. And social scientists may not be able or may not want to do what is necessary to make research useful. The papers in this volume describe field research projects that have found ways around many of these problems to generate research and relationships useful in promoting change.

Some argue that there are fundamental differences in the theories and methods of "applied" and "abstract" anthropology. Our view is that all anthropologists utilize the same array of theoretical frameworks and research methods. If the methodology is carefully articulated, there can be no question about the soundness of anthropological research in an applied setting. The differences between applied and abstract anthropology lie in the *processes* of selecting the problem, deciding on appropriate methodology, analyzing the results, and utilizing the information.

What are these processes? First is the selection of collaborators. The identification and selection of collaborators stem from the personal interests, values, and commitments of the researcher vis-a-vis social change and social problems.

Equally important is the selection of topic, which arises from a social problem central to the interests of the collaborators. The problem may or may not fit within a *current* theoretical or methodological issue of anthropology.

Third is the involvement of a variety of people in designing the research strategy within the limitations of the field setting. This often requires considerable flexibility and innovation in research design, particularly if funders are rigid in their demands for "traditional" research design.

All field research projects are subject to constraints that may necessitate change in research design, modification of the sample, and so forth. These constraints can be overcome more easily in a collaborative setting, however, because actors in that setting have a vested interest in the best possible results. Thus, they may go to considerable lengths to ensure the maintenance of rigorous research methodology under difficult field situations.

Fourth, transformation of the research into usable materials for policy and practical purposes may mean limitations on time available for publication in professional journals, which in turn limits access of the scientific community to research results.

In sum, collaborative research represents a dialogue between university-trained researchers and policy makers at the community, regional, national, and international levels. From this dialogue arises a more profound understanding of pressing social problems as well as greater insight into the ways these problems may be addressed. Testing such insights contributes to social welfare on the one hand and theory building on the other. At its best, this process results in the ongoing sharing of appropriate scientific information and technology in the quest for social and political equity.

The present volume emerged from a session on "Collaborative Research and Scientific Method" at the annual meeting of the American Anthropological Association in Los Angeles in 1981. This session, chaired by Jean Schensul, brought together a panel of applied anthropologists to discuss problem definition, research design, and difficulties in collaborative field research. The following spring Donald Stull chaired a session on "Universities, Professionals, and Communities: Developing Linkages for Effective Social Action" at the annual meeting of the Society for Applied Anthropology in Lexington, Kentucky. Subsequently, Jean Schensul, Gwen Stern, and Donald Stull decided to bring the issues raised in these two symposia to wider attention. A conference at the 1982 meeting of the American Anthropological Association on "Anthropological Theory and Collaborative Research" brought together the first draft of a book combining theoretical papers and case studies on collaborative research. Given the length and quality of the papers, the editors decided to publish two sets of materials. The theoretical papers were published in 1985 in the *American Behavioral Scientist* (Schensul and Stern). This collection of case materials gives closure to our effort to bring thoughtful, self-critical analyses of collaborative research projects to the field.

The anthropological literature is replete with success stories. A major contribution of this volume, however, is the willingness of the authors to discuss openly the shortcomings as well as the successes of their work. We feel strongly about this since most of these case materials involve long-term field commitments. For this reason, they offer the opportunity for historical review of the progression of projects in their wider social, economic, and political contexts. We have tried to promote, both in our discussions and in the writing of these case materials, an analysis of the difficulties involved in establishing a collaborative field setting, funding research activities, and finding effective ways of utilizing research results.

The case studies are presented in two parts. The first contains projects in which American anthropologists work with communities "at home." These papers are organized geographically, moving from the Northeast through the Midwest to California. In each instance, the anthropologists and their collaborators concentrate first on building a strong base, then on advocating with wider social institutions. The second section takes us into the arena of collaboration with international colleagues. In these settings, the work of American anthropologists and their colleagues ranges from strengthening community bases (as in the case of Vicos) to advocating for the housing and developmental needs of the urban poor. The volume concludes with comments on the politics and process of collaborative research.

PART ONE

Collaborative Research in the United States

In the United States, collaborative research can be traced to the work of Sol Tax and his students with the Fox Project in the 1940s and 1950s. While the visible accomplishments of this project were limited, it nevertheless established many of the principles of collaborative research. These principles include:

1. *Developing and testing theory on an ongoing basis in interaction with interventions or action (what Tax called "learning and helping").*
2. *Ensuring consistency between project means and desired ends.*
3. *Basing ends and means on guidelines established by the host community.*

These principles were utilized throughout the 1960s and 1970s by "action" or "advocacy" anthropologists as they applied research to community development in ethnic minority communities in the United States. Such anthropologists were successful in making research useful, but were less successful in involving community actors directly in research activities as a tool for change. By the mid-1970s this had changed somewhat as ethnic minority communities began to see the need for information in the advocacy process. This perception permitted the development of a new configuration in the integration of research and action in which anthropologists became collaborators with community activists in research directed toward social change.

The projects discussed in the following chapters all reflect this basic philosophy (for example, all but one of the accounts are coauthored by anthropologists and their collaborators). In each case, the anthropologists approached a local community with an interest in collaborating in the use of research for change purposes. Although these communitites--reservation Indians, urban Puerto Ricans, Punjabi immigrants--are diverse, they are representative of populations that have been the focus of traditional anthropological concern. In this regard, Barger and Reza's approach is noteworthy by introducing action research in a majority community to improve working conditions for a minority group.

Each case differs in the degree to which research was successfully introduced, carried out, and utilized in a collaborative manner. The work of Schensul and her associates in the Hispanic Health Council and the bilingual/bicultural education program undertaken among the Hualapai by Watahomigie and Yamamoto both reflect close cooperation between outside professionals and community representatives, resulting in highly successful outcomes. But in spite of sincere efforts on the part of both anthropologists and their community collaborators, project results may be mixed. The projects carried out by Stull, Schultz, and Cadue among the Kansas Kickapoo and Gibson among the Punjabis in "Valleyside," California suggest that "successful" projects are, as often as not, ones that only satisfy some of the people, to some extent, some of the time.

While these efforts vary in scope and duration, the anthropologists share a common bond in their lengthy associations with the communities or populations in which they work. Their experiences point to the great importance of long-term commitment by both anthropologists and community collaborators. It is this commitment, the authors suggest, that ultimately results in funding, quality research, and productive use of results for community institution building and positive social change.

1

Urban Comadronas: Maternal and Child Health Research and Policy Formulation in a Puerto Rican Community

*Jean J. Schensul, Donna Denelli-Hess,
Maria G. Borrero, and Ma Prem Bhavati*

"Collaborative research" refers to a process in which university-trained researchers bring their skills and interests to bear on a community or institutional problem. The initial problem is often, though not always, identified by members of the institution or community. Once identified, it is negotiated and translated into researchable terms. Community or institutional participants then work with researchers through operationalization of concepts, research design, collection and analysis of data. Utilization of the information is planned and carried out jointly, often leading to "next steps" in the action research process (Schensul and Stern 1985).

This process is relatively clear-cut and described in the action research literature, when the emphasis is on research and action as separate though related phases of the same effort. In such projects, collaboration refers to the relationship between researchers and actors in the setting. Problems revolve around the methodology for empowering nonresearchers to engage in all aspects of the research process in the belief that full participation will lead to active and informed participation in its use (Borrero, Schensul, and Garcia 1982). Using research results is nowadays referred to in anthropology as "knowledge utilization."

The process is somewhat less clear-cut, however, when the interest of the researcher is to integrate research into intervention or ongoing social change programs and to encourage participants in an already existing social change network to see and utilize the value of research in interdisciplinary program design, implementation, and evaluation.

This paper will explore the latter situation. In so doing, it will refer to case examples from the Puerto Rican community of Hartford, Connecticut. The specific purposes of the paper are:

1. To explore the notion of collaboration in applied research.
2. To discuss a complex research and intervention program as an example of this approach.
3. To extract principles of collaborative research applicable to other efforts in which applied social scientists are involved with community and institutional representatives to bring about social change.

ANTHROPOLOGY AND APPLIED RESEARCH

Since anthropology is fundamentally a research-based discipline, applied anthropology must be understood as the application of anthropological research in the solution of human problems (cf. Kimball 1978). Over the past 50 years, the discipline has developed a number of terms to describe this process. For example, "applied anthropology" is associated with George Foster's (1969) original text and those times when anthropologists have been called upon to work either with national governments or international change agents in the implementation of change programs. Anthropologists have utilized research to reconcile local community needs, beliefs, and behaviors with these programs and to assess and explain program efficiency.

"Action or advocacy anthropology," on the other hand, stems from the work of Sol Tax and his students (cf. Gearing 1960; Peattie 1968) and later on Peterson (1974), Schensul and Schensul (1978), and others. It refers to the association of anthropologists with ethnic minority community activists in the United States and the use of research to facilitate the empowerment of local communities.

In most cases, however, regardless of their base, anthropologists interested in using anthropological knowledge for social change generally find themselves brokering between local communities and larger sociopolitical entities (Stull and Moos 1981). In so doing, they attempt to ensure that policies and programs are created or changed to suit the needs of local communities and are effectively implemented (Chambers 1985; Heighton and Heighton 1978; Hicks and Handler 1978). This process of negotiated change takes place in an environment--whether in the United States or elsewhere--in which the populations of concern have limited power, influence, and resources (cf. Bee 1982).

In this competitive environment, an effective strategy available to anthropologists is participation in the formation of community institutions that strengthen the involvement of Third World communities in national and international dialogue (J. Schensul 1985a). There currently is a sizeable body of literature that demonstrates how research can be an effective tool for initiating this process by: (1) enhancing a group's knowledge base; (2) integrating university and community resources around a common problem; and (3) training knowledgeable community research staff to take on leadership roles in further research and development (see Schensul and Borrero 1982; Stern 1985).

The 1960s and 1970s saw a flourishing of such community institutions, each advocating its own view of community needs. More recently, local community groups have found it less effective to advocate independently and have sought to form coalitions around social issues. Some have termed these coalitions "policy clusters" (Pelto and Schensul 1986; J. Schensul 1985b). Policy clusters cut across sectors to bring networks of people with different resources together to try to solve common problems on a broader basis.

The policy cluster is essentially an urban phenomenon. It is usually found in primary and secondary urban environments where multiple sectors vie for limited local and national resources. When policy clusters cut across class lines, they generally are responding to needs of the urban poor, assisted by "sympathetic sectors" among the local and national middle and upper classes.

When these coalitions systematically utilize research, they may be termed "policy research clusters." These policy research clusters include: (1) different disciplines; (2) different sectors; (3) different assumptions about research methods and what constitutes legitimate "data"; (4) different opinions as to the relative weight of research versus intervention; and (5) different opinions as to "theories of intervention."

Policy research clusters provide a context for collaborative research. Those interested in the collaborative research process must either form such coalitions or participate directly in their formation. Otherwise it is unlikely that social science research will be seen as central in the process of policy formulation.

Theories guide the policy cluster. These theories may be termed "theories of action" in that they are meant not only to direct research but to suggest directions for social change. It is quite common to find policy clusters in which several theories of action or intervention are active simultaneously. Confusion in discussion, planning, and policy generation most often arises when theories of action are unclear and conflicting. A commitment to research requires a theoretical framework. Thus, research can "force the issue" in the clarification of theoretical diversity in the policy cluster. It can do this in several ways, each appropriate for a particular problem and setting. For example, when information is required to arrive at decisions concerning program or legislative direction, one or a combination of theoretical frameworks guide research. Or a program may be established to test a theoretical proposition, and an evaluation research design is generated to determine its effectiveness (Cook and Campbell 1979). The evaluation design then becomes an important part of the program's logic.

In the following section, we will discuss the applicability of the concepts "policy cluster," "collaborative research," "knowledge utilization," and "theory of action" in the context of a maternal and child health program in the Puerto Rican community of Hartford, Connecticut. This program began with a policy cluster consisting of local and state representatives working together to plan a local program. Throughout the life of the program its reference shifted back and forth from local to state and national levels. At various points in the program's history, different members of the original policy cluster came together to influence opinion about the program, to shape the direction of the program and of information collection, and eventually, in some instances, to oppose it. This paper will describe the program, the history of shifts in the program, policy clusters, and research strategies. It will conclude with implications for collaborative research in intervention programs.

HISTORY OF THE COMADRONA PROGRAM:
CONCEPTUAL FRAMEWORK AND PROGRAM STRUCTURE

In August 1982, representatives of the Maternal and Child Health Section of the Connecticut State Health Department, the Hartford City Health Department, and the Hispanic Health Council met to define maternal and child health problems in the Puerto Rican/Hispanic community of Hartford and to respond to a request for proposals for a Title V national demonstration grant in the area of maternal and child health (MCH). Included in this meeting were a number of physicians, a Puerto Rican community activist, and a medical anthropologist. The city health department offered statistics on Hispanic maternal and child health; the Hispanic Health Council provided data on the importance of social supports in access to and compliance with prenatal care (Schensul and Schensul 1982); and the state health department offered technical assistance with grant writing.

Two sets of assumptions were combined into a program model. The first was medical in origin and argued that early and continuous prenatal care was central in influencing positive birth outcomes for pregnant high-risk, low-income Hispanic women. The second, sociological in origin, argued that social supports were central in influencing prenatal health behavior, including access, compliance, and health maintenance. They were combined in the concept of the traditional birth attendant in Puerto Rico, the *comadrona*, a powerful cultural symbol combining good prenatal care with strong social and community supports.

The two assumptions were to some extent, however, contradictory (see Figure 1.1). The sociological perspective led to a model for intervention and evaluation in which the primary emphasis lay with the relationship between the independent and intervening variables. The intervention, as carried out by the *comadrona*, involved the development of community and family supports during the prenatal and postnatal periods. Measurement of success in this model did not require a large sample; instead, it required careful documentation of the building of support systems and the relationship between social support development and access to care.

The medical framework, on the other hand, emphasized the relationship between the intervening variables and the dependent variables. The role of the *comadrona* was defined as improving access to and continuity of care. The test of success was the degree to which improved service access would influence stated outcomes; measurement of success in this model--in conformity with standard epidemiological research and health services practices--was seen as requiring a large sample size.

The crucial distinction between these two models was unclear in the design phase. While the program staff came to advocate the first model, in reality the second model, with its associated large sample size, was selected by the policy cluster as the basis for the program. In addition, the second model was attractive because of the policy cluster's interest in collecting data on pregnant Hispanic women. The larger sample size was seen as providing more data.

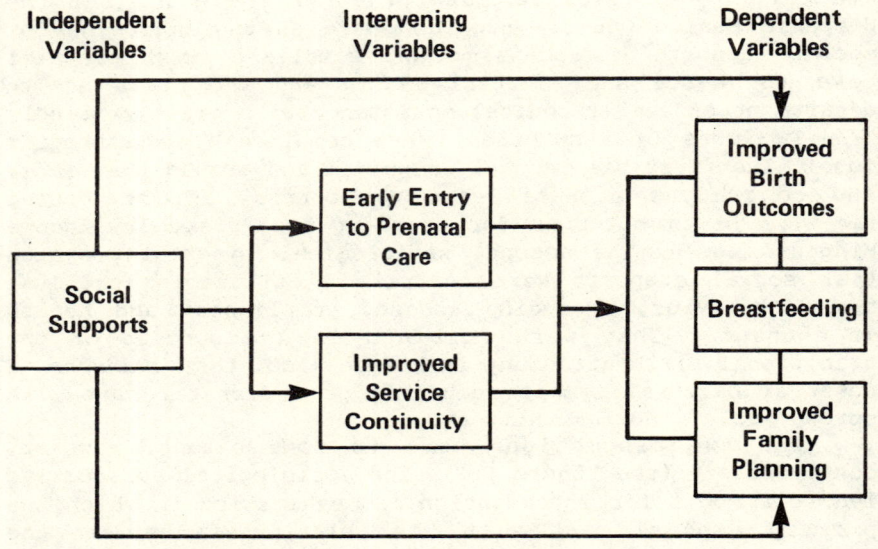

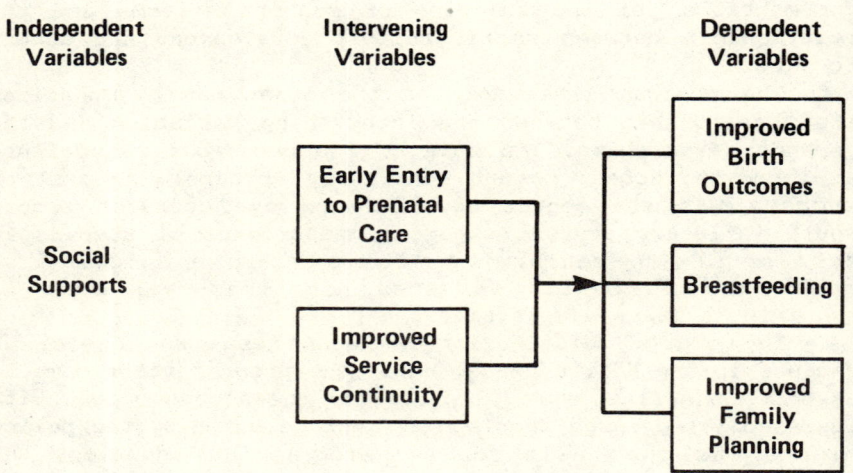

Figure 1.1 Alternative Models for Research and Intervention to Improve Maternal and Child Health

The policy cluster submitted a grant application based on the still unclear combination of first and second models, and in September 1982 the Connecticut Department of Health Services (DHS) received a three-year grant for the Hispanic Maternal and Child Preventive Health Network, the Comadrona Program. The Community Health Division (CHD) and the Maternal and Child Health Section of the state health department contracted the funds to the Hispanic Health Council (HHC) of Hartford, Connecticut. The policy cluster was differentiated into two bodies--the administrative team, consisting of members of the state Maternal and Child Health Section and the HHC, and the technical advisory team, consisting of members of the city health department and other MCH programs in the city.

PROGRAM THEORY: THE COMADRONA REINSTATED

The stated overall purpose of the Comadrona Program was to prevent perinatal and child health problems in low-income Puerto Rican families and to enhance pregnancy outcomes for mother, child, and family by developing and strengthening support networks in the community. The model was derived from an understanding of: (1) the importance of social supports in affecting perinatal behaviors and health outcomes for mother and child (Gottlieb 1981; Schensul and Schensul 1982); and (2) the traditional role of the birth attendant in Puerto Rico, which combined biomedical, social, and psychological services to women, their families, and the new baby.

The *comadrona* was the traditional midwife/birth attendant in Puerto Rico prior to the introduction of U.S. health care delivery systems. The *comadrona* was available for consultation during pregnancy, for delivery of the child, and for provision of postpartum support for the family, particularly during the 40-day period after birth referred to as the *cuarentena*.

With the introduction of hospital-based health care, the role of the *comadrona* shifted from providing direct care to providing linkages to the health care system for pregnant women. The primary responsibilities of the *comadrona* over time have been to provide women and their families some aspects of perinatal health care in both rural and urban areas, links to other forms of health care (indigenous and contemporary), health education, and to facilitate the mobilization of family supports around the care of the mother and child during the birth and postnatal periods.

The work of the *comadrona* in local communities, particularly in small towns and rural areas, was complemented by family, friends, and community-wide supports. This supportive network offered information, help with children, and other material and social resources to pregnant women and their families. In addition, the *cuarentena* offered an organizing framework for family members as well as friends during the crucial transition period after the birth of the child (cf. Stern 1985).

The combination of *comadrona*, community social networks, and the *cuarentena* came into active coordination especially during periods of crisis, such as the death of the mother or the child, abnormal birth, or severe illness. These cultural supports also provided an opportunity to accumulate informally information concerning the care of pregnant women, preparation for birth, the care of infants, and methods of family planning. Finally, local community settings offered numerous indigenous health care resources and, later, the addition of those introduced through Western medical influences. Access to both domains of care was also facilitated through this combination of cultural supports.

The contemporary urban setting in the United States offers a very different set or resources and dynamics in which to integrate a redefined role for the *comadrona*, or traditional birth attendant. These include the following characteristics:

1. Disruption of traditional support networks, including the family, long-term friendship networks, and the *compadrazco*, or godparent relations.

2. Diffusion, disruption, or discontinuity in traditional cultural supports providing guidance, protection, and support for new mothers and their infants. Such supports would include the *cuarentena*, a 40-day period after birth in which the mother must follow rules that maintain bonding and in which members of the family rally to support the household while the mother concentrates on the infant.

3. A shift from birth at home to birth in the hospital. The consequence is that the birthing process is separated from family life and, depending on the hospital, the mother may be separated from the new infant. This is more likely to occur with low-income, recently arrived, and non-English-speaking mothers who do not have access to, or information about, "rooming-in" arrangements and are discouraged from breastfeeding.

4. The absence of indigenous health providers, such as the *comadrona*, who are well known and trusted in the community and who can act as reliable and respected sources

of maternal and child health information. Outreach workers do not perform this role since they usually extend the individualized care of the clinic or hospital to the patient, but do not become involved in the day-to-day life of the community.

5. Lack of easily accessible information and support in the area of family planning. Most health care facilities do not offer the time or the linguistic and cultural capabilities necessary to fully inform Puerto Rican women and their spouses about family planning alternatives that meet their specific needs.

6. The existence of a variety of factors impeding regular use of prenatal health care. These include distrust of hospital and clinic settings and personnel, conception of pregnancy as a status to be managed by the woman and not by the health care system, and the custom of using the hospital for birth rather than for prenatal health care (in some cases).

7. Changing and unclear cultural rules about pregnancy, sexual activity, and male-female relations. Clear rules no longer exist, since they rested on close family ties and frequent family gatherings, chaperoning, clear role distinctions between men and women, and other aspects of community social life that have been disrupted with the transition to urban and U.S.-based life styles.

Reintegrating the role of the *comadrona* in the urban environment of Hartford involved the following steps:

1. Learning about the reproductive health care needs of Puerto Rican women.
2. Facilitating community-based support networks which included groups of neighborhood residents, friends, family networks, and self-help groups.
3. Reinstating key aspects of the *cuarentena*; for example, beliefs about the importance of bonding to foster the family unit after the birth and the general health and mental health of the mother.
4. Becoming involved with health care services to understand how to function effectively as broker and advocate.
5. Using the above to facilitate early, positive, and continuous involvement of pregnant Puerto Rican women in prenatal care and positive health management.
6. Developing alternative community-based social-support or self-help groups (such as Lamaze training, breastfeeding support groups, and labor room accompaniment) for Puerto Rican women.

The predicted results of the process were early entry and consistent use of prenatal care. Those behaviors usually associated with good prenatal care, including better birth outcomes, breastfeeding, and fertility control, would follow as expected.

THE PROGRAM PHASE

Development of the program required operationalizing the concept of the urban *comadrona*, training core staff, identifying and training a number of volunteer *comadronas* who constituted community support staff, establishing links with health care facilities and community resources, developing a case intervention strategy, creating appropriate bilingual/bicultural resource materials, and developing a documentation system. The state MCH policy oversight committee and the program's advisory committee assisted in these activities. These committees also helped promote the image of the program in the city and the state.

The program was viewed as interesting but controversial in the local and state MCH network. As a health program, its base was in the community rather than in a hospital or clinic. This was viewed as a threat by some, as confusing by others. The local nurse midwives saw the introduction of *comadronas* as threatening because their own status in the community was under question. They felt that a new and different role would only confuse community residents and interfere with their attempts to authenticate the licensed midwife role at the state level. The established health educators questioned the ability of a community agency to provide accurate health education to community residents. The specific ethnic focus of the program concerned public health personnel who felt the program "did not serve everyone."

The program began with ethnographic interviewing to obtain women's perspectives on pregnancy, prenatal care, the *cuarentena*, pregnancy management, and the role of the *comadrona*. Former *comadronas* living in the Hartford area were interviewed about their activities in Puerto Rico and changes in their role both in Puerto Rico and in the U.S. While program developers believed that interviewing was crucial in establishing a well-rounded conceptual framework, there was division of opinion among staff as to whether the "priority" of the program should be research, service, or community organizing around MCH. The staff included one trained health educator/community researcher, one case-oriented social worker, and one social work community organizer, each with her own perspective. This dialogue was made more difficult by increasing pressure from the state to fulfill the obligations of the second conceptual model by expanding the program's case load more rapidly. These debates went on at the level of the advisory and oversight committees as well; while in the larger city, the program held the spotlight in the arena of MCH services.

Program administration finally summarized the situation by asserting the sociological model over the medical/ epidemiological model. This was done with the recognition that state and city committees supported the second model and that problems with expected outcomes were sure to occur. The program made a clear commitment to the extensive development of community and volunteer support networks and a concomitant reduction in case load. During the second and third years, far greater amounts of time were spent in network building in the community and in the training of volunteers than in case finding. By the beginning of the third year, this network was working effectively to refer and provide continuing support to Puerto Rican women in crisis during pregnancy, and the case load was growing accordingly. Nevertheless, the decision to build the network resulted in a 50 percent reduction in anticipated case load at the end of the second year. This was enough to bring about a loss of support for the program by the now two independent policy clusters associated with it.

A further debate within the program had to do with "how much" and "what kind" of information to collect on clients. In the program itself, administration viewed information collected on clients from the point of view of research on pregnancy in the Puerto Rican community. This meant preparation of a standardized, precoded instrument for use with all program participants and ethnographic evaluation of the program for preparing a training manual. Social work staff were at least indirectly opposed to the idea of collecting research--i.e., systematic--data on program participants and argued for service-oriented case files to meet their own needs. This position was supported by the program advisory committee, which consisted primarily of MCH service providers. The state committee viewed information collection as a program-monitoring function, was not concerned about "additional information" or client profiles, and had no understanding of the utility of qualitative documentation.

This set of confusions was resolved, finally, by the completion of a precoded instrument and administrative insistence on its systematic use. A medical anthropology student was hired to act as data manager. In addition, she teamed with a second medical anthropology student to use data from the project in the preparation of a series of "fact sheets" on the central problems of infant mortality, teenage pregnancy, breastfeeding, low birth weight, and high-risk pregnancies. They illustrated these problems in the Puerto Rican community and ways in which the Comadrona Program was organized to address them. They were used for training purposes and to advocate for the program in an increasingly competitive environment.

By the end of its second year, although sample size was small, the Comadrona Program could claim: (1) an increase in first trimester entry to health care; (2) improvements in continuity of care and compliance with medication; (3) decreases in numbers of low birth-weight babies; (4) increased rates of breastfeeding; and (5) improvements in familiarity with and use of family planning methods.

In addition, referral to the program shifted from agencies and clinics in the first year to Comadrona Program staff and volunteers in the second. Agencies and clinics referred "difficult" patients with whom their staffs could not cope; the shift in referrals in the second year suggested the effectiveness of the program's community support network in identifying those patients early, well before they encountered problems in the health care system.

THE EVALUATION PHASE

The "evaluation phase" of the program began in the third year with a site visit from the Boston Regional Office of the Bureau of Community Health Services. This visit was prompted by the office's interest in advocating for the program regionally as well as at the state level. The Boston office defined effective advocacy as involving "outcome evaluation," for which they wished to provide technical assistance. For the Boston team, positive outcomes revolved around the degree to which the program had built community support networks to improve service use. In demanding outcome data, the team shifted the model to be evaluated back from the medical model supported by the state to the sociological model supported by the program.

Program research was then defined as "outcome evaluation data," including documentation of the "program methodology" (i.e., the creation of community support networks). To further the shift from the medical to the sociological model, the Boston team requested that programmatic goals and objectives and the information collection procedures be rewritten to meet current case-load realities and the informational needs of the now new policy cluster--the regional team. This further frustrated the state team which, still operating within the framework of the medical model, took the position that the program had failed because it had not seen sufficient clients to demonstrate epidemiologically or medically acceptable outcomes.

In the final evaluation report, program staff stated the contradiction in the following manner:

> The principles to be evaluated in the program are:
> a) that it is possible to locate, strengthen and/or build community networks which will identify women at risk in a difficult-to-reach population.
> b) that a combination of culturally relevant and community-based social supports, and biomedical support for women at risk will improve pregnancy outcomes, service utilization and family planning.
>
> If the purpose of the program was seen as improving the pregnancy outcomes of a certain number of Hispanic women in a designated period of time, the program did not meet its quota of pregnant women. If the purpose of the program was to test a model for attracting high-risk women into prenatal care, providing a combination of social and biological supports to improve pregnancy outcomes, and sustaining this support system in the community, the program can be seen as successful insofar as it:
> - more than doubled first trimester entry and continuity in prenatal care
> - nearly doubled the rate of breast feeding
> - slightly reduced the low birth weight rate
> - reduced diagnosed prenatal anemia
> - introduced the first Lamaze classes in the region for Puerto Rican women
> - demonstrated the utility of volunteers and community support networks in assisting women into early and continuous prenatal care
> (Final Comadrona Report 1985).

In the meantime, while support was deteriorating in the original policy clusters, program staff were building an extensive citywide network of support through their participation in many health-related committees. These included a school health task force, an infant mortality/teen pregnancy committee, and a child advocacy committee. The program's methods and results were shared with these committees while heated discussions were going on in the city concerning infant mortality and teen pregnancy.

In 1981, the local health systems agency had produced a report demonstrating that Hartford had the fourth highest infant mortality rate among the nation's cities. The report indicated as well that Puerto Ricans showed a high incidence of low birth-weight babies and teenage pregnancies. These data attracted the attention of the citywide committees, many of which included members of the policy clusters originally associated with the Comadrona Program. Public health officials and medical personnel argued that infant mortality could be addressed best through improved prenatal care and general health education. The medically oriented direction of these committees was supported by the state's public health programs. Committee members representing community organizations did not have sufficient power to obtain funding for themselves. Nor did they have the philosophical or theoretical framework to promote alternative policies, centering on the expansion of social support networks and appeal to ethnic identity, as a means of enhancing utilization of health services.

Soon after, private donor organizations (corporate givers) indicated their interest in a clearly focused program. A citywide plan for maternal and infant health care was developed that called for public- and private-sector monies to be amalgamated in a service and outreach program for high-risk poor women. To appease those concerned with "community involvement" in maternal and child health care, the program was modeled after the Hispanic Health Council's maternal and child health program, insofar as it involved home visits and health education. It did not, however, include central aspects of the program, such as the creation of social support networks, volunteer groups of health promoters, and ethnically specific health education materials. Nor did it target services in the neighborhoods served by the Comadrona Program.

The above arrangement was opposed by the independent Black and Hispanic organizations that had been excluded from the decision-making process and from fund raising in the city. In addition, they were dissatisfied with the plan's apparent inability to acknowledge that cultural factors and social networks played a significant role in enhancing the management of pregnancy and postnatal care. These groups formed a new local policy cluster to address these problems.

Comadrona Program staff were able to play a central role in this debate by utilizing program data within the framework of the sociological model to demonstrate the ability of an ethnic organization to promote better health outcomes. The program evaluation materials used simple frequencies to show the development of social support networks for pregnant women. The availability of social supports was then associated with continuity of prenatal care and breastfeeding. Finally, it demonstrated that health outcomes for mothers and infants with the social and educational supports offered by the Comadrona Program were significantly better than outcomes citywide.

During the evaluation phase, then, new policy clusters formed around the program to provide support and exposure for the sociological, or social intervention, model. As the debate raged in the wider city, regional evaluators described their needs for data for advocacy purposes. This convinced program staff of the importance of systematic data collection, and they began to cooperate actively in its collection. Medical anthropology staff assisted in the organization and analysis of program data for advocacy purposes in this new setting. The outcome was a citywide, multiethnic emphasis on maternal and child health education and targeted funding for special-interest community-based programs.

The regional policy cluster's strategy for ensuring continuity of the program was to assist in convincing the state that within the framework of the sociological model, the program had been successful. The policy cluster did prevail upon the state to continue the program after federal support was over, to fund a training manual, and to provide money for a staff person to disseminate the program statewide. The state team, however, was never convinced that problems could be prevented during and after pregnancy through social supports. Thus, the community education, self-help, and volunteer components of the program were lost and, with them, the community base that made the program unique. These components have lately been funded by the private sector and are being rebuilt.

THE FORMATION OF NEW THEORY

The Comadrona Program was based on the initial proposition that social supports enhance the likelihood of early (first trimester) entry to prenatal care. This proposition has been generally acknowledged in the literature on prenatal service utilization since the early

1970s, although it has not been confirmed for Puerto Ricans. A second important proposition asserted that traditional cultural elements, redefined as appropriate for the same population in a new environment, could be an important vehicle for bringing about positive social change (J. Schensul 1985c; Stern 1985). In this case, the cultural element was the traditional birth attendant, or *comadrona*. The program began with the further assumption that all Puerto Rican women were at risk for inadequate social supports and prenatal care as well as problematic pregnancy outcomes. These concepts were refined and changed during the course of the program as data pointed in new directions.

The program utilized a standardized instrument to obtain data on 129 cases. Some important results are summarized below.

CLIENT PROFILE

The population served by the program was poor (57 percent were on government assistance); young (70 percent were in their teens or early 20s); either very recently arrived or long-time residents (47 percent were recent arrivals; 36 percent had lived more than 10 years in the city); urban in background (67 percent had been raised in an urban area); and, with the exception of recent arrivals, predominantly English-speaking. Recent arrivals and urban dwellers were highly overrepresented in this sample, compared to the results of previous random sample survey research in the same community.

Eighty-nine percent of the clients came from neighborhoods of private run-down inner-city housing in predominantly Puerto Rican areas; 78 percent of all clients came from the south end of the city, in the heart of the Puerto Rican community.

The client group was highly mobile during the previous five years—79 percent had moved twice or more during this time. Moving in the Puerto Rican community can be considered a general indicator of stress, since it disrupts the household, support networks, jobs, schooling, and resource acquisition, and is often associated with eviction, urban renewal, and loss of job. Clients reported that they moved to Hartford for family reasons, either to be with family, to help with a family problem, or to get away from a family problem. Eighty-eight percent of all reasons given for migration were related to family members.

Of those reporting on their education level, 69 percent had not completed high school. Eighty-nine percent of the clients were not working at the time of entry into the program. Well over half had male partners. An unexpectedly high percentage lived in dual rather than single-parent households (61.2 percent compared to 45-48 percent in other samples). Nuclear households, either dual- or single-parent, far outnumbered other types. Extended family households generally included either siblings, parents, or friends. This can be attributed to difficulties in locating adequate private housing and the regulations governing family size in public housing units.

Crowding is a problem in Hartford, since gentrification has eliminated the majority of low-cost private rental housing, and little new housing is being constructed for lower-income residents. Using the definition of crowding as two persons per bedroom, 63 percent of households were crowded.

Crowding brings a variety of social, emotional, and health problems. It is further exacerbated by the presence of small children. The number of children under five in a household is associated in the target community with higher rates of economic, health, and mental health problems (see Schensul, Nieves, and Martinez 1982). Half of all households included one or more children under five, excluding the new baby. Many mothers were very young when they first became pregnant. Fifty-seven percent of the clients in the Comadrona Program had their first child as a teenager, and 35 percent had, or were having, their first child between the ages of 12 and 17.

Pregnant women in the sample cited having one or more close relatives in Hartford and seeing them regularly: 72 percent report seeing their mother daily or weekly; 71 percent report seeing sisters daily or weekly; 35 percent report seeing brothers daily or weekly; and 27 percent report seeing female relatives daily or weekly.

Although clients reported the presence and availability of these relatives, they did not report seeking them out for specific assistance, such as sympathy, money, transportation, babysitting, information, advice, or translation. For these purposes, they seek out spouses/partners or friends and neighbors.

In this regard, it is important to note that clients described a series of nonmedical problems during pregnancy. The most important of these in order of salience are: (1) depression—63 percent; (2) conflict with spouses or partners—44 percent; (3) conflict with children—30 percent; (4) conflict with other family members—12 percent; and (5) situational problems (economic, housing, etc.)—10 percent. These findings suggest that although clients have family members to turn to, the relationships are fraught with difficulties, and they may feel quite alone during their pregnancy, particularly if they are in conflict with spouses.

These sociodemographic characteristics confirmed a client population at risk for poor service utilization and health outcomes. Findings also correspond to earlier research suggesting several household types at increased risk: monolingual, recently arrived, young, single-parent female-headed households with two or more young children and limited supports; long-term residents with older children, a history of difficulties in the urban environment, and limited supports; and dual-parent, unemployed households. (Schensul, Nieves, and Martinez 1982; Pelto, Roman, and Liriano 1982).

Pursuing the matter of "high risk" further, "risk" was conceptualized as two separate variable domains: social risk and medical risk. A third variable domain, pregnancy outcome, was defined as term, weight at birth, and quality of delivery (normal versus abnormal). Pregnancy outcome was defined as successful if birth weight was 5 pounds 5 ounces or more, the birth process was rated normal, and the pregnancy was defined as full term. Of the large number of variables in the "social risk" domain, only income level, presence of mother in Hartford, seeing sister daily, and seeing mother daily were more than weakly associated with positive pregnancy outcome (lambda, contingency coefficient, or phi between > .3 and < .6). Among the variables in the "medical risk" domain, month of entry into prenatal care, age of mother, and high-risk label by caseworker were weakly associated with negative pregnancy outcome.

Factor analysis did not identify significant factors in either domain that could account for more than 66 percent of the total variance. However, in the medical domain, medical problems accounted for 33 percent of the total variance, and in the social domain, having a mother and sister in Hartford accounted for 35 percent of the total variance.

In predicting pregnancy outcome, those characteristics associated with social high risk were most significant, and within the domain of "social high risk" those factors associated with family situations were the strongest predictors of pregnancy outcome. Having a mother or sister in Hartford and seeing them once a week or more appears to have a positive effect on pregnancy outcome (Denelli-Hess 1986).

The combined effect of community support network and female relatives appears to be early entry into health care: 77 percent of pregnant clients entered prenatal care in the first trimester and only 33 percent were referred to prenatal care by Comadrona Program staff. Most of these referrals were in the first year of the program. The staff concluded that by the second year, the community support network was taking care of referrals into prenatal care. The program was offering continuing support and crisis intervention for pregnant women who were either recently arrived, and/or undergoing their pregnancies in conflict with family members, and stressed by young children and lack of support in the house. The women in the program sought help through the program network because they saw it as an opportunity to solve deeply rooted family problems and create life options during an important transition in their lives.

Returning to our initial theoretical framework, the data suggest that sociocultural and economic risk factors can be mitigated by the presence of maternal relatives. The presence and availability of mothers and sisters both enhances the likelihood of early entry to prenatal care and the likelihood of positive pregnancy outcome. Women at risk during pregnancy, therefore, are those who do not have these specific supports available. It also suggests that effective health education offered through a reinstated social role and set of cultural attributes can enhance perinatal health behavior such as breastfeeding and medical compliance and can, to a certain extent, replace the social support function of female relatives. The data also pointed to age and medical problems as contributing to medical risk and to teens as a second high-risk category.

These data have been used to argue for a second program which is now building social support networks and offering individual support to pregnant teens in family conflict situations.

THEORETICAL PRINCIPLES AND MATERNAL AND CHILD HEALTH POLICY

This case illustrates the ways diverse interest groups, or policy clusters, converged to develop policies and programs in the area of maternal and child health. It points clearly to the way policy clusters may be marked by pronounced differences in theoretical perspective. In this case, association with medically versus sociologically shaped theories of action strongly influenced the beliefs, expectations, and behavior of policy cluster members. In addition, it shaped views of what data should be collected.

The case materials indicate that community members have strong preferences about approaches to community health needs. MCH programs directed to particular ethnic minorities are unlikely to achieve long-term success unless members of these groups are included in policy-making bodies, such as health committees, city health departments, and legislative task forces (Hicks and Handler 1978).

The case also illustrates the ongoing nature of policy formulation and the changing configurations of policy clusters in relation to this process. What began as one cluster in the early phases of the program, dispersed into two as the program was implemented. Throughout the course of the program new clusters came into existence in relation to specific internal and external issues.

Each of the policy clusters wished to have data available for its use and supported certain research. Research was only supported, however, when its relationship was clear to the monitoring, evaluation, or advocacy needs of either the cluster or individual members. While policy cluster members supported information collection, there was considerable lack of appreciation for the research process among client-oriented service staff, since from their point of view it was time consuming and not directly related to service provision. Only when these staff were forced to advocate for the program did they appreciate the utility of systematic data collection. Eventually they came to agree that health programs directed to particular urban ethnic minorities were unlikely to achieve success unless the programs included considerable investment in research on specific conditions and features in local communities.

Finally, successful management of the data and analysis required both the input of program staff and the collaboration of a university-trained data manager, in this case a medical anthropology student. Collaboration involved team development of the instrument, joint interviewing, checking for data quality control, coding, data input, and utilization of qualitative data in the preparation of a training manual now in use.

COLLABORATIVE RESEARCH AND POLICY CHANGE

The previous discussion described the complex relationships between shifting maternal and child health policies, competing theoretical frameworks for program development, changing policy clusters, and alternative directions for information collection. Based on this case example, we may define collaboration in the context of the policy research cluster as including the following elements:

1. Interdisciplinary, intersectoral agreement on the basic problem to be addressed (see Parades 1985). It may be quite difficult for persons of different backgrounds and experiences to perceive a situation in sufficiently common terms to permit agreement on the existence of a problem. In the case described here, the initial policy cluster was able to agree on the problem because of the virtual absence of programing for pregnant Hispanic women. In addition, two sets of data were convincing. The first pointed to the importance of social supports in prenatal-care utilization in the Puerto Rican community; the second, collected by the city health department, indicated that Puerto Rican women were behind in indicators of pre- and postnatal health status, including entry to care, continuity of care, low birth weight, and breastfeeding.

2. Group articulation and clarification of the theory or theories of action underlying explanations of the problem. Once a problem is defined, it must be explained. The explanation of the problem—which may well be a statement of proposed causality—is a theoretical proposition. Collaboration involves group agreement on the theoretical propositions underlying the defined problem. This is often the arena in which negotiations break down and differing positions are seen as irreconcilable. A more subtle problem arises, as in the case of the Comadrona Program, when there is agreement on the basic elements in the model, but not on their hypothesized relationships. This agreement is sufficient to proceed with program development, but can result in serious breakdowns in communication later on. At such junctures only the formation of new policy clusters supportive of one or the other approach can resolve the problem. In other words, the problem is resolved through the political rather than the scientific arena.

3. Agreement that research will be useful to the process and/or the products of the group's work. There needs to be an understanding that information collection must be systematic and rigorous in order to be valid and reliable (e.g., Hessler, New, and May 1979). This agreement is relatively easy to obtain in the design phase of a program. It is more difficult to obtain as the program moves into the implementation phase and program implementors must juggle the constraints of systematic data collection with the daily demands of service. Only when implementors clearly see information collection as being in their best interests, and when the process is monitored closely by a

collaborative researcher, can data be collected in a rigorous manner.

A further problem arises when the various audiences for a program see the role of research and the information to be collected differently. The result can be confusion concerning what information is to be collected, for what purpose, and to meet whose interests. The audiences for information change continually throughout the life of a program. These changes can and should be discussed openly and negotiated within the program and associated policy clusters. If this discussion does not take place, research advocates find themselves responding to multiple interests simultaneously and placing unnecessary demands upon an already reluctant service staff.

4. Utilization of research results serves the purpose of promoting a group's interests. Utilization can take place through lobbying, policy formulation, publication of materials, presentations through educational events, and similar activities. The public presentation of research results is a political process. The degree to which the presenter is questioned depends on the level of sympathy of the audience and the degree to which the presenter is seen as having power in the community or the wider environment. Unsympathetic audiences look for design flaws, statistical errors, simple calculation errors, and differences of interpretation. In such cases, the advocate should be accompanied by the "technician" or methodologist. It should always be kept in mind in preparing research results for an audience that the data can be used in a supportive or oppositional manner later on.

5. Finally, it should be understood that outcome evaluation as a subset of research utilization is a highly political process, somewhat distinct from knowledge utilization in general. The difference lies in the fact that the audiences for an outcome evaluation are usually clearly defined as the evaluation is in process. The interests of these audiences may change, but it is possible to establish the sort of relationship with them that permits negotiation of the evaluation design to best enhance the overall picture of the program. Evaluation audiences may be the best critics and the strongest supporters of a program. This is unlike the ongoing nature of knowledge utilization in which new audiences and new arenas for presentation appear unpredictably, and their interests are unknown and difficult to assess in advance.

This paper examines collaborative research within the ongoing process of a complex maternal and child health program in a changing urban environment. Collaborative research by definition involves the "juggling" of methodological requirements with the demands and constraints of the sociopolitical context of the problem in question. In this case example we have tried to articulate more clearly what these demands and constraints are and how they may be managed in order to carry out sound research and rational program planning and development. Central to the argument has been the role of theory and model building. It is in this arena that the reputation of applied anthropology has fallen short. We believe that not only is this reputation unnecessary, but that, as Kimball (1978:286) pointed out: "Speaking out on public issues does not a policy scientist make." Without careful articulation of theory in the planning and development process, anthropologists have little new to offer the policy sciences.

2

In the People's Service: The Kansas Kickapoo Technical Assistance Project

Donald D. Stull, Jerry A. Schultz, and Ken Cadue, Sr.

INTRODUCTION

The late 1960s and early 1970s were exciting and important years in U.S. Indian policy. Young activists brought the concerns of Indian people to the nation's attention. Presidents Johnson and Nixon delivered special messages on American Indians to Congress. Major government studies issued recommendations for sweeping reforms in Indian affairs, while the courts upheld tribal reassertions of treaty rights. Congress, between 1968 and 1978, enacted no less than nine pieces of major legislation that addressed past grievances and promised to usher in a new era of "Indian self-determination." Indian people and communities made significant strides in health, education, professional training and employment, and energy development (Stull, Schultz, and Cadue 1986). A new era seemed about to emerge; one that offered hope of ultimately transforming Indian tribes from "administered communities" (Castile 1974:220) to self-sufficient, self-ruling governments.

This same period also proved to be significant for American anthropology. Increasingly, it was coming under attack both from representatives of traditional "subject" populations and from within its own ranks. Major criticisms centered on the motivations of anthropologists, how their findings were disseminated, and, most importantly, the lack of tangible benefits of their research for the populations under study (Maynard 1974:402). Anthropologists responded by seriously reevaluating their discipline. One such response was the reemergence of action anthropology. Influenced, at least in part, by the Fox Project (Gearing, Netting, and Peattie 1960), a new generation of anthropologists began collaborating with local groups to foster community development and empowerment (J. Schensul 1985b:

187-188). Internal pressures for reform and demands from hosts for accountability led many anthropologists to develop new political and research relationships with their communities of study (van Willigen 1981).

From Indian demands for sovereignty and self-determination and anthropologists' rediscovery of action research, a confluence of interests emerged, spawning a number of projects (Schlesier 1974; Efrat and Mitchell 1974; Parades 1976; Willard 1977; Borman 1979). This chapter describes one such effort--the Kansas Kickapoo Technical Assistance Project. It began with one anthropologist working sporadically and alone, but over the course of a decade came to include a number of professionals and students working closely with the tribe. The project grew in scope from traditional ethnography to technical assistance to active participation in tribal affairs. The working relationship between anthropologists and tribal members grew from tolerance to loose cooperation to a formal contractual agreement between tribal government and the university.

The goal of the Kickapoo Tribe was to use federal programs and funds to build an autonomous reservation community. They hoped to develop the infrastructure, social services, and employment opportunities needed to provide a base from which to move toward economic and political self-sufficiency. The goals of the anthropologists were (1) to provide the tribe with research and technical assistance that would enhance community development and foster the revival and maintenance of native language and traditional culture; and (2) to develop long-term research and training opportunities in applied anthropology. Anthropologists and tribal leaders sought these goals amid an ever-shifting and often tumultuous landscape of federal policy. Their lengthy experiment in collaboration helped change not only the reservation community, but the individual participants as well.

The authors, each intimately involved in the project, examine its outcomes from both anthropological and tribal perspectives. A brief description of the Kansas Kickapoo is followed by a chronology of the project. The authors conclude by discussing the factors, both internal and external, that influenced their collaborative effort and its implications for the practice of anthropology.

THE KANSAS KICKAPOO

The Kickapoo Tribe in Kansas, one of three federally recognized Kickapoo groups, is centered on a small reservation in the northeast corner of the state. They belong to the Central Algonquian language family and lived around the Lower Great Lakes when first encountered by the French in the late 1600s. Over the next 150 years, intertribal conflicts and European expansion led to tribal migrations and dispersal as emerging autonomous Kickapoo bands scattered widely throughout Indiana, Illinois, and Missouri. In 1832 the followers of Kenekuk, a prophet who advocated accommodation to the dominant society, were removed to northeast Kansas. Conversion to Kenekuk's teachings and intermarriage led many of the nearby Prairie Band Potawatomi to take up residence on the Kickapoo Reservation. In 1937 the Kickapoo adopted a constitution and bylaws under the Indian Reorganization Act, resulting in their present council form of government (Stull 1984a).

With a reservation population of slightly more than 600, the Kansas Kickapoo are in many ways similar to other tribal enclaves. The group is young, with a median age of 20.5 years, and characterized by low income, endemic unemployment, low educational attainment, and major health and social problems. Life expectancy is less than 50 years.

Located 40 miles from the nearest city (Topeka), the reservation itself is also fairly typical. A classic case of "checkerboarding," only 37 percent of the 19,200-acre reservation (6 X 5 miles) is under Indian ownership. Indian land is divided about equally between acreage held communally by the tribe and that held by individual Indian allottees. Much of the allotted land is leased to non-Indian farmers. There are no significant natural resources in the area (United Indian Tribes of Western Oklahoma and Kansas 1975; Menninger Foundation 1978).

PROJECT EVOLUTION

Initial Contact

In the spring of 1976, shortly after joining the faculty of the University of Kansas, Donald Stull began conducting research for Indians in northeast Kansas. The tribes wanted basic demographic data to use in seeking federal funds, and, working through an intertribal organization, Stull began conducting a census/needs assessment for two groups--the Prairie Band Potawatomi and the Iowa.

As his work got underway, Stull approached the Kickapoo about the study. He initially met with Ken Cadue, Sr., a planner and "gatekeeper" for the tribe. Although the tribal administration declined to participate in the census, they were interested in developing a bilingual/bicultural program.

Over the next few months discussions focused on appropriate strategies for linguistic and cultural revival and maintenance. Tentative agreement was eventually reached to investigate the persistence of Kickapoo language and traditional culture. By this time, however, it was too late to obtain external funding, and the project was left up in the air.

The mid-1970s were an exciting time on the Kickapoo Reservation. The federal government was implementing its new policy of Indian self-determination: tribes were to contract directly for and administer programs and services previously provided by the federal government. This transfer of programs and a concomitant increase in federal spending promised opportunities to develop reservation economies. These opportunities attracted young Kickapoos back to their reservation. Many who returned, such as Cadue, had worked in urban Indian centers and gained experience with federal programs. Soon they were occupying key positions in tribal government.

When Stull began to visit the reservation in 1976, the Kickapoo were embarking on an aggressive program of infrastructural development. Over the next five years, grants from the Department of Housing and Urban Development (HUD) and the Economic Development Administration (EDA) enabled the tribe to build 75 homes; a gymnasium-multipurpose center; a shopping center housing a gas station, laundromat, cafe, and general store; a library-cultural heritage center; a print shop; a senior citizens center; a daycare center; and a swimming pool. The tribe developed a reservation water treatment and distribution system, formed its own construction company, started a farm and livestock operation, and founded a tribal school (grades K-12). Adopting a policy designed to regain tribal lands within the reservation boundaries, the Kickapoo eventually repurchased approximately 2,400 acres (Stull, Schultz, and Cadue 1986).

The commitment of the Kickapoo tribal government to an active program of economic and social development was infectious. Stull decided he wanted to be part of this adventure: it provided an ideal setting to apply the principles of action anthropology (Tax 1958; S. Schensul 1974; Schlesier 1974).

In the fall of 1977, Ken Cadue again contacted Stull about the native language/culture project. Federal funding was still unavailable, but Stull obtained limited financial support from the University of Kansas and, later, from the Kansas Committee for the Humanities and the Center for Applied Linguistics. These grants supported preliminary ethnographic and linguistic research as well as the publication and public dissemination of research findings.

In January 1978--one and a half years after the initial discussions--the project got underway when two graduate students began linguistic fieldwork. Assisted by three young Kickapoo women, Stull began ethnographic research in the summer of 1978 on remembered or extant native cultural practices. The research team engaged in participant observation, open-ended interviews, and intensive work with key informants, collecting information on both "memory culture" and current practices.

Linguistic research resulted in an orthography (writing system), a basic vocabulary list, and initial data for a reference grammar. Ethnographic research produced a modest body of old and new photographs and a number of transcribed interviews with tribal elders. Photographs and examples of material culture (borrowed from tribal members) formed the basis for a multimedia exhibit at the newly completed tribal library-cultural heritage center. The manuscript for a "Foxfire-type" book on Kickapoo oral tradition and language was prepared for publication by the tribal press. However, a constellation of factors, including inadequate funds, tribal politics, and inexperience and mismanagement on the part of the press's staff, delayed publication of the book for several years.

The most substantial research product to come out of this period was a 30-minute ethnographic film (Stull, Bernofsky, and Hirsch 1979). It combined original footage from the 1930s with interviews of elderly Potawatomi and Kickapoo conducted in 1978 and 1979. Although the film focused on the Prairie Band Potawatomi, the raw footage was discovered in the course of the research among the Kickapoo, and much of the sound track was derived from interviews with residents of the Kickapoo Reservation.

By fall 1979, initial work with the Kickapoo was winding down. The tribal council was immersed in its program of economic development and had little time to devote to what were viewed as "esoteric" and "small-time" efforts at cultural revival and maintenance. But the groundwork had been laid for further collaboration between anthropologists and the tribe.

Initial work with the Kickapoo conformed to what Agar (1980) has called "informal ethnography." The research was more or less a "fishing expedition" in which the anthropologist canvassed the community to identify and collect whatever bits of oral tradition he could. Research was carried out in the traditional "Lone Ranger" ethnographic style, with the researcher collecting the bulk of the data, assisted by native interviewers.

Stull attempted to convince tribal administrators that he could be helpful in their development efforts; in fact, his interests and training were better suited to such a role than that of "traditional" ethnographer. Nevertheless, they relegated him to a role that conformed to their stereotype of what an "anthro" should do. The tribal council wished to strengthen contacts with the university; the salvage ethnography to which he was assigned was relatively harmless and made good political capital with the tribe and non-Indians alike. But they did not see the products of the initial research as essential to their overall development plan. They had yet to discover the value of anthropological input in tribal development.

For better or worse, the Kickapoo now had their very own "pet anthro"--a more or less permanent fixture on the reservation, to be welcomed, tolerated, or avoided depending on individual inclinations or situational circumstances.

Interim Period

By late 1979 tribal interest in further work on Kickapoo language and traditional culture had waned. From time to time, however, anthropology graduate students found research and planning positions with the tribe. As they executed their duties in grant procurement, administration, and research, tribal administrators became increasingly aware of the potential usefulness of anthropologists in tribal affairs.

In the summer of 1980, Stull helped place an anthropologist, Steven V. Lutes, with the tribe. Lutes's previous experience with grant procurement and administration made him especially well-suited for his new position; soon he was playing a vital role in tribal planning and administration. Shortly after his arrival, a voter-initiated referendum closed the public school that served the reservation. The school had always suffered from interethnic tensions, and as the number of Kickapoo students increased during the 1970s Anglo parents began removing their children.

The vote to close the school fell along ethnic lines, and in spite of an active effort the Kickapoo narrowly lost their bid to keep the school open. Undaunted, the tribal council, under the chairmanship of Keith Keo, immediately moved to secure the school facilities. The Kickapoo vigorously pursued their goal on several fronts--the state legislature, the governor's office, the state school board, the Bureau of Indian Affairs (BIA), Congress, and the media. Working under the council's direction, Lutes managed the details of the campaign, from gathering support data to preparing oral and written arguments. Overcoming what seemed at times like insurmountable odds, agreements were finally reached with all parties involved, and the tribe signed a contract with the BIA to operate the school. The Kickapoo Nation School opened in the fall of 1981.

During the late 1970s the Kansas Kickapoo became a model of successful adaptation to the new policy of Indian self-determination. Between 1972 and 1980 the number of tribal employees rose from 2 persons to 142; the tribe's annual budget rose from $30,000 to $1.7 million. The tribal government was achieving its short-term goal of building a reservation infrastructure and work force. From this base they hoped to pursue their long-range goal of economic independence by establishing tribal enterprises. The cafe, gas station, and general store represented their first tentative steps in this direction. But their success proved a mixed blessing: federal programs provided rapid development and jobs for a growing number of tribal members; they also produced an increasing dependency on Washington.

Increased dependency began to take its toll in the fall of 1981. Moderate reductions in support for Indian programs began in the final year of the Carter administration (FY 1981); however, the Reagan administration's first budget in FY1982 brought a 32 percent reduction in the tribe's income and a concomitant loss of programs, services, jobs, and planning money. Tribal employees were reduced by one-third, and the planning staff was cut in half!

Faced with mounting losses of funds and personnel, the tribal council desperately needed to maintain its planning capacity. A possible solution presented itself in the fall of 1981 when Lutes was offered a part-time teaching position at the University of Kansas. After discussions with Stull, Lutes suggested to the tribal council that he accept the offer, reduce his time commitment to the tribe, and use the freed funds to hire two part-time graduate assistants. These students already possessed credentials comparable to those of previous tribal planners; they would be closely supervised by Lutes and Stull and be paid the rather modest wage of graduate research assistants. By making their jobs "internships" in applied anthropology, they would also earn research, thesis, and dissertation credits.

The council approved the plan, and two graduate students in anthropology, Jerry Schultz (a first-year doctoral student) and Lindy Grell (a first-year master's student), were recruited in October 1981. Such was the beginning of KKTAP--the Kansas Kickapoo Technical Assistance Project.

The Kansas Kickapoo Technical Assistance Project (KKTAP)

Laying the Foundation. At first the project acted as a stopgap to provide the tribe with necessary professional and technical services during an acute fiscal crisis. The newly formed team knew it faced serious problems--budget cuts were staggering and small tribes, such as the Kickapoo, are always at a competitive disadvantage. Nevertheless, they were convinced they could continue to successfully "hunt the federal buffalo," as the Kickapoo liked to put it. What the tribe didn't know was that for them, like their 19th century ancestors, the "buffalo" were rapidly disappearing.

By January 1982, three months after the new project had begun, the Kickapoo faced a crisis of staggering proportions. The extent of the Reagan administration's first funding reductions and the subsequent lengthy delays in final congressional approval of the FY1982 budget brought the tribal economy to its knees. The number of tribal employees plunged from an all-time high of 142 in August 1980 to 16 in January 1982--in a mere 18 months the unemployment rate had soared from 34 percent to 93 percent!

That same January a severe winter storm struck the reservation. With over 90 percent of the tribal employees out of work, people were unable to buy propane to heat their homes. Because of budget reductions and delays the tribal treasury was virtually empty. Many houses and most public buildings on the reservation were without heat: evacuations, frozen water pipes, and the threat of major health problems ensued. The nearby BIA agency office promised to investigate the situation but refused to allocate emergency funds. The anthropologists and tribal administrators worked feverishly to alert the media, charitable organizations, and state social service agencies. National attention focused on the "plight" of the Kickapoo, and a major disaster was avoided. Spring brought relief from the bitter cold and the release of long-delayed funds for tribal programs, but the reductions in federal funding forced the closing of the gymnasium, library, and shopping center.

While the acute circumstances of the winter of 1982 subsided, the tribal difficulties proved to be chronic. Even with the approval of their budget for FY1982, unemployment remained at approximately 70 percent. The responsibility for tribal planning now rested solely with Lutes and the two interns.

Over the next several months the interns became increasingly familiar with tribal and federal procedures and goals. They were gradually given greater responsibilities, and Lutes worked more closely with Stull and the tribal council to develop and refine the overall goals and structure of the emerging technical assistance project.

Formalizing the Project. For the tribe, the goal of the project was to provide competent, cost-effective, culturally sensitive services, including grant writing, planning, basic and applied research, and advocacy. The project would also allow the tribe to draw upon the resources of the University of Kansas, especially those of the Center for Public Affairs (an interdisciplinary research and service unit now known as the Institute for Public Policy and Business Research) and the Department of Anthropology, in which Stull held joint appointments.

For the anthropologists, the project promised ongoing opportunities for employment, research, and publication. The close, formal relationship with the tribe presented an unusual opportunity to gain insights into the daily workings of tribal government and the federal agencies responsible for Indian affairs. Furthermore, the relationship might well provide access to funding sources not usually available to either party.

For both the Kickapoo and the anthropologists, the ultimate goal of their collaboration was the development of a self-sustaining tribal economy. The institutional arrangement was to be more than just a scheme to save the tribe money and gain greater access to federal funds. It was envisioned as providing the necessary institutional linkages from which the tribe could draw on the expertise of a wide variety of specialists in such areas as public administration, business management, economic development, education, and information processing. It was hoped that these specialists, working in concert with the anthropologists, who had learned the intricacies of tribal government, might improve tribal living standards by promoting economic growth compatible with the tribe's desire to revive and maintain its traditional culture.

To this end, in June 1982, almost nine months after the project began, an agreement was signed defining the scope and objectives of the Kansas Kickapoo Technical Assistance Project (KKTAP) and its relationship to the Kickapoo Tribal Council and the University of Kansas. The agreement went to great lengths to guarantee the tribe's right to self-determination, while assuring KKTAP workers the right to carry out objective inquiry and publish their findings (Lutes and Stull 1986). In short, the agreement codified the arrangement that had been in operation for almost a year.

The arrangement between the tribe and KKTAP had been quite successful. In FY1982, Lutes and the two interns were paid a total of $21,777 (Stull's services were provided at no charge). Project staff obtained $620,633 in federal program funds--nearly one-half of the tribe's income and almost 70 percent of its payroll. Thus, the project consumed less than 4 percent of the funds it generated. The cost-benefit advantages of KKTAP were even more striking when compared with the record of earlier tribal planning staffs, whose combined salaries consumed 38 percent of the total income they generated (Lutes and Stull 1986).

The marked decrease in costs in relation to revenues produced was in large measure built into the project. By creating a training program, the university was used to subsidize the operation by making available skilled professional labor at student rates of pay. But the university linkage is not sufficient to explain the increased cost effectiveness. The project also minimized the need for professional workers.

The Kickapoo Tribe is organized into a number of semi-autonomous subunits with responsibilities for basic services such as tribal government and administration, housing, health, education, and social services. Previously, the tribe employed one or more persons to manage each of these programs and one or more to actually provide the basic services. Such specialization resulted in a top-heavy bureaucracy with an over-abundance of administrators. A community of 600, operating on inadequate and insecure revenues, simply could not sustain such an organization.

KKTAP consciously set out to develop a generalized managerial and planning competence so that one person could handle the work of several programs. By decreasing the hierarchical specialization within the tribe's planning staff, KKTAP was able to increase productivity while dramatically reducing costs.

During its first year, KKTAP procured funds for education, health care, research and planning, and economic development. Throughout FY1982 and FY1983, KKTAP continued to demonstrate its effectiveness in grant writing. As the students became more comfortable with their duties, and as some degree of normalcy returned to Indian country, KKTAP branched out to other forms of technical and research services. External funding was obtained to support several research projects, including a videotape documentary on the impact of the Indian Self-Determination Act on the Kansas Kickapoo (Stull and Kendall 1982) and a tribal studies text for use in the Kickapoo Nation School (Stull 1984a).

Unfortunately, performance successes were offset by institutional problems within the tribe and the university. The tribe continued to suffer from funding reductions and delays; as a result the KKTAP staff sometimes did not receive their paychecks on time. Resentment of non-Indians on the tribal payroll during hard times undoubtedly played a roll in this as well. Efforts to provide Lutes with a secure university appointment were unsuccessful. Although university administrators encouraged the project, they would only provide a courtesy research appointment.

Efforts to address some of these problems led to a purchase-of-services agreement, signed in March 1983, between the tribe and the Center for Public Affairs. The agreement covered salaries, travel, and miscellaneous expenses of the students. In return, KKTAP was to provide grant writing and planning services to the Kickapoo Tribal Council and the Kickapoo Nation School. Payment was to be divided equally between the council and the school. With the signing of this agreement, it appeared that KKTAP was firmly in place and financially secure. *In reality, the project was beginning to unravel.*

KKTAP's Demise. The fiscal difficulties that had plagued the tribe since the winter of 1982 brought longstanding political dissension to the surface. In the spring of 1983 a recall campaign was mounted against five of the seven members of the tribal council. Supporters of the recall, including the remaining two council members and many of the tribal elders, accused them of illegally passing tribal resolutions, improperly disposing of government property, and misappropriation of tribal funds. When the tribal council rejected the petition, the "dissidents" elected their own council and took over the tribal office.

The "old council" obtained a restraining order and the matter went to Federal District Court. The court ruled it had no jurisdiction. The BIA refused to intervene, leaving the "old council" in power. Mounting pressure from the U.S.

attorney general's office and the congressional delegation led to a freeze on some new program funds and audits of existing programs (Stull, Schultz, and Cadue 1986).

At the same time, the school was becoming a battleground in the dispute. While the tribe's treasury was being steadily depleted, the school's budget was increasing. The school was governed by an elected board, and its budget was not under the council's control. In April 1983, the tribal council attempted to gain access to school funds by dissolving the elected board and appointing a new one. The elected school board was controlled by the faction that opposed the council and had steadfastly resisted the council's attempts to appropriate school funds. The newly appointed school board fired the school's superintendent, a Kickapoo, and hired a non-Indian with a background in educational planning and administration, but lacking experience in Indian education.

In spite of everything they could do, the KKTAP personnel became embroiled in the tribal dispute. In order to establish and protect his turf, the new superintendent made it clear that he had no need of KKTAP's services. Although ongoing contracts prevented him from terminating the relationship, the superintendent attempted to discredit KKTAP, refused to work with Lutes and Grell, and made only limited use of Schultz's services.

Meanwhile, the movement to recall the tribal council was heating up. Having worked closely with the tribal council for three years, Lutes was unable to escape the controversy. Events at the school, and an ultimatum by the "old council" that he sever his ties with members of the "dissident" group, led Lutes to resign his positions with the tribe and KKTAP. Subsequently, he left the state to take other employment.

Lutes's departure was a serious blow to KKTAP; it could have proved fatal had it not been for the strong ties and diverse networks each of the KKTAP workers had developed with tribal members. These ties, and the willingness of the remaining staff members to continue to perform their duties in spite of ongoing difficulties, kept the project in place.

The school superintendent's high-handed style and insensitivity to local customs and circumstances soon alienated the council and the school board. His position was further imperiled as the dispute between the tribal factions intensified. After a series of confrontations involving school employees, members of the tribal council, and the school board, the superintendent was fired. His dismissal was followed by a teacher walkout that brought outside attention to the disputes within the tribe. A tribal member, the late Lindreth ("Bud") DuPuis, contacted Senator Nancy Kassebaum, who prevailed upon the BIA to force the tribal council to dissolve the appointed school board and hold a special election. BIA officials exacted a promise from the tribal council to leave the operation of the school to the newly elected school board. The new board upheld the superintendent's dismissal (Hiawatha Daily World, November 1983).

By this time the school was in a state of utter chaos: enrollment plummeted and several faculty and administrators were either dismissed or resigned. KKTAP's relationship with the newly elected board was amicable due to Stull's long-term friendships with several of the new members, such as Ken Cadue and Bud DuPuis. Stull met with the new school board and offered KKTAP's assistance. Schultz, a KKTAP intern and certified teacher, was hired as acting superintendent/principal to help stabilize the situation.

All other KKTAP activities were immediately suspended while the staff worked to help bring the school back to normal operations. Because of its access to university resources, KKTAP was able to provide the school with much needed personnel and materials. Rapid reestablishment of the school program was imperative since further deterioration would have resulted in closure of the school. The reputation of Schultz and KKTAP with both the tribe and the BIA allowed them to meet this tribal crisis and rapidly stabilize the situation. By the beginning of the spring 1984 semester the school was running "normally."

Ironically, this drastic turn of events allowed KKTAP to make progress toward its ultimate goal of establishing a viable research function with the Kickapoo. In 1982, the school had been awarded a three-year grant from the Department of Education to develop materials for a tribal studies program, and the school subcontracted to KKTAP to develop these materials. Progress in this area had been hampered by the difficulties with the previous superintendent. With KKTAP now playing a central role in the operation of the school, the way was paved to move ahead in this area.

Unfortunately, smoother relations at the school were offset by further difficulties with the tribal council. Payment for KKTAP's grant-writing services was to be divided equally between the tribal council and the school. While the school honored its financial commitment, the tribal council did not. The steadily declining resources of the embattled tribal council left it unwilling or unable to pay. Lingering hostilities from Lutes's departure and the increasingly apparent alignment of KKTAP with the "opposition" faction, who now controlled the school, also contributed to the council's recalcitrance. Through KKTAP's efforts, the bulk of the tribe's contracts had already been awarded for the coming year, and the council saw little immediate need for their services. After repeated attempts to secure payment, KKTAP was forced to terminate the agreement with the tribal council in January 1984.

Later that month, the tribal chairman was removed from office (subsequently, he was convicted of misappropriating tribal funds); however, his ouster left the council split and impotent. It took another nine months before the remnants of the "old council" were voted out of office and a unified tribal council emerged. During this time many program funds were held up and several new projects were cancelled (Stull, Schultz, and Cadue 1986). Although the new council was on good terms with KKTAP, they were confronted with the large debt left by their predecessors and were unable to repay their creditors (including KKTAP).

Withdrawing from commitments to the tribal council, KKTAP focused its efforts on the school's tribal studies program. Expanding activities and Schultz's continuing employment at the school allowed the addition of four new student assistants. What had begun as the writing of a single tribal studies text for use at the secondary level, quickly expanded on several fronts. In the next two years, the KKTAP team produced a feasibility study on Kickapoo language instruction in the school (Vantine 1984), language materials and lesson plans (Folarin 1985), a book on Kickapoo oral traditions (a revised version of Stull's [1984b] earlier manuscript), two tribal studies texts for use by middle-school students (Stull, Grell, and Weston 1985; Stull n.d.), four short videotapes on traditional culture (Schultz and Kendall 1985), and a one-hour videotape documentary on off-reservation Indian boarding schools (Stull, Schultz, and Kendall 1985).

In 1984 and 1985 KKTAP finally achieved the goals for which the anthropologists had struggled for the past decade: they were working with and for a tribal institution to produce materials of use to both the tribal and the scholarly communities. They looked forward to implementing a program designed to introduce Kickapoo language instruction into the curriculum. Unfortunately, continued factional disputes led to the resignation of KKTAP's supporters from the school board. The reconstituted board grew increasingly resentful of the use of "school funds" to support the work of KKTAP. In fact, KKTAP's funding was quite modest and left the bulk of the grant monies for the school's discretionary use. Nevertheless, the board ignored the fact that the Department of Education grant had been written by KKTAP for the school and was designed specifically to underwrite such efforts. In spite of prior board approval, they resisted and undercut project activities.

The belligerence of the school board, combined with fatigue and the disaffection of KKTAP staff, resulted in the project's termination. The students were drifting away as they completed their studies or found more stable and less stressful employment. With completion of the last of their contract commitments, the Kansas Kickapoo Technical Assistance Project was disbanded at the end of 1985.

DISCUSSION

We look back over the past decade with mixed emotions. The collaborative effort that ultimately evolved into KKTAP was unusual in its intent, longevity, and structure. Unlike so many efforts in both abstract and applied anthropology, it did not focus on testing specific hypotheses. While it lacked a specific problem focus, it was, nevertheless, problem oriented. Following in the tradition of action anthropology, it sought to put anthropology "to use" by helping the Kickapoo achieve their own community goals through the provision of research and professional services.

The project's output over the course of a decade was substantial. Yet, in many ways, the anthropologists viewed these research products as almost incidental. Increasingly, their interests turned to the factors that enhanced or impeded their ability to collaborate successfully with the Kickapoo. Shifts in federal policy and funding, university politics, the history of tribal relations with non-Indians, individual ambitions and personalities, and cultural differences all played a part. Although space does not permit a detailed discussion of each of these factors, three bear further consideration--the internal dynamics of the research team, the interaction between the anthropologists and the tribe, and the federal policy milieu in which they operated.

The Anthropologists

Starting with Stull, and later expanding to include Lutes, Schultz, and Grell, a core team took shape. As needed, the core expanded to include additional members with special expertise such as filmmaking and linguistics. Small size and commonalities of interest minimized the problems that often plague team research. Even so, there were such problems.

The fact that the team's codirectors, Stull and Lutes, were based primarily in the university and the reservation community respectively often led them to place conflicting demands on the students. The situation was problematic in large part because the students who were available and interested in the project were still engaged in coursework and other formative aspects of their training. As they became increasingly involved in their internships, progress toward degree requirements suffered. While the codirectors tried to minimize this problem, it was a major flaw in the training aspect of the project.

Team members commuted to and from the reservation, and the 150-mile round trip undoubtedly took its toll. Although some members stayed on the reservation for varying lengths of time, other commitments prevented them from living in the community. The team tried to minimize this shortcoming by staggering their visits and by weekly debriefing sessions. This approach proved moderately successful and, at times, advantageous in avoiding periods of potential difficulty on the reservation.

In spite of the "commuter" nature of their research presence, burnout was a major problem. As Agar (1980) points out, constant movement in and out of a field situation may in itself prove stressful. The major cause of burnout, however, was the ebb and flow of support and animosity toward KKTAP and its individual members that attended the increasingly pervasive factional disputes within the tribe. While the KKTAP members developed strong personal bonds with many Kickapoos and tried to avoid taking sides in disputes, identification with various factions was unavoidable.

A final internal source of tension stemmed from the nature of anthropological tradition. By training and inclination, anthropologists are "Lone Rangers"--they have traditionally worked as independent researchers in single communities and have jealously guarded "their people" from incursions by other researchers. Stull was committed to developing a team project. But as his role shifted away from field research to administration and writing, he suffered feelings of personal and professional loss. These feelings contributed to his ultimate disaffection.

The Tribe

While internal team relations are important, it is in the interaction between the team and the tribe that the key issues are to be found in assessing the project. Clearly, KKTAP was immensely successful in achieving its stated goals--the team provided vital assistance to the tribe during several crises (e.g., the acquisition of the school), successful grant procurement at minimal cost, and a series of research products that were valuable to the school's educational mission and enhanced the tribe's image. Why then did the Kickapoo grow increasingly antagonistic to what had become a highly successful project?

Some of the reasons are readily apparent. KKTAP was identified with certain tribal members and factions; ironically, not always with the same ones with which the KKTAP members identified themselves. As their influence waned new actors emerged who were antagonistic to KKTAP for personal and political reasons. Centuries of mistreatment by and subordination to non-Indians have made the Kickapoo, and indeed most American Indian communities, extremely suspicious of and hostile toward outsiders. This posture was effective in resisting past encroachment, but it proved counterproductive when cooperative relations with outside professionals became both possible and necessary. Even after years of mutually beneficial association with the tribe, the anthropologists were still mistrusted by many.

Tribal politics works indiscriminately against lasting relationships with outside professionals. The inadequacy and uncertainty of tribal funds, combined with endemic unemployment, set up fierce competition for staff positions in tribal government. Tribal leaders are forced to decide between investing salaries and positions in outside professionals who *may* help the tribe achieve long-term goals, or providing employment for relatives who *will* provide political support in upcoming elections (tribal council elections are held annually and council members serve staggered two-year terms). In times of scarcity, they almost always choose the latter. As jobs and resources are used to satisfy the short-term needs of tribal members, the tribe's long-term adaptive capabilities suffer. The need to use their scarce resources as political capital creates a cycle of inefficiency that opens avenues for opposition leaders to criticize the status quo. Yet, when new leaders come to power they repeat the "sins" of their predecessors. This vicious cycle leads to dissipation of funds, a scarcity of skilled workers, inefficiency and poor management, as well as ineffective use of professionals.

The "catch-22" of scarce resources and high unemployment was at the heart of the ultimate failure to develop a successful ongoing collaborative relationship between the tribe and KKTAP. While the anthropologists saw the acquisition of program funds as a means to achieve long-term goals of tribal self-determination, the tribal government saw these programs as sources of jobs. The anthropologists were seen as laborers whose primary purpose was to produce jobs for tribal members, not as researchers working together with the tribe to achieve common long-range goals. There was little serious commitment to project outcomes, such as the tribal studies materials; rather, these products were seen as "hooks" to "reel in" additional money for the tribe and its members. As a result, such products have not been utilized to their full potential.

This basic difference in outlook results in distrust and hostility toward outsiders, even if they produce visible results for the tribe. It also explains the strong resistance to financial arrangements with outside institutions and individuals. Subcontracts are looked upon with disfavor, even when subcontractors have good "track records," because control of the funds passes out of tribal hands. Although such arrangements are advantageous to the tribe in terms of goods and services received, the costs are too great in terms of lost income in the short term. However, the tribe does not have the personnel to produce many of the products for which contracts are awarded.

In the end, the systemic difficulties that confronted the tribe precluded the development of a truly collaborative effort. Although the anthropologists saw themselves as producing products *for* the Kickapoo, the tribe saw these same products as *belonging to* the anthropologists. Thus, there was little real tribal input into or identification with the products produced by the project. The ultimate fate of KKTAP was to be one-half of an ambitious but flawed collaborative project--"the sound of one hand clapping."

Federal Policy

Federal Indian policy has provided only a shadowy background to this narrative. In reality, however, it played a pivotal role in determining the fortunes of the tribe and the ultimate fate of KKTAP.

Throughout the 1970s the Kickapoos, and the anthropologists, rode the "up-escalator" of emerging Indian self-determination. All over Indian country, reservations became "boom towns" as the increase in federal funds and programs created new jobs and housing. The out-migration that had characterized reservations since World War II was reversed as Indians saw the opportunity for socioeconomic development of their homelands.

Like many tribes, the Kansas Kickapoo enthusiastically embraced the rhetoric of Indian self-determination. They believed they could "determine their own destiny" through skillful acquisition of federal funds and programs. Indeed, the very nature of the government's policy of self-determination encouraged them to adopt an adaptive strategy built on increasing dependence on the federal government. They had little real choice in setting their short-term goals, since federal agencies established funding categories and priorities.

Long-range goals and attempts to establish tribal business enterprises notwithstanding, three factors conspired to keep the Kickapoo from gaining a foothold on self-sufficiency. First, there was no incentive to actively pursue less lucrative but more stable sources of private support as long as they could successfully compete for an abundance of federal funds.

Second, the federal government's "edifice complex" led to an overemphasis on infrastructural development. Undoubtedly, the need for such development was great, and construction provided employment for many tribal members. But when the buildings were erected, the funds for program activities and maintenance were not forthcoming. All too often they soon stood empty.

Finally, the nature and location of the community itself worked against the tribe. They attempted to attract investors to an "industrial park," but governmental constraints and tribal politics, the remoteness of the reservation, the lack of a skilled labor force, and the absence of an adequate infrastructure (poor roads, limited water and utility lines, etc.) failed to offset any incentives the tribe could offer.

The tribe's strategy of increasing reliance on federal program monies worked so long as the escalator of federal spending continued to go up. But it reached its apex all too rapidly--barely had the new age of Indian self-determination begun when federal support was sharply curtailed. Although the rhetoric of Indian policy continued to speak of self-determination, the reality was that the Kickapoo (and Indian tribes in general) were given neither enough money nor enough time to develop the foundation for a diversified and self-sustaining economy.

In the 1970s the Kickapoo "successfully" pursued self-determination by increasing their dependence on federal programs. But when the escalator of federal spending started down in the 1980s this same dependence quickly became disastrous. They had made great strides toward building a reservation infrastructure, but they had yet to build the necessary institutions to allow the tribe to begin to operate programs and enterprises that were not totally dependent on federal subsidy.

When the escalator was going up, technical assistance from outside professionals was an important catalyst in helping the tribe achieve its short-term goals. By the time KKTAP was formed, however, the escalator was already starting down. KKTAP was skillful and resourceful, but neither it nor the tribe could change the direction of the escalator. KKTAP provided a "safety net" that helped ease the tribe's transition while the escalator changed directions, but in so doing it also required a portion of the tribe's economic resources. The tribe's frustration with its shrinking resource base ultimately turned inward, surfacing in increased factionalism, and toward the only non-Indians over whom they had any real control--KKTAP. There is no doubt that KKTAP was ultimately done in by forces over which neither the anthropologists nor the Kickapoo had any control--changes in federal Indian policy and funding.

Implications for the Practice of Anthropology

While the collaborative effort with the Kickapoo ultimately came to an end, it nevertheless taught us a great deal about the practice of anthropology. One of the most important lessons involved the very nature of participant observation and how it should be carried out. No one denies that participant observation requires a certain amount of involvement by the researcher in what is being observed. However, in anthropology's attempt to achieve "objectivity," we have emphasized observation and deemphasized participation. The line of reasoning has been that we need to develop good theory about how cultures function based on empirical knowledge--this knowledge should be based on observations of "naturally" functioning cultural processes. Only after we have such knowledge, most anthropologists have argued, should we attempt to apply our skills to foster, or in some cases impede, culture change (cf. van Willigen 1981).

Our experiences with the Kickapoo lead us to question this time-honored truism. We feel that we have learned far more about the Kickapoo, the institutions of the larger society with which they interact, and the processes of cultural change and maintenance by being active participants in the day-to-day workings of tribal institutions.

Our participation evolved out of a steadily growing commitment to and understanding of the Kickapoo people, and we became active participants with tribal members in formulating and implementing tribal goals and objectives. As advocates for the Kickapoo and active partners in their affairs, we abandoned the facade of "objectivity" and left ourselves vulnerable to criticism from the tribe and anthropology alike. Yet our participation afforded us the opportunity to gain a depth of understanding of Kickapoo culture, current Indian policy and affairs, and the processes and methods of directed change that would not have been possible otherwise.

A central aspect of active participation, and for anthropologists perhaps the most troubling one, is that of decision making. A canon of "traditional" action anthropology (and to a lesser extent applied anthropology as well) asserts that anthropologists do not make decisions, they provide the group with alternatives from which to choose and allow them the freedom to make mistakes (Piddington 1960:205). Noninterference and the resulting reduction in responsibility are proposed for both ethical and pragmatic reasons (Hinshaw and Young 1979:516). In fact, however, anthropologists very often exert considerable influence in action projects (see Stucki's [1967] critique of the Fox Project). Even if action anthropologists are able to avoid such influence, there is a question as to the propriety of those who take such a position (Naylor 1973:368).

The dilemma of decision making was for each KKTAP member a matter of considerable frustration and guilt. As a result of professional training, they invariably sought to avoid substantive decision making. Yet constant pressure from the Kickapoo forced them into substantial roles in policy making and implementation. This increased involvement ultimately brought a fuller understanding of both the Kickapoo and themselves.

Collaborative research by its very nature is a partnership that requires a sharing of responsibility and risks, of successes and failures. Anthropologists who wish to collaborate with host communities in action-oriented projects must be willing to participate in policy decisions and bear the consequences of their decisions.

In its attempt to maximize benefits for the Kickapoo, KKTAP developed a model for collaborative research involving formal linkages between university-based and community-based anthropologists. Working in isolation, neither the university-based nor the community-based anthropologist has adequate access to the full array of institutional or community networks, resources, and supports needed to provide the host community with optimal benefits from his services.

Enhancement of collaboration between university-based and community-based social scientists seems necessary to the evolution of a truly applied discipline. A continuance of antagonism between "practicing" and "academic" anthropologists, wherein each camp espouses its own superiority, promises only stagnation and decline for the discipline as a whole. Anthropologists in each setting have much to offer each other in the way of resources, theoretical and practical insights, and network linkages--cross-fertilization seems necessary if action/applied anthropology is to develop a set of basic issues, principles, and methods.

Finally, it seems to us that KKTAP's greatest contribution was its attempt to establish a mutually beneficial relationship between outside professionals and the host community. The agreement signed by the tribe and KKTAP established a formal relationship that maximized the benefits of professional services to the Kickapoo people, while respecting tribal sovereignty and protecting the rights of the anthropologists. While the Kansas Kickapoo Technical Assistance Project ultimately foundered, it left the Kickapoo people not only with a substantial body of tangible products, but also with the knowledge that anthropologists were willing and able to use their skills "in the people's service."

ACKNOWLEDGMENTS

The authors are grateful to the many members of the Kickapoo Tribe in Kansas and the faculty, staff, and students of the University of Kansas who supported our efforts over the last decade. We specifically wish to thank Jeannette Biggoose, Marilyn Jessepe, Carol Yazzie, Geoff Gathercole, Sonia Manuel-Dupont, Genie Trapp, Tim Weston, Liess Vantine, Antonia Folarin, Dave Kendall, and Ward Bryant, all of whom, although not mentioned by name in the narrative, made significant contributions to this project. We also wish to thank Jean Schensul, Akira Yamamoto, and Steven Lutes for their comments on the first draft of this paper. We are especially grateful to Robert Hackenberg for his critical review and thoughtful guidance in our conceptualizations.

3

Community Action and Social Adaptation: The Farmworker Movement in the Midwest

W.K. Barger and Ernesto Reza

When politicians, bureaucrats, revolutionaries, prophets, community groups, and social scientists take on the task of trying to initiate social change, the concepts they hold about what change is and how it works have serious implications for action. Ideas about change influence the goals, planning, methods, and outcomes of efforts to implement policies and programs, thereby affecting the lives of many people. Impacts are made at the community level, the societal level, and even the global level. Directed change, where there is conscious and organized effort to implement specific goals, thus provides a unique opportunity to develop both theory and practice (Arensberg 1978; Partridge and Eddy 1978; Thompson 1965). Practice tests the validity, predictability, and comprehensiveness of concepts. It also provides new ideas and empirical information to expand conceptual understandings about change.

Concepts of sociocultural change include specific ideas about what changes occur and what influences these changes. These perspectives are useful in planning and implementing directed change. Even more important, however, is an understanding of *how* changes occur. Many concepts of change inadequately address the *processes* involved and can therefore limit the achievement of change goals and produce unforeseen and sometimes unfortunate consequences.

A review of the literature illustrates marked differences in the degree of success of models used to initiate and direct change. A dialectical systems concept of change represented by Marxian revolutionary ideas has had global impacts in initiating social changes, even though these changes have not necessarily produced the economic and social orders envisioned. On the other hand, applied change activities based on a trait-replacement model of acculturation have produced many examples of what went wrong and comparatively few examples of what went right. We believe that such inconsistency in the impact of applied efforts is due largely to inadequate models of sociocultural change. We also believe that those who seek to initiate changes have a basic responsibility to understand change itself.

Collaboration between social scientists and community groups in applied change programs provides an excellent opportunity to better understand the processes of change. Such collaboration establishes conditions for both conceptual and practical awareness of how changes occur. This report examines such a case of collaboration, where one conceptual framework of change, a systems model of social adaption, was used in a specific case of directed change--a community action project in support of the farm labor movement. In discussing this case, we will review the model that guided the project, the farm labor movement in the Midwest, and then describe the community action project in support of the farmworkers' cause. Finally, the implications of the project for community-academic collaboration and for conceptual models in applied change will be discussed.

SOCIOCULTURAL ADAPTATION

A systems concept of sociocultural change considers how the content and direction of changes are governed by the interaction of different forces within an integrated system. Such ideas are evident in the concepts of innovation, syncretism, and mazeway reformulation (Barnett 1953:49-56; Wallace 1956:270-273). The interaction of a group with its environment is seen in Steward's (1955) multilinear evolutionary model and in concepts of cultural ecology, though these schemes have focused more on the maintenance of a system than on its development and alteration (Geertz 1963, 1972; Harris 1966; Moran 1979; Rappaport 1968, 1971). The main contributions of systems models derive from their active consideration of the *process* of change; that is, how related forces interact and direct events toward a particular outcome as well as the sequence of events involved in the interaction.

Perhaps the most dramatic examples of systems models that provide a framework for directed change are the dialectical and conflict models of Hegel and Marx (Marx 1904; Dahrendorf 1964). The global effects of these models speak to their influence, and, while the change outcomes have not necessarily conformed to revolutionary visions, they nevertheless indicate that a systems perspective can provide a powerful set of guidelines for directed change.

One systems model that we believe has great potential for guiding applied change is sociocultural *adaptation*: changes made by a population in interaction with its environment which enhance its survival and continuation (Barger 1977, 1982). Adaptation is essentially an evolutionary concept, but one that emphasizes the processes involved in change rather than particular traits or directions. Adaptation is also a group process, since it is populations that evolve rather than individuals. Similar processes, however, do occur within an individual and at other levels of living systems (Miller 1978; Mazess 1975, 1978; Stini 1975). When applied to sociocultural systems, the focus can be on changes in a group's behavioral patterns, morphology, and/or environment, as long as these changes are initiated by cultural processes.

The concept of adaptation calls for empirical measures of the adaptive success of changes (Barger 1982; Alland and McCay 1973). Adaptation is relative, where a change is most adaptive when it fully maximizes group continuity and is most maladaptive when it results in a group's extinction. Intermediate criteria of adaptation, like population growth and health, have also been posed (Alland 1970; McElroy and Townsend 1979; Dubos 1965; Mazess 1975, 1978).

The Process of Adaptive Change

Adaptation is a dynamic *process*, a continual and evolutionary interaction between a population and its environment (Alland 1967, 1972, 1975; Alland and McCay 1973; Barger 1977, 1982; Parsons 1964; Mazess 1975; Dubos 1965; Moran 1979). This process involves two sets of factors, the internal resources of a group and the external challenges of its environment, which interact to direct changes during the time frame in which adaptation occurs.

1. A group's internal *potentials* for adaptation involve the collective functioning of its characteristics and members. The focus here is on the needs and resources a group brings to a particular change situation. Its traits and members must function together in a compatible manner in order for the group to maximize its potentials for adaptation.[1] A group's traits must enhance both its internal functioning and its collective functioning in relation to particular environmental challenges. Internal resources and needs, then, set the possible alternatives for adaptation.

When used to guide applied change, the adaptation concept calls for an estimate of group needs and resources in terms of change goals and methods. Such an assessment should ideally be conducted before initiation of changes, but it is equally important during the change process to evaluate how well the group's needs are being met and how effectively its resources have been mobilized.

2. A group's external *environmental challenges* direct the actual course of adaptation from among the different alternatives set by its internal potentials. Challenges include both limitations and opportunities. A limitation is a condition, imposed by the environmental setting, without which the group cannot survive. An opportunity is something that can enhance a group's survival, depending on its utilization. Thus a group's traits that meet particular *environmental challenges*, in addition to their *internal functioning*, increase its chances for survival and continuation. It should be stated here that "environment" includes not only physical and ecological conditions, but also a group's larger societal setting. This is particularly relevant with reference to minorities within a larger national society (Barger 1977, 1982; Barth 1956). The adaptation model calls for an evaluation of both limitations and opportunities in a group's social, economic, and political environment, given the goals of directed change.

3. The *interaction* of a group's potentials and its environmental challenges is at the core of the process of adaptation. The needs and resources that a group brings to a particular environmental setting must be considered in the context of the particular limitations and opportunities of that setting. Events at both the internal and external levels can affect events at the other level, and the optimal functioning of a group's traits at *both* levels is generally necessary for the group to maximize its chances for survival and continuation (Williams 1966; Stern 1970). In making adaptive changes, a group can modify its internal characteristics, its external conditions, or, as is usually the case, both.

The basic process of adaptation is thus a *synthesis*, or *reorganization*, of a group's traits and abilities to better meet environmental challenges. This reorganization is to better meet internal needs, to better utilize internal resources, and, in general, to enhance internal functioning, given the group's environmental limitations and opportunities. Synthesis can include development or adoption of new traits as well as the elimination of old ones. It should be noted that the process does not mandate that the same form be continued or that characteristics be indigenous.

Changes may be conscious and purposeful, at other times unconscious and even accidental. To be adaptive, however, changes must contribute to an overall optimal balance in a system where many internal traits and external challenges are interacting simultaneously. This balance is assessed in terms of the group's survival and continuation.

In applied change, it is important to examine the change *alternatives*, given the group's needs and resources and its environmental limitations and opportunities. In order to ensure that changes are as constructive as possible, an evaluation of how the internal and external factors are likely to interact and direct events should be done before interventions are implemented, as well as during the course of changes.

4. Another consideration in the process of adaptation is *time*. Since no system is in complete balance, some characteristics and members of a group are in conflict with others, and this incomplete homeostasis stimulates a continual process of reorganization (Parsons 1964; Marx 1904; Dahrendorf 1964). The adaptive balance of changes can therefore vary or even reverse over a period of time, and for this reason, it is important to clearly specify time frames involved in a particular case, especially where applied change is involved.

In summary, we believe a systems model of social adaptation offers the greatest potential for use in applied change. This model allows for a flexible focus on the level of analysis and time frames, so that a specific subsystem can be investigated for a specific time depending on the particular change issue being considered. It also provides a greater understanding of the change *process*, how related forces interact and direct events toward a particular outcome which can make an important difference in the effectiveness of applied change. Moreover, collaborative applied projects can foster both the practical application of concepts and the further refinement of theory based on actual experience. This mutual development of theory and practice is illustrated in an applied project in support of the farm labor movement in the Midwest.

THE FARM LABOR MOVEMENT IN THE MIDWEST

It is a paradox that the migrant and seasonal farmworkers whose labor helps feed America are themselves members of one of the most socioeconomically deprived groups in this country. The disadvantaged living and working conditions of farmworkers have been documented for generations (Burnaway 1976; Coles 1970; Coye 1985; Friedland 1969; Goldfarb 1982; Harper, Mills, and Parris 1974; McWilliams 1939; Moore 1965; Sosnick 1978; U.S. Senate Subcommittee on Migratory Labor 1970). These conditions include deforming labor, poverty-level wages, child labor, substandard housing and sanitary facilities, poor health, and constant exposure to dangerous pesticides. Despite such conditions, health care and other services are frequently unavailable or inaccessible, and farmworkers generally do not receive those fringe benefits, such as workers' compensation and medical insurance, that are taken for granted by other American workers.

The 65,000 farmworkers who each growing season enter the central Midwest states of Indiana, Ohio, and Michigan generally share these deprived conditions (Barger and Reza 1984a, 1984b; Carlson 1976; Indiana Advisory Committee 1974; Johnson 1976; Rubel 1966). Most are Mexican Americans, native or naturalized U.S. citizens, though some are in the country as legal immigrants. Most originate in the lower Rio Grande Valley in Texas, although in recent years some have moved their base to Florida where they can work citrus crops during the winter. In the Midwest, they work mostly with vegetable and fruit "table crops," such as tomatoes, cucumbers, cherries, and apples.

One of the greatest injustices suffered by farmworkers is denial of the opportunity to participate in decisions that affect their well-being, a consequence of the economic and political system in which they work (Burnaway 1976). Farmworkers are either specifically excluded from key labor laws, such as the National Labor Relations Act, or have legal standards reduced for them, as with many child labor laws (Craddock 1979; U.S. Senate Subcommittee on Migratory Labor 1970). The tomato industry in the Midwest is a good example of exclusion from participatory rights. This industry is dominated by large multinational corporations, whose policies and operations are based on annual production and profit goals. These corporations stipulate unilateral contracts with growers before the spring planting season, specifying such conditions as price structures, strains of tomatoes, and pesticide use. The growers receive comparatively high returns from tomatoes, though they are subject to weather and other risks. Growers in turn arrange with crewleaders (labor contractors) to recruit field workers, for which crewleaders receive returns usually based on the earnings of their workers. At the bottom of the system are the farmworkers, who perform the actual labor in producing the crop but who are subject to a host of decisions made at higher levels which affect their living and working conditions. They have had little opportunity for input into these decisions and, at best, can only react to them once they learn of impending or actual events.[2]

When the various alternatives for improving farmworkers' living and working conditions are considered, only the farm labor movement led by the United Farm Workers of America (UFW) in California has proven truly effective (Barger and Reza 1985b; Chavez 1976; Denny 1979; Friedland and Thomas 1974; Goldfarb 1982; Hoffman 1978; Jenkins 1985; Levy 1975; London and Anderson 1970; Majka 1981; Majka and Majka 1982; Rudd 1975; Sosnick 1978; Walsh and Craypo 1979). A typical social reform movement, the UFW has utilized nonviolent means like grassroots organizing, strikes, and marches to achieve strong internal support among farmworkers, who overwhelmingly support the UFW as the most viable alternative for improving their lives (Barger and Reza 1984a, 1984b, 1985b). The UFW has been successful in mobilizing considerable external support from church, labor, political, and civic groups; it has also organized widespread popular participation in UFW-sponsored boycotts (Barger and Haas 1983; Jenkins 1985; Jenkins and Perrow 1977; Majka and Majka 1982). This external support has counterbalanced the relative powerlessness of farmworkers in the face of the political and economic power of agribusinesses.

As a result of this combined internal and external support, the UFW has achieved greatly improved living and working conditions for farmworkers in the areas where it has been active, even for those farmworkers who are not members of the organization. For example, all farmworkers in California are now covered by the state's Agricultural Labor Relations Act. And farmworkers under UFW contracts no longer endure poverty, child labor, and exposure to dangerous pesticides. Instead, UFW workers receive such benefits as medical insurance and retirement pensions, and they have reported experiencing personal and social growth.

An allied reform movement, led by the Farm Labor Organizing Committee (FLOC), has sought to achieve improved rights and conditions for farmworkers in the Midwest (Barger and Reza 1984a, 1984b, 1985a; Valdes 1984). FLOC was founded in 1967 by Baldemar Velasquez and in 1979 was formally organized as a labor union of farmworkers working in the Midwest. One innovation of the FLOC movement was a call for three-way negotiated contracts, which would ensure that all major parties in the agricultural system (food processing corporations, farmers, and farmworkers) participate equally in making necessary decisions.[3]

After unsuccessful attempts to establish a dialogue with Campbell Soup Company, FLOC workers voted in 1978 to strike all Campbell's tomato field operations in northwestern Ohio. When strikebreakers were brought in and the corporation moved some of its operations elsewhere, FLOC called for public support in the form of a citizens' boycott of all Campbell Soup products. Like the UFW boycotts, the rationale behind this strategy was that a boycott is one of the few nonviolent means available to offset the relative powerlessness of farmworkers. FLOC reasoned that the widespread socioeconomic power of the public at large can effectively counterbalance the economic and political power of large agribusinesses. In 1983, FLOC began an extensive public information campaign to strengthen the boycott and to bring greater social pressure on Campbell Soup. In 1984, FLOC added another strategy to its efforts: a "corporate campaign" to gain support for its cause among Campbell Soup's stockholders and investors. In that same year, FLOC also began organizing pickle workers involved with the corporation's Vlasic pickle products.

In February 1986, after two years of on-and-off talks, FLOC, Campbell Soup, and Campbell's tomato and pickle growers in Ohio and Michigan signed a unique three-year labor contract (Cleveland Plain Dealer 1986, New York Times 1986, and Toledo Blade 1986).[4] The agreements included union recognition for about 800 farmworkers, wage rates of $4.50 an hour, major medical insurance, a paid Labor Day holiday, a 48-hour grievance resolution procedure, paid union representatives, and dues check-off added to regular wages. Compensation was also provided for those farmworkers who went on strike in 1978. Of historic importance were two unique features in these agreements. The first was a multilateral contract among all three of the major parties concerned. The second was the contractual establishment of the "Dunlop Commission," a private labor relations board composed of representatives of each of the three parties concerned, with the power to review, arbitrate, and, as necessary, resolve complaints. The Dunlop Commission provided a way to resolve the complex situation of farmworkers working across various states with different laws and agricultural structures. Baldemar Velasquez attributes these achievements primarily to the boycott and to the social pressure on Campbell Soup by church, labor, political, and citizen groups.

A number of citizen support groups were organized around the country to advocate for the farmworkers' cause and the Campbell Soup boycott, to raise money and goods for the striking farmworkers, and otherwise to work for FLOC's success (Barger and Reza 1985a). The Indianapolis Farm Worker Support Committee was one such volunteer group, founded in 1980 by teachers, clergy, former farmworkers, union members, lawyers, social workers, and other local people concerned with farm labor issues. In addition to public education activities, the committee was instrumental in enlisting the first statewide labor organization (the Indiana AFL-CIO) and the first statewide religious organization (the Indiana Council of Churches) in support of FLOC. It also worked with local schools to encourage support of Midwestern farmworkers by not participating in the Campbell's labels program—the focus of the community action project (Barger and Reza 1985a).

Farmworker Adaptation

When the farm labor movement in the Midwest is seen from the perspective of a systems view of adaptation, several major influences in change are evident. The adaptation model calls for examination of the internal needs and resources of the FLOC movement and how these interact with the larger socioeconomic system. Examining internal factors, Midwestern farmworkers aspire to the same rights and benefits as other American workers (Barger and Reza 1984a, 1984b). But being a disadvantaged minority they have not had sufficient resources to make meaningful socioeconomic changes, and their efforts have focused on achieving social solidarity and the formation of a farm labor organization. This internal means of adaptation has been effectively achieved, and recent research documents that farmworkers believe the most effective means for improving their conditions and rights is the farm labor movement led by FLOC and the UFW (Barger and Reza 1984a, 1984b, 1985b).

When external factors are considered, farmworkers have been constrained by their socioeconomic environment, particularly the structure of American agribusiness. This structure has benefited the large food processing corporations at the expense of farmworkers' conditions and rights. Midwestern farmworkers have lacked the resources to influence directly such multinational corporations as Campbell Soup.

But it must be remembered that agribusiness is only one factor in the farmworkers' social environment and that one alternative in adaptation is for a group to attempt to change its environment. FLOC sought to change its environment by obtaining support from other entities in the broader social arena within which farmworkers and agribusiness operate--consumers, churches, labor unions, political bodies, and local citizen support committees such as the Indianapolis Farm Worker Support Committee. In particular, FLOC sought their endorsement and, more important, their active boycotting of Campbell Soup products.

As group after group gave its support, the balance of power between Midwestern farmworkers and agribusiness steadily shifted in favor of the farmworkers. The interaction of internal and external forces is evident in this process, where limited internal resources have proven most effective in mobilizing external support. According to Baldemar Velasquez, the boycott was the primary force in achieving farmworkers' formal participation in the socioeconomic system that sets their conditions.

THE COMMUNITY ACTION PROJECT: PUBLIC SCHOOLS AND THE FARMWORKERS' BOYCOTT

Collaboration between FLOC and its local support groups was an important factor in achieving the farmworkers' goals. Two types of relationships were involved in the action project considered here. One was the relationship between FLOC and its local support groups. FLOC established general and specific goals, such as broadening the boycott and raising money to support striking farmworker. It then asked its supporters to help meet these goals. But support groups exercised considerable initiative in how they contributed to FLOC's efforts, drawing upon the strengths of their particular members, resources, and settings.

The other type of relationship was that between the authors. At the time of the project (1981-1982), Ernesto Reza was a FLOC staff member working with the boycott campaign and a doctoral student in organizational psychology at the University of Michigan. Ken Barger was an associate professor of anthropology at Indiana University at Indianapolis and coordinator of the Indianapolis Farm Worker Support Committee, a citizens' group involved in social action and advocacy on behalf of FLOC. We met in 1980 on a bus of FLOC farmworkers going to a UFW convention in Texas, and on that trip we actively discussed ways in which FLOC and academics could cooperate. Contributing to our relationship were the personal values and views we shared that led us both to become involved in the farm labor cause. We also shared common academic interests in applied change.[5]

The Labels Project

The community action project considered here was an effort to encourage local schools in Indianapolis to honor a farmworkers' boycott (Barger and Reza 1985a). This project was somewhat unusual in that the applied change focus was not on the particular social group of concern (Midwestern farmworkers), but rather on the larger socioeconomic environment in which that group exists. That is, our purpose was to make an impact on agribusiness to facilitate achievement of the farmworkers' goals. Applied work often focuses on initiating changes within a particular "target" group, usually in conjunction with social programs designed to serve such groups. In our case, the task was to facilitate external adaptation by organizing support in the larger social system to empower farmworkers in their relationship with agribusiness.

The labels project began in 1981 when Reza drew up a FLOC plan to generate support among school systems through the Campbell's labels program, which provides educational and athletic equipment to schools and churches in exchange for a designated number of labels from the company's products. Participating schools and churches obtain needed equipment, and Campbell Soup benefits from tax deductions, promotion of its products, and a positive public image. In Reza's plan, local support committees were asked to survey schools and determine how much awareness and support existed for the boycott. Barger organized the local effort in Indianapolis and, in coordination with Reza and FLOC, developed an intervention campaign based on the results of the survey. The Indianapolis committee thus supported the boycott by encouraging local public schools not to participate in the labels program.[6] The general method was to win over public support by informing people about the issues in a manner that was compatible with and relevant to those being addressed.

In the initial survey conducted in November 1981, 130 public and Catholic schools in the central city and suburban townships were contacted. This survey revealed that 33 (35%) of the schools were participating in the labels program. Support committee members who were involved in local schools as teachers and parents then got together and, in coordination with FLOC and Reza, discussed the survey findings, the school systems involved, and strategies for introducing the boycott issue.

An immediate task was to determine as realistically as possible *where* (structurally) in the school systems to focus efforts, given limited time and resources. The support committee decided to concentrate on the central city public schools because this was the largest school system and had the largest number of schools collecting labels (31). Thus, an impact here would have the broadest effect.

Drawing upon personal experience as teachers and parents, committee members felt that little cooperation was likely to be received from school boards, superintendents, or principals.[7] Parent groups, on the other hand, were considered an optimal level at which to focus efforts, since in most cases they were running the labels programs. Also, social dynamics in such volunteer groups predispose people to avoid issues of conflict, and this could work toward *non*participation in the labels program if they were informed about the issues in a compatible manner.[8] So it was decided to focus the labels project on the parent groups.

After coordinating with FLOC and Reza on the social unit to be addressed, the next task was to determine *how* to effectively stimulate change. The first challenge was to develop a conceptual explanation that would be most relevant for parents. After some discussion, it was apparent that *their* issue was not the farmworkers' cause, but whether or not to participate in the labels program in light of the farmworkers' cause. Given this, the support committee needed to emphasize those issues that were most compatible with their concerns. After assessing parents' views and values, five issues were identified.

1. Farmworkers are fellow Americans, who help produce our food but who experience deprived conditions in the process.
2. Child labor begins a disadvantaged life, to the distress of those parents who need their children's help in supporting the family at the expense of their education.
3. Farmworkers are a hard-working people, but they do not have the same basic rights as other American workers.
4. Farmworkers are seeking through negotiated contracts an equal voice in those conditions that affect their lives; but since Campbell Soup has refused to negotiate, they have had to turn to other Americans for support of a boycott to counterbalance their relative powerlessness in dealing with the giant corporation.
5. School parents have a unique opportunity to set a positive example of citizenship for their children by openly and responsibly examining the issues.

A conscious effort was made to be credible and reasonable in approaching the parents' groups. They were not asked to drop the labels program, but were rather presented with a positive request to openly discuss the issues, which were admittedly complex. The groups' right to participate in the labels program was recognized and respected, but they were asked to make an *informed* decision. They were even urged to write to Campbell Soup and to FLOC to learn both sides of the issue, and addresses and materials from both parties were provided for this purpose.[9]

After coordinating with FLOC and Reza on the conceptual approach, materials were drafted to present these points in a concise manner and "pretested" on parents and even on people who were unsympathetic to farm labor issues. A picture of migrant children working in the fields was included along with an offer to discuss the issues. The materials were then printed for free by a local labor union.

Having decided on the content of the appeal to the parent groups, the next challenge was how to reach them. It was felt that school officials would be reluctant to give materials to children to take home to their parents (as is done with the Campbell's labels promotion materials), so a multichannel approach was developed to reach parents by crosscutting different community settings. As an initial effort, a general letter with enclosed materials was sent to the parent groups of all schools as well as to principals, superintendents, and boards of every school district.[10]

The main effort focused on utilizing the internal communication channels of community-based organizations to reach parents. During the winter, local teachers' associations, interfaith church organizations, labor unions, and other community groups were approached and asked to help inform their members about the issues. Over 5,000 pieces of literature were distributed through these crosscutting channels. In addition, a supplementary effort was made to inform the community through press releases and appearances on radio and television talk shows concerned with religious and minority affairs. In several cases, support committee members who were teachers and former farmworkers spoke to parent groups. Reza and other FLOC staff were kept informed about these events, and their suggestions were incorporated into activities. On a couple of occasions, FLOC representatives came to Indianapolis to meet with local groups concerned about boycott issues.

In the spring of 1982, a followup survey of all 180 Indianapolis schools was conducted to evaluate the impact of the labels project. This second survey revealed that significant changes had occurred. In the central city schools, participation in the Campbell's labels program had decreased from 39 percent to 23 percent; that is, 43 percent of those schools collecting labels had dropped the program, a statistically significant change ($X^2 = 36$, $p = .0002$). Furthermore, awareness of the boycott had risen from 9 percent in the fall to 82 percent in the spring. Most important, 52 percent of those schools that had learned about the boycott issue had stopped collecting labels. The labels project had contributed to the desired social changes.

Informal feedback from parents and teachers also indicated that the boycott was a crucial factor in dropping the labels program, even where other issues (such as opposition to commercialization of school children) were involved. Also, public awareness of the farm labor cause increased substantially throughout the larger community, and a number of church and other groups took public stands endorsing the boycott.

An important impact was on Campbell Soup itself. The company's concern was evident when the executive responsible for addressing the farmworker issue wrote a local newspaper giving the company's views. He later came to Indianapolis to meet with an interfaith organization when it was considering endorsing the boycott. In public discussions, he admitted that the boycott had made the company more aware of farmworker conditions, and a local sales representative later informally said that sales in the central Indiana area were down because of the boycott.

Another impact could be seen on the farm labor movement. The labels project clearly increased FLOC's public and organizational support in the region, including formal endorsements of the boycott by community groups and new active members in the support committee. FLOC farmworkers have told us that the visible popular support for their cause gave them encouragement in their struggle. FLOC staff members also participated in an analysis of principles for use by other support committees. The labels project helped shift the balance of socioeconomic power between farmworkers and agribusiness in a direction more favorable to farmworkers.

Social Adaptation in Community Action

From a broader perspective, the Indianapolis schools constitute a subsystem of the larger society in which both Midwestern farmworkers and agribusiness are also subsystems. Where the Indianapolis schools are considered, an attempt was made to initiate internal changes from an external position. As a part of the larger community setting, the support committee sought to change schools' participation in the labels program. Evaluation of the internal structure of the school system indicated that the parents' groups were a crucial unit in terms of the change objectives.

The final level of a systems analysis, then, was the parent groups. An evaluation of their internal structure and norms suggested the messages that would be most effective, and an examination of their larger setting indicated the most effective means for reaching their membership.

A series of systems changes were thus initiated. The labels project made an impact in the parent groups; this in turn altered the schools' relationship with Campbell Soup, which took on the new function of serving as a social sanction against agribusiness where farmworkers were concerned. The ultimate change was a reorganization of the socioeconomic system that balanced the relationship between FLOC workers and agribusiness. It should be noted that the collaborative relationship between FLOC and the Indianapolis support committee was at the heart of these systems changes. FLOC and Reza generally set the change goals in terms of long-term, practical outcomes, and the support committee and Barger provided the local application, specific strategies, and time and energy to implement FLOC's goals. In the labels project, neither party could have succeeded without the other. FLOC did not have the internal resources to achieve the applied changes, and without FLOC's involvement the support committee's efforts would have been aimless and shortsighted. The ongoing coordination and complementary roles between the two parties ensured the greatest effect on the farmworkers' social adaptation.

APPLIED CHANGE AND SOCIAL ADAPTATION

Different theories of sociocultural change have been posed for over a century, but there is still a need for an empirically grounded and predictive model of change. The need for a valid and reliable theory is particularly critical where applied change is concerned. Those who try to initiate changes have an ethical, social, and professional responsibility to understand change itself. Since they are impacting on the lives and well-being of others, it is most important that they understand the *process* of change, how related forces interact and direct events toward a particular outcome, and the empirical testing of theory with practice. According to Thompson (1965:278):

> Success in the practice of applied anthropology involving predictive skills is measured in the long run by empirical test, not by consensus of professional colleagues, administrators' prejudices, political expediency, or any other nonscientific criterion. In turn, the empirical test may serve as a corrective to theory and a spur to greater refinement of method.

We believe that a systems perspective of sociocultural change has great potential for effectively developing and implementing applied change. The adaptation model calls for consideration of a group's internal potentials (needs and resources), its external challenges (limitations and opportunities), and how these two sets of forces interact over time. The potential of this model for understanding and directing change is illustrated in the Indianapolis community action project in support of the farm labor movement.

The adaptation model calls for a focus on the internal-external systems processes, and several levels of focus were involved with the labels project. The first level involved the FLOC movement as a part of a larger socioeconomic system. Where internal needs and resources are concerned, Midwestern farmworkers have aspired to the same rights and benefits as other American workers. But as a disadvantaged minority, they have not had sufficient internal resources to make meaningful changes. Their primary internal potentials have consisted of emerging social solidarity and the formation of a farm labor organization (Barger and Reza 1984a, 1984b, 1985b).

One alternative in adaptation is for a group to change its environment, and this is essentially what the FLOC movement has sought to do. Part of farmworkers' environment is the socioeconomic structure of American agribusiness, which has largely benefited the food processing corporations at the expense of farmworkers' conditions and rights. With insufficient resources to influence directly such multinational corporations as Campbell Soup, FLOC did have the ability to mobilize external support in other segments of society to counterbalance the farmworkers' lack of socioeconomic power.

In this light, a systems perspective leads to another level of focus, the larger societal environment of *both* FLOC and Campbell Soup that includes consumers, churches, labor unions, political bodies, and schools. FLOC has sought the endorsements of these groups and, more importantly, their active boycotting of Campbell Soup products. As group after group gave its support, the balance between Midwestern farmworkers and agribusiness steadily shifted in favor of the farmworkers.

When the Indianapolis labels project is considered, a series of subsystems were involved, including the parent groups, the local schools, agribusiness, and Midwestern farmworkers. And a series of changes occurred across these subsystems: from more informed parents to reduced school participation in the labels program to a greater sense of social responsibility on the part of Campbell Soup to, finally, the eventual active participation of farmworkers in socioeconomic decisions affecting their lives. With each subsystem, the basic process of change was resynthesis, or a reorganization of the interactive factors in the system. The end result brought reorganization of the larger socioeconomic system in a direction more favorable to farmworkers.

The ultimate change outcome, then, was the greater social adaptation of Midwestern farmworkers. The change model calls for a measure of adaptive success, which is ultimately the survival and continuation of the group. The 1986 labor contracts formally establish FLOC farmworkers as an equal party in the Midwestern agricultural system and as a continuing force in farmworker affairs. A more balanced relationship between FLOC workers and agribusiness, in terms of socioeconomic power, has thus ensured the continuation of the farm labor movement as an effective means for improving farmworkers' living and working conditions.

Throughout the adaptive process, the collaborative relationship between FLOC and its local supporters helped direct the course of change. FLOC could set the change goals, but its internal resources consisted primarily of solidarity and a deep and lasting commitment to justice. It did not have sufficient resources to bring about changes in the larger socioeconomic system. However, FLOC was able to mobilize considerable external support, and so its efforts were supplemented by the resources, time, energy, and networks of local supporters. On the other hand, the reason for the existence of groups such as the Indianapolis support committee was the presence of FLOC, and local efforts were guided by FLOC's goals. The labels project could not have succeeded in the absence of either party. The ongoing coordination and complementary roles between FLOC and the local committee made an impact upon the larger socioeconomic system. Together, these organizations were able to maximize the success of the labels project and enhance the ultimate social adaptation of Midwestern farmworkers.

In summary, we have argued that an adaptive systems model has the greatest potential for understanding change, and that in turn such a conceptual framework offers the best guidelines for applied change. One of the best means for developing a grounded theory of sociocultural change is collaboration between social scientists and groups attempting to alter their life conditions. This method serves both to test and refine concepts in actual life events and to ensure that the applied changes will be as constructive as possible.

ACKNOWLEDGMENTS

This project was conducted from October 1981 through April 1982. We wish to thank Ann Barger, Rena Dunn, Melinda Paniagua Riddle, Karen Smith, Errol Stevens, and other members of the Indianapolis Farm Worker Support Committee, whose efforts made the project possible and who contributed to its success. Our gratitude also extends to the church organizations and labor unions who supported the project and the parents and teachers in the Indianapolis local schools who were responsive to the social issue of farmworker justice when it was raised. Finally, we would like to express our appreciation to the FLOC leaders and farmworkers, whose dedication and sacrifices inspired the project and who have taught us a deeper meaning of "applied" regarding changes in people's lives.

NOTES

1. Characteristics can include both morphological traits, such as physical endurance and neurological development, and behavioral traits, such as values and social norms. The characteristics of individuals taken together constitute the group's collective resources for adaptation. Some traits might provide only a limited resource, while others might provide a range of responses for adaptation.

    Internal characteristics can range from *fixed* to highly *plastic*. A fixed trait is one that has few alternatives for expression. Such traits cannot be modified to any degree by environmental influences and so are more "innate." A plastic trait is one that has many alternatives for expression. The more plastic a trait, the more it can be modified by environmental influences. From fixed to highly plastic, the collective characteristics of a group's membership determine its adaptive potentials.

2. We have heard people say that if conditions are so bad why don't farmworkers find other kinds of jobs, and indeed this is the premise of some government service programs for farmworkers. But this presumes that a variety of desirable jobs are available in the national economy, when even a "normal" unemployment rate is over 6 percent of the work force. This perspective also ignores the fact that farm labor is essential in agricultural production of many foods, so when one person does leave farmwork another steps in to take his place. Thus deprived conditions persist for decade after decade, regardless of who performs the actual labor. Also, many farmworkers have told us that they really prefer their occupation. Not only have they developed the necessary job and life skills for this kind of work, but many enjoy working outdoors, having their families together, and other aspects of farmwork. The main challenge, then, is how to make farmwork an occupation with acceptable conditions for those people whose labor produces food for other Americans, rather than to cycle people through an occupation that inherently involves deprived conditions.

3. FLOC initially focused its attention on local growers, since they were directly involved with farmworkers. But after winning contracts, FLCC discovered that large canning corporations set conditions for the farmers that in turn affected farmworkers. In fact, both FLOC and the UFW have been careful to distinguish between individual family farmers and the economically large and politically influential agribusinesses. They see family farmers as also jeopardized by the structure of the agricultural system dominated by the large agribusinesses.

4. Two sets of contracts were involved in this settlement. One was a contract between FLOC, Campbell Soup, and the Michigan Vlasic Pickle Growers Association. The other involved individual contracts between FLOC, Campbell Soup, and 16 Ohio tomato growers supplying Campbell Soup. The agreements also set up committees to study and recommend improvements on pesticides, housing, health care and safety, daycare programs, and, for the pickle operations, share-cropping arrangements.

5. Our relationship has continued beyond this particular project to further applied research for FLOC and the UFW among Midwestern and California farmworkers.

6. A year and a half earlier, the committee had worked with local Catholic schools and found that once people became informed they readily sympathized with the farmworkers' cause and did not participate in the labels program. The hierarchy of the Archdiocese school system was sympathetic to the issue and encouraged their schools to evaluate the collection of Campbell's labels in light of the boycott issues. As a result of these and subsequent efforts all the Catholic schools stopped participating in the labels program.

7. School systems are hierarchial in their organizations, and the attitudes of administrators can greatly influence events. When the Catholic schools had been approached the year before, sympathetic administrators actively encouraged schools to examine the issues. However, public schools are more political in nature, and administrators tend to be cautious about social issues. This produces a tendency towards inertia, if not opposition, in addressing new issues.

8. In deciding to focus on the parent groups, several crucial points were considered. If parents decided not to collect labels, the program could not be conducted, and school administrators simply could not oppose or reverse the parents' decision. The internal structure of parent groups also presented several opportunities. These are

volunteer groups: leadership is largely self-selective and decisions tend to be made on a consensus basis. Since such groups have to maintain internal cohesion, norms emphasize cooperation and avoidance of conflict. These norms initially work against the raising of issues, particularly where the group is already involved in an activity, such as collecting labels. But if several members raise the issue together in a compatible manner, then these same norms foster taking the course of least resistance, in this case, not becoming involved in a controversial activity and *non*participation in the labels program.

9. We recognized that parent groups would decide their actions for themselves and that the support committee's most effective role was one of raising the issues, calling upon the parents to become informed, and appealing to predominant social norms like fair play and democracy.

10. Materials were sent to school officials primarily to maintain openness and credibility, since a response from the hierarchy of the public schools was not really expected. No responses were received.

4

Linguistics in Action: The Hualapai Bilingual/Bicultural Education Program

Lucille J. Watahomigie and
Akira Y. Yamamoto

INTRODUCTION

In the usual approach to the study of American Indian languages, anthropological linguists obtain their data directly from native speakers of the languages involved. Such research may take either the form of "linguistics-on-the-spot," in which the linguist works in the community where the language is actually used, or "linguistics-at-a-distance," where speakers of the language under study are imported to an academic setting (Voegelin and Voegelin 1972). In either case, the linguist generally remains monolingual in English, while the native speakers become bilingual in their native language and English. The native language is documented and reconstructed, but it is not "revitalized."

This chapter describes the development of the Hualapai Bilingual/Bicultural Education Program (HBBEP). In this program, the goal of the linguist/anthropologist is to become bilingual and bicultural, while the native professionals may or may not become bilingual. Bilingualism/biculturalism is viewed as part of a process in which the linguist/anthropologist learns to become useful to the local community and is invited to develop linguistically and culturally relevant programs with native professionals.

HBBEP began in 1975 as an effort to document the Hualapai language and culture. At that time there were virtually no written materials in Hualapai. Once the language was transcribed, the program began producing bilingual/bicultural materials suitable for use in native education programs. In less than 10 years, this program developed into an Indian Bilingual National Demonstration Program with over 30 major publications.

The program has proved unusual in several respects. Early on, traditional linguistic investigation developed into an education program that eventually became an integral part of the public school system. This program has grown continuously both in scale and content during a time when bilingual programs on the whole have faced gradual reduction in federal funding. It has become a place to train academic professionals to work with native educators to assume varied roles as language specialists, curriculum designers, and materials developers. It has also provided native speakers and school personnel with continuous training in bilingual/bicultural education. The linguistic work began as an association between a linguist and a native Hualapai speaker. During a decade of association and a number of projects, this relationship has developed into a fully collaborative effort in which university-based linguists and native professionals work together on all aspects of program development, curriculum, and evaluation. It has been a long, slow process, but we have been rewarded by the establishment of trust, friendship, and most importantly, a feeling of professionalism that allows each and every member of the team to contribute to shared goals.

APPLIED LINGUISTICS AND CULTURAL MAINTENANCE

Applied linguistics for the purpose of cultural maintenance stems from several sets of related theoretical assumptions:
1. Individual identity is confirmed by sharing cultural and linguistic elements. Disconfirmation of these elements through time, either through negation or prejudice, has negative psychological consequences which may include depression, substance abuse, violence, and poor educational and job performance. Enhancement of these elements may result in more positive learning and a reduction in individually harmful behaviors and beliefs.
2. Minority ethnic programs frequently have inadequate internal resources with which to mobilize more effective interactions with their larger socioeconomic and political environment. Strengthening of cultural and linguistic traditions provides one mechanism around which members of such groups can organize to address environmental restraints such as lack of access to economic resources.
3. Cultural diversity is adaptive. The preservation and/or revitalization of cultural elements add to the store of cultural alternatives available for use, improving the

overall viability of human populations in relation to their social and physical environments.

Kenneth Hale (1972:384-385) points out that the anthropological linguist "depends upon native speakers of the language he studies. The study of American Indian languages is primarily in the hands of non-Indians," and while "there is nothing wrong with studying the language and culture of a community other than one's own: it is essential that the people who inhabit this planet come to know one another intimately, and the study of languages and cultures has an obvious central role to play in achieving this goal." Anthropologists and anthropological linguists "are often motivated by this consideration, as well as by a deep respect for, and abiding loyalty to, the people whose languages and cultures they study." What needs to be addressed, however, is the gap between the ideal of the anthropological linguist and the reality of the situation. Hale (1972:388) concludes that:

> ...the future of such fields as American Indian and Australian Aboriginal linguistics will depend critically upon the extent to which they come to be in the hands of scholars who are native speakers of the languages involved. I do not mean to imply that linguists should cease work on languages other than their own--I tend to agree with those who say that there are certain real advantages to being a detached observer. But a native speaker's control of linguistic data is critical..., and it seems to me essential to the future of the field that the state of affairs represented by present-day American Indian and Australian Aboriginal linguistics be reversed.

It is vitally important that anthropologists and anthropological linguists undertake the responsibility of training native researchers and work with them to develop collaborative language and cultural revitalization and/or maintenance programs. The Hualapai Bilingual/Bicultural Education Program pioneered this approach. The model that has emerged over the last decade promises to serve as an exemplar both for native communities and anthropological linguistics.[1]

THE HUALAPAI INDIANS

The Hualapai Indians, together with the Havasupai and the Yavapai, form the Upland language group of the Pai branch of the Yuman language family. For well over a millennium, the Hualapai and Havasupai, often referred to as the Northeastern Pai, inhabited northwest central Arizona at the western edge of the Colorado Plateau. Their lifestyle was classified as the "basin-plateau" type: they hunted wild game and gathered seeds, roots, berries, nuts, and fruits, while cultivating gardens with relatively scant water resources. They apparently had close contacts with the Puebloan peoples, especially the Hopi, and the Mojave, trading peacefully for manufactured goods and garden produce. Their relationship with the Yavapai to the south remained hostile, however.

In the 1820s Anglo fur trappers and prospectors entered the Northeastern Pai territory. Initially these intruders were few in number, and they were either ignored or attacked by the Indians. Beginning in the late 1840s, however, white miners and settlers began to stream into Hualapai territory. Hualapais and Havasupais began working in the mines and soon became a reliable, cheap source of labor. By 1869 conflicts between Hualapais and whites had destroyed the traditional Hualapai way of life. In 1874 the Office of Indian Affairs removed the Hualapai to the Colorado River Indian Reservation, far to the south of their aboriginal territory. Two years later they were allowed to return to their homeland. White cattlemen opposed the Hualapai's return, but mine owners supported the move since the Indians were their only source of dependable labor. On January 4, 1883, by a decree of President Chester A. Arthur, their present reservation was established--some 997,045 acres of deep canyons and high plateaus (Dobyns and Euler 1976; Spicer 1962).

The Hualapai people voted to organize the tribe under the Indian Reorganization Act of 1934 and, in 1938, a constitution and bylaws were adopted. The tribal membership was established, an elective nine-member council was created, and the Peach Springs settlement was designated the tribal capital (Manners 1974; Weaver 1974).

Currently the Hualapai Tribe occupies 991,680 acres of range and forest land in northwestern Arizona. Their territory ranges from 2,000 to 7,000 feet in elevation and from densely wooded to barren desert areas; rainfall varies from 5 to 15 inches per year.

The tribal headquarters of Peach Springs lies along the main line of the Santa Fe Railroad and U.S. Highway 66, about 120 miles northwest of Flagstaff and 50 miles northeast of Kingman. Peach Springs has one public school (grades K-8), a post office, a small general store, two gas stations (one is open only "on call"), the tribal office complex, and an Indian Health Service clinic. On both sides of the Santa Fe Railroad tracks lay clusters of homes--modern houses, built in the last decade with funds from the Department of Housing and Urban Development, interspersed with a few one- or two-room huts.

In 1983, the Bureau of Indian Affairs (BIA) estimated the reservation population to be 946. The population is young and rapidly growing--only 4 percent of those who live on the reservation are over 65 years of age, while 48 percent are under the age of 16. Only 28 percent of the labor force has been able to find work on the reservation, and their jobs are primarily with the tribe and the federal government. The Peach Springs School has always been a source of jobs for tribal members, but its importance as an employer has increased significantly since the inception of the bilingual/bicultural program, currently one of the major sources of work in the community.

PEACH SPRINGS SCHOOL

Peach Springs School (Peach Springs School District Number 8) is the only educational institution on or within 40 miles of the Hualapai Reservation. Established in the mid-1950s, it has 10 classrooms, an arts and crafts center, a library, a computer center with 20 microcomputers (in addition to three microcomputers in each classroom), two special-use classrooms, a science and home economics building, and an office complex which includes the headquarters of the Hualapai Bilingual/Bicultural Education Program. There are 12 certified teachers and 7 instructional assistants, supervised by a principal/superintendent and an assistant principal/bilingual education program director. Three members of the certified staff and five of the instructional assistants are Hualapai.

In 1983 there were 159 pupils enrolled in the school, of whom 152 were Hualapais. Enrollment has stabilized at about 175 for the last three years. Preschool children attend the Hualapai Early Learning Program and Hualapai Headstart, staffed by seven noncertified teachers and six teacher's aides, all Hualapais. There are about 60 children in these programs, ranging from infants to four-year-olds.

ESTABLISHMENT OF THE HUALAPAI
BILINGUAL/BICULTURAL EDUCATION PROGRAM

During the summer of 1972, while working on his dissertation on language use in a community in Japan, Akira Yamamoto participated in the Indiana University Summer Field Station in Flagstaff, Arizona, headed by the late C.F. Voegelin. During a weekend seminar, Voegelin suggested that Yamamoto study Hualapai. At that time, Hualapai was the only Upland Yuman language not actively under study by Voegelin's students. At the close of the summer, with Voegelin's encouragement, Yamamoto contacted linguists who had studied Hualapai or related languages.

In June 1973, with the help of these linguists and the Hualapai Tribal Council, Yamamoto visited Jane Honga and Maude Sinyella--potential teachers of Hualapai. He explained that he wanted not only to learn their language but also to record it so that their children and grandchildren might become literate in Hualapai. In so doing, Yamamoto expressed his desire to make a contribution to Hualapai history and identity and his willingness to enter into a dialogue with members of the tribe toward that end. Jane Honga was most enthusiastic about the idea; she proved a superb teacher and an advocate of community involvement in education. With his other teacher, the late Maude Sinyella, the work of recording the language and presenting it in an easily readable form began.

From the outset, Mrs. Honga and Yamamoto worked together as a team--Honga functioned as a language resource person and evaluator of Yamamoto's work. Together the two went throughout the community visiting people. This approach gave them several advantages. Honga not only enjoyed working for her people even when there was no financial reward, but she was also recognized and respected as a superb educator and social worker. As a result, whatever this team produced became a model to be followed by others. She could convince almost anyone of the need for such linguistic maintenance and recruited many people to assist the project.

At the beginning of the summer of 1974, Mrs. Honga organized a session with the elders of the community to discuss their ambivalent and sometimes suspicious feelings toward Yamamoto. The meeting lasted several hours as the elders aired their feelings. Some believed that linguists were "making a bundle" by publishing materials obtained from the Hualapai. From their point of view, anyone who wanted to "work with" Indians had some hidden motivation. This initial meeting with tribal elders was necessary to allow Honga and Yamamoto to continue their work. Yamamoto had to be completely frank to convince them of his sincerity. The elders who were skeptical remained so, but there was no further objection to Yamamoto remaining on the reservation or returning in the future.

In 1974, the first year of their collaboration, Mrs. Honga and Yamamoto prepared the first orthography of the Hualapai language and two reading texts with accompanying tape recordings. The products were distributed to the tribal council, the school, and persons who had assisted them. The orthography was published in the newsletter issued by the tribal council.

Fortunately, Mrs. Honga's son-in-law, Earl Havatone, a Hualapai educator, replaced the non-Indian principal of the school in 1974. When Mrs. Honga introduced Yamamoto to him, his children were already using the orthography and reading the storybooks that Mrs. Honga and Yamamoto had prepared. Mr. Havatone's excitement with the Hualapai written language spread among key individuals in the community. Earlier, he had completed the groundwork for a Title VII (bilingual education) proposal and launched a strong community-based education campaign.

The following year, Havatone's proposal for the Title VII program was funded, and Lucille Watahomigie, a Hualapai with a master's degree in education from the University of Arizona, was hired to direct the program. Watahomigie was named director for several reasons: she was the only Hualapai with an advanced degree; she had extensive teaching experience in elementary education and with minority students at the University of Arizona; she had previously taught at the Peach Springs School; and she was from a respected family in the community. Together Havatone and Watahomigie formulated the Hualapai Bilingual/Bicultural Education Program.

During this formative period, Yamamoto worked indirectly with Havatone and Watahomigie through Mrs. Honga. In the summer of 1975 Yamamoto and Watahomigie met briefly to discuss possible future contributions that each might make to the development of HBBEP. This was an informal interview in which Watahomigie and her staff wanted to see if Yamamoto would talk "linguistics" and if he would want them to work as his "informants"; Yamamoto, on the other hand, wanted to find out if he could be incorporated into HBBEP as a partner. The meeting resulted in an agreement to work together.

In 1976, Havatone resigned his post and subsequently became chairman of the Hualapai Tribal Council (1977-1979). Since 1976, a non-Indian has served as principal/ superintendent of the school district, continuing the educational philosophy of Havatone and Watahomigie. The new principal appointed Watahomigie assistant principal; she continues to serve as director of the Hualapai Bilingual/Bicultural Education Program as well.

DEVELOPMENT OF THE HUALAPAI BILINGUAL/BICULTURAL EDUCATION PROGRAM

In 1976, when HBBEP had been in operation for a year, the attitudes of the children and their parents toward bilingual/bicultural education were surveyed. The results showed that parents and children were overwhelmingly in favor of the program. In the same year, 143 Hualapai pupils were tested using SEARCH, a language dominance test for Hualapai and English developed by Dr. Gena Harvey of Northern Arizona University.

These data allowed us to formulate both long-range program plans and specific course designs. For example, half the student population (48.9 percent) spoke Hualapai as their first language, so teaching "Hualapai as a second language" was not appropriate. On the other hand, 45 percent of the student population spoke English as their dominant language, and the question of teaching English as a Second Language (ESL) had to be considered. The data also indicated that there was a group of students (6.3 percent) who spoke English as their mother tongue and had no command of Hualapai. Although the number was small, we could not bypass these students if the educational policy was to be one of bilingualism and biculturalism. These questions, dealing with a population with complex linguistic backgrounds, are crucial to any language teaching program, yet they surface clearly only with data such as those derived from a home language survey and language proficiency tests. In order to deal with such diverse and complex language situations at Peach Springs School, extensive in-service training has been provided to the instructional staff, both certified and noncertified teachers and instructional assistants.

Administrators have also made serious attempts to involve the community in school affairs. A parent advisory committee was established in 1975 and meets regularly. Approximately 120 parent visitations to classes take place annually. HBBEP staff has provided special activities to encourage parent involvement, such as Indian dances, hand games, footraces, arts and crafts displays, parades, and theatrical performances. Approximately 75 percent of the parents have participated in these events.

Several linguists have studied Hualapai and others have worked on related dialects in neighboring areas. These linguists have engaged in basic research from which they hoped to reap traditional academic benefits--dissertations, academic publications, and the like. In the course of their studies, some have approached HBBEP to cultivate their potential role as linguists. Essentially, they proposed a "trade-off": the linguists would do something for HBBEP (e.g., provide data) if the program in turn would do something for them (e.g., find informants, lodging, or other facilities).

In some cases, friction developed between linguists and the Hualapais because of conflicting needs and expectations. For example, the program developed its writing system based on the principle of one phoneme-one symbol, which was more convenient for teachers and students. The system is essentially phonemic-based and, therefore, will not distinguish subtle allophonic differences. The linguists wanted to use their own transcriptions for all data they were collecting, including those to be donated to the program. This meant that program staff had to convert the linguistic transcriptions into their own writing symbols--they simply did not have the necessary time and energy. As a result, valuable data were left untouched.

From the outset of Yamamoto's involvement with the Hualapai people, several factors helped develop a successful collaboration in action linguistics. First, the Hualapai research was not his dissertation; thus, he was not subject to the theoretical and temporal pressures that generally attend such research. Second, he was an educator with research interests, not a researcher with an interest in education. His major concern was educating himself and others. Third, his first encounter with the Hualapai was with a group of people interested in education: the late Jane Honga, an educator and social worker in the Hualapai community; her son, Earl Havatone, principal of the Peach Springs School; and Lucille Watahomigie, an educator and enthusiastic advocate of native education. Watahomigie shared Yamamoto's basic philosophy of education. These initial encounters reinforced Yamamoto's belief that he could play an important role as a coeducator in the Hualapai community. Finally, he met Margaret Langdon and Leanne Hinton, linguists of Yuman languages who have been strong supporters of linguistic education for Indian people. They have consistently encouraged his efforts.

Reconfirming their commitment to education, Watahomigie and Yamamoto set the goals for his work: (1) he would work directly with the Hualapai people; (2) the most crucial component of his efforts would be to train native linguists/ ethnographers; and (3) when native speakers become skilled in linguistic research, he would gradually change his position from *the* linguistic specialist to *a* member of the Hualapai language research team. His long-range goal was to help the Hualapai develop and implement *their own* research and educational program for their native language.

Once these goals were established, they had to be communicated to the Hualapai people. Watahomigie and Yamamoto approached the tribal council, the school principal, and the community (especially the elders). Communicating these goals was a tedious process. People were skeptical that a linguist would do so much work without any obvious personal reward. Many were suspicious of Yamamoto's motivations since they differed from those of the academicians who had previously come to the reservation to "study" the language. Through Mrs. Honga's efforts in 1974, many of the elders accepted Yamamoto as a member of HBBEP and allowed him to record the language for the program. But it was the school administrators and the HBBEP staff who needed to know Yamamoto better. It took almost four years (1975-1978) before they would fully accept him as a member of their team. It was not so much a matter of persuading them that he could be useful, but of demonstrating that he would produce materials that were immediately useful and applicable for the teaching of language in the classroom.

Yamamoto conducted sessions in which he instructed the HBBEP staff in linguistic and ethnographic field methods. During this "probationary" period, Yamamoto, Watahomigie, and her staff often worked after-hours and on weekends. For such overtime, Yamamoto provided the staff with some financial compensation. He could do so because Watahomigie arranged free lodging and the staff often provided him with meals. These savings in turn became a source of compensation for the staff.

In spite of modest financial resources Watahomigie and Yamamoto remained committed to the project, and they managed to find the financial resources and time to work together. This may be one of the most significant factors in the project's success. For action-oriented work, obtaining funds from traditional sources is difficult unless proposals emphasize the scholarly contributions of the research (cf. Schlesier 1974).

In 1980, however, Yamamoto received grants from the American Philosophical Society Phillips Fund and the National Endowment for the Humanities. Supported by these grants, the HBBEP staff and Yamamoto spent the summer cleaning up fieldnotes from previous years, organizing their linguistic data, and writing up their work. The effort resulted in the *Hualapai Reference Grammar* (Watahomigie, Bender, and Yamamoto 1982). The following year, Yamamoto received support from the University of Kansas General Research Fund to prepare a second volume of the grammar. Thanks to these awards, he did not need to ask the Hualapai for financial assistance; instead he could provide modest financial support for the team.

This last point is crucial. If academic linguists or anthropologists wish to engage in action work, they need some outside funding to support their activities, and they should develop a separate area of academic publications. They cannot, and at least initially should not, rely on action work for their publications for two reasons. First, the goal of this approach for both the local and the academic professionals is to train each other to become a team that will eventually produce publishable materials *together*. Second, the process of cultivating mutual trust is a slow one, and the linguist/anthropologist may be delayed in publishing the results of his work.

Once HBBEP was running smoothly, Watahomigie insisted on paying for Yamamoto's services. This was a natural outgrowth of mutual trust. It renewed the linguist's conviction that when one shows a genuine interest in the life and future of a people, rewarding feedback, financial or otherwise, will eventually follow. These payments have been converted to a Hualapai research fund from which Yamamoto compensates the HBBEP staff for extra efforts.

As stated above, during and after the "probationary" period, the HBBEP staff and Yamamoto held formal and informal sessions over a wide range of topics from phonetics to syntax to Hualapai orthography to story telling.[2] In 1978, while such training sessions were being carried out, Watahomigie, the Yuman linguist Leanne Hinton, and the late John Rouillard, then chairman of the Department of Native American Studies at San Diego State University, submitted a proposal to the National Endowment for the Humanities to conduct an intensive summer linguistic institute for native teachers of Yuman languages. The proposal was funded for three years, and the 1978 institute was held at San Diego State University. Since 1979, in addition to the NEH grant, the Office of Bilingual Education, Minority Language Affairs and Title VII have provided funds to continue the American Indian Languages Development Institute (AILDI).

AILDI has been instrumental in the development of the HBBEP staff and the community resource people. These institutes have been organized and coordinated by Watahomigie (curriculum coordinator), Yamamoto (linguistics coordinator), Dr. Ofelia Zepeda (Papago) of the University of Arizona, and most recently by Dr. Teresa McCarty of the Arizona State Department of Education.

Linguistic instruction at the institute is structured to meet the needs of students at different levels. First-year students are introduced to linguistics by emphasizing the relationship of sounds to writing symbols for various tribal languages and the comparative study of English and the students, native languages. Second-year students study morphology and syntax, while third-year students focus on sociolinguistics and creative writing in their respective languages. All students are involved in developing techniques for assessing native language proficiency and tribal language policies.

Courses in curriculum development are divided into three levels. First-year students learn the basics of curriculum development by writing unit and lesson plans. Development of curriculum plans is based on linguistic classes and is integrated into the school program. Second-year students develop units and lesson plans as well as a framework for curriculum content and skills development. Third-year students, in addition to curriculum framework development, work on community projects such as dictionaries, readers, and instructional guides. All students are involved in micro teaching sessions that help them implement and integrate linguistic and cultural content into teaching activities. They are also taught to cultivate their confidence as language and culture teachers.

In addition to the institutes, during July 1986 Watahomigie and Yamamoto taught two courses through Northern Arizona University to 12 teachers and instructional aides at Peach Springs School. Watahomigie's course, "Principles of Indian Curriculum Development," emphasized design and development of curriculum units and accompanying lesson plans. Yamamoto's course, "Principles of English Linguistics," covered the structure of English and teaching English as a Second Language.

As a result of such formal and informal linguistic sessions, since 1978 Watahomigie, her assistants (Malinda Powskey, Jorigine Bender, Josie Uqualla), and Yamamoto have begun participating in professional linguistic meetings. They have presented coauthored papers, opening the opportunity for native linguists without higher degrees to participate professionally in academic activities. Such efforts have been supported and encouraged by most capable Yuman linguists (Margaret Langdon, Leanne Hinton, and Pamela Munro, among others). This last point is another significant factor in the success of HBBEP. The cooperation of professional linguists cannot be overemphasized for the successful planning, implementation, and evaluation of any bilingual/bicultural education project.

SUCCESS OF THE HUALAPAI BILINGUAL/BICULTURAL EDUCATION PROGRAM

The success of HBBEP may be measured in several ways: by higher achievement scores of school children in statewide tests, increased involvement of parents and community members in school activities, and effective incorporation of new educational technologies (e.g., microcomputers) in learning and teaching processes. In the following sections, we discuss some of the major factors that have contributed to HBBEP's success.

Role of the Native Leader

It is imperative that a bilingual program cultivates the community environment: the linguist cannot, and indeed should not, do all the work. Community members must be trained to participate as partners, not merely as "informants," and eventually assume the major role in the project themselves. If the linguist does all the work for the people, his departure from the community may spell the end of the project. For this reason, in any successful action work the most important factor is the role of key individuals in the community--in this instance the director of HBBEP, Lucille Watahomigie, was centrally involved.
1. If there occurred any conflict or problem within the program or between the linguistic team and the community, Watahomigie resolved it before it became serious. After the unfortunate death of Mrs. Jane Honga in 1976, Watahomigie, who became a member of the tribal council in 1978, became a major force in advancing the education of the Hualapai people and in encouraging close ties between the school and the community. From the onset, community involvement was sought through the tribal council, the parent advisory committee, and individual contacts.
2. The director has been successful in recruiting future native linguists/educators and has continuously provided them with in-service training. Tribal elders are systematically invited to school as resource persons to work directly with children or the HBBEP staff; parents are invited to classes to observe their children and participate in classroom activities; and the staff makes periodic visits to parents to show them what their children are reading and

writing in Hualapai. Through these activities, eager members of the community are identified and invited to further participate in various training sessions.

3. The director has been successful in obtaining federal funds to continue and expand the program. Such funds enable the program to hire community people, thus providing one of the few employment opportunities on the reservation.

4. The director has eagerly recruited outside linguists and education specialists to assist the program. She has been an advocate of action linguistics and, at the same time, aggressive in utilizing those professionals who are willing to work *for* the program.

5. Finally, she has taken the initiative in sending her staff and parents to linguistic institutes and nearby colleges to obtain teacher certification.

Lucille Watahomigie's enthusiasm and diligent efforts have brought her both local and national recognition.

Community Development

Since the establishment of HBBEP in 1975, the program has proven instrumental in bringing all segments of the community together with outside professionals to work toward a common goal. Through continued interaction with the teachers, the program staff has become involved in the general education processes of the school. Consequently, noncertified staff started enrolling in teacher certification programs at various colleges and universities. This means that within a few years there will be certified Hualapai teachers to actively continue bilingual/bicultural education even when federal funding is no longer available.

The parent advisory committee was established in 1975, and it remains an important component of the program. HBBEP not only permits, but requires, an active involvement of parents in the educational process. Parent participation in school activities has changed from uncooperativeness or indifference to passive interest to an enthusiastic involvement in policy making and bilingual/bicultural teacher-training sessions.

The program has maintained its close ties with the reservation community, both on the individual level and on the level of local government. In our view, this is of extreme importance. Munson (1983:2) warns of problems that local professionals may encounter as a direct result of contact with outside academics:

> We of the western world speak of "self-determination" in regards to native peoples. We

laude demonstrations of what *we* consider to be manifestations of this attitude and strive to create environments in which it can further develop. We willingly allow ourselves to function as vehicles for ideas and influences which we consider to be beneficial in this change process, which will result in "self-determination" on the part of the native groups with which we associate. We need, however, to recognize both the ethnocentric origins and focus of our ideas and actions as well as the fact that there is conflict in all cases of social change. We must anticipate this conflict because our actions frequently place our associates in untenable positions vis-a-vis their own communities.

HBBEP has eliminated such potential isolation by maintenance of close ties with the community. On the individual level, program staff has recruited elders for classroom activities and materials-development projects. On the group level, program staff has consulted with the tribal council and other organizations, requesting their assistance in materials-development projects, recruitment of community resource persons, preparation of grant proposals, and dissemination of program information and materials. As a result, the community has been provided with meaningful opportunities for direct involvement in the educational process.

Other Factors Facilitating Program Success

HBBEP has been very successful in producing published materials, ranging from primers to how-to texts, from essays on historical events to contemporary practices in cattle ranching to basket weaving, from scientific books on ethnobotany and geography to collections of legends and stories, from Hualapai translations of English accounts of historical events to creative writing. American Indian Languages Development Institutes and subsequent follow-up training sessions on language analysis and general linguistics have enabled the staff to transcribe oral literature, engage in creative writing, edit students' work and their own writing, and produce a new genre of literature in Hualapai and English.

All bilingual programs must be able to assess children's language proficiency in both the native language and English. HBBEP has adapted two existing language assessment instruments to meet the needs of the program. The first, the Hualapai Oral Language Test (HOLT), assesses the students' language proficiency. HOLT is important for improving program planning and teaching strategies and meeting the children's needs for language development. It consists of five categories, each designed to measure Hualapai language ability in the areas of (1) oral language comprehension, (2) vocabulary comprehension and production, (3) understanding of grammatical rules, (4) questioning skills, and (5) communication skills. In this set of tests, only responses in Hualapai are recorded; those in English are noted for reference. HOLT is administered at the end of each school year. To maintain consistency, the tests are administered by Hualapai language instructors. Each score is recorded and used to measure gain or loss from one year to the next. The HOLT test scores for the past three years correlate positively with other test results.

The second instrument, the Language Assessment Scale (LAS), is used to identify limited or non-English-speaking children. It evaluates oral English language proficiency and contains sections on sound discrimination, lexical comprehension, sentence comprehension, and story retelling. LAS is administered individually once a year to all students, and each score is recorded and measured for gain or loss from year to year.

In addition to these two instruments, the Comprehensive Test of Basic Skills (CTBS), is given to identify Hualapai student proficiency levels in comparison to national norms. A comparison of test scores from 1975, when the program began, and 1978 shows a marked improvement in students' academic performance.

Table 4.1
Comprehensive Test of Basic Skills Scores of Students at the Peach Springs School Compared with the National Average, 1975-1978

Grade	Grade Equivalent 1975		Grade Equivalent 1978		Deficiency Score	
	Hualapai	National	Hualapai	National	1975	1978
2	1.7	2.9	2.1	2.9	-1.2	-0.8
3	2.3	3.9	3.0	3.9	-1.6	-0.9
4	3.1	4.9	3.6	4.9	-1.8	-1.3
5	3.7	5.9	3.5	5.9	-2.2	-2.4
6	4.0	6.9	4.8	6.9	-2.9	-2.1
7	4.2	7.9	7.8	7.9	-3.6	-0.1
8	4.9	8.9	6.7	8.9	-4.0	-2.2

The following is a summary of comparative data for three current project years, reporting normal curve equivalent scores. The California Achievement Test was administered for the first time in April 1982. The previous year's test results form the baseline. Only students with pre- and posttest results are included here.

Table 4.2
California Achievement Test Scores for
Peach Springs School, Grades 2-8, 1982-1984

	Normal Curve Equivalent Mean Gain/Loss on A Scale of 100	
Test Date	Reading	Language
4/82 N=86	- .67	- .20
4/83 N=91	+3.11	+10.10
4/84 N=116	+1.62	+ 6.80

The results indicate a slight loss on the reading and language subtests of April 1982, probably due to the use of new tests. Results of April 1983 and April 1984, however, show significant gain on both subtests.

Tests and survey results point to HBBEP's effectiveness and the positive cumulative effects of participation in the program. These findings suggest that as staff members become better trained through capacity-building activities, they will become better able to serve students.

The success of this curricular approach is reflected in the repeated positive responses of parents, community members, classroom teachers, students, and outside professionals. In 1981 and 1983, the Arizona Department of Education conducted a formal Program Quality Review Inventory and reported that HBBEP was one of the most innovative programs they had observed. Special commendation was made for the program's scope and the design of the Hualapai curriculum and materials-development component.

The program deals directly with the need for students to develop English language proficiency while participating fully in their own language and culture. The program provides a learning environment that is familiar, relevant, and supportive. As a result, the curriculum developed by the program staff has greatly increased students' motivation and interest in learning. Through ongoing training activities, the program develops the capacity of local people to meet students' special needs. In particular, program success has been facilitated by:

1. Long-term support from the school board and school administration.
2. Commitment to development and training in bilingual and bicultural education, not only for staff members but also for the community. Involving parents, elders, and others in training sessions has served to increase their feeling that the program "belongs" to them. Bilingual aides see a future with the school because the skills they acquire are applicable in the local context. Consequently, instructional staff turnover rates tend to be relatively low--less that 20 percent annually--resulting in continuous and consistent instruction for students. In general, students who exit the program after the eighth grade have received comprehensive and uninterrupted instruction in an organized curricular sequence.
3. Commitment to quality materials development.
4. Commitment to effective instructional methods through training workshops for staff and parents, especially in the areas of teaching English as a Second Language and language assessment.
5. Frequent and thorough evaluations of the program. Baseline data are collected on all students in language and academic areas; English and Hualapai language assessments are conducted yearly; all instructors maintain individualized performance records; posttesting determines achievement of objectives; and an external evaluator periodically monitors program development, management, and attainment of project goals.

CONCLUSIONS

The past decade of collaboration between Yamamoto and the Hualapai offers several important lessons. Chief among these is that the action linguist must adopt long-range plans for involvement with the host community. Such an approach raises several issues:

1. The action linguist must first enter the community as a specialist who knows the dos and don'ts in the study of language. He must, however, approach the people with the conviction that he will eventually bow out as the specialist in that language in that community. One goal, in other words, should be to train community members to be native linguists and researchers. The training period may be long, and it requires patience and talent on the part of both the

linguist and the trainees. One problem rests in how to recruit native speakers *who will continue* to work on the project. Recruitment calls for cooperation of the community, the tribal government, and the school personnel with the professional linguist. Continuity requires funding for those who undertake linguistic training as well as ongoing opportunities to work on the language. National Multifunctional Bilingual Centers, in particular, provide funds for consultants with special skills in curricular development, planning bilingual education programs, organizing workshops for teachers, and writing grant proposals. Thus, the action linguist may not be the only one who works with the team. Whenever a chance arises, he must encourage recruitment of other specialists--the project is not the action linguist's exclusive "property."

The problem here is that the philosophy and conviction of the linguist may not be shared by other professionals. He may have established a smooth working relationship with the community and planned long-range activities. The local people, however, may find that some other individuals can do the same work, and eventually these others may be invited to complete the work. On his return to the community, he may find that many of the activities he planned with the rest of the team have already been carried out--his feeling of "being needed" diminishes. Although his long-range goal was to work himself out of a job, it still has a demoralizing effect. The action linguist must remind himself that such developments are a consequence of the process he is trying to foster--self-determination, not only in language but in decision making as well.

2. As an important part of the training process, the linguist must encourage trainees to become professionals who can eventually participate in academic dialogue by attending professional meetings and publishing in academic journals. One of the ways to achieve this is for the linguist to write papers *with* them. It is easier for the linguist to write academic papers *on their behalf*, but he must keep in mind that he is not helping them by doing so. Such an approach defeats the purpose of his involvement as an action linguist. When the people involved in writing these papers can genuinely claim them as their own, the action linguist has succeeded.

3. Another important aspect in this process is the linguistic fieldwork method. Although trainees are the native speakers of that language, they must seek as many and as varied speakers as they can--it is especially important to encourage older speakers to become involved in language maintenance efforts. When those involved in the project

succeed in recruiting their elders as resource persons, the future of the project is bright. If, on the other hand, they begin to claim that they are the language specialists, the project is doomed.

As an action linguist, then, it seems most important to be willing to be *invisible*, to be able to convince other professionals of the importance of action work, and to share linguistic knowledge and talents. In order to do this, the linguist must become familiar with the work of colleagues. He must also have a means of survival that does not rely solely on the project or community resources. To be able to survive independently of the action work may be a key factor, at least initially, in providing the freedom that in turn promises objectivity and wholehearted involvement. If he is hired to work for the community (i.e., is paid to do the work that the community has designed), he may be constrained in his research design, procedure, and results. In other words, he may be obliged to report only those results that will please the community. For these reasons, the approach that HBBEP has chosen seems to work: initially Yamamoto obtained funds that allowed him to travel to the community and live there for varying periods of time. Over the past several years, he has continued to live and work in the community on an intermittent yet regular basis. Meanwhile, whatever work he does is as a member of a team.

Not every linguist is willing to do such work. Some may want to engage in an action project, but their personality may not be suitable. Some may be constrained by academic demands (publish or perish), others may find that their host communities are not receptive to action work (see Stull, Schultz, and Cadue in this volume). They must, as professional linguists in academic settings, give their students humanistic and interdisciplinary training if those students are to engage in fieldwork in local communities rather than in linguistics-at-a-distance. In some cases, this may mean bearing an extra burden in addition to that of providing traditional linguistic training. When he takes an interdisciplinary posture, the anthropologist/linguist cannot continue the idea that he alone can do everything (Cochrane 1976:3). This kind of training must instruct students to be "humble." Rider (1976:72-73) writes of his experience:

> I was an applied anthropologist working in an educational setting. I was doing much more than applying an anthropological perspective.... An anthropologist, I was taught, doesn't play politics; he or she usually observes them being

played. In administration this could lead to a very high mortality rate.... My anthropological training had improperly prepared me for the role I was playing, and this did curtail my usefulness to the bureaucracy.... My point of view was not as objective as it should have been. Nowhere in my training,...has anyone been able to convince me that there is only one right way or best way either "anthropological" or "educational" to accomplish a task.

I experienced conflict between educational and anthropological values....Training in anthropology teaches you that there are many sets of values and beliefs, but not that one set is better than another, just more or less appropriate given the total cultural context. An educationalist must inculcate specific values. Can anthropologists even be teachers? This is the kind of human problem that interdisciplinary work presents.

Over a decade of involvement in HBBEP, we have learned how important it is for the anthropologist/linguist who wants to be useful and effective to his host community to have skills and knowledge beyond his own discipline. Furthermore, we learned from each other the educational process; we learned the hows of curriculum development and lesson planning; and, more importantly, we learned the necessity of making and implementing decisions, even if the team did not always agree (see Watahomigie, Bender, and Yamamoto [1981] for a more detailed discussion on this point). Finally, program staff have learned much from the linguist--ethnographic methods and the skills necessary to the study of language. As long as we *share* the feeling that we are pooling our knowledge, skills, and resources, and continuing to learn from one another, our collaboration will continue.

In this chapter, we have described the importance of teamwork between local and academic professionals in building and maintaining a successful community-based bilingual/bicultural education project. Such programs require that local professionals provide academic professionals with continuous training so they may become integrated into the local community, while academic professionals commit themselves to educating local professionals in research techniques. Such a mutual educational process results in solid teamwork, leading to a successful program. We believe that the kind of teamwork embodied in HBBEP is the best way to implement an enduring and successful program. We offer it as a model to be considered by local and academic professionals elsewhere.[3]

ACKNOWLEDGMENTS

We are deeply indebted to Donald D. Stull and Jean J. Schensul who have spent numerous hours reading our manuscript in its many stages, providing critical comments and suggestions.

NOTES

1. In 1983, Yamamoto and Watahomigie organized a session entitled "Doing Research in Indian Communities" at the 11th International Congress of Anthropological and Ethnological Sciences at Vancouver, British Columbia. In 1986 at the annual meeting of the Society for Applied Anthropology, William Leap organized a similar session. As far as we know, these are the first signs of academic interest in collaborative linguistic work with American Indian people.

2. The staff continues to meet twice a week for language study. Participants in these training sessions receive college credits, and topics include Hualapai language structure, sociolinguistics, historical linguistics, and ethnography of communication. For application of such linguistic training, Hualapai texts (stories, legends, autobiographic and ethnographic texts) are prepared and presented for their study.

3. In April of 1985, we visited the Oklahoma Kickapoo Bilingual/Bicultural Education Program upon the request of its director, Shirley Brown. We laid out to her and her staff the teamwork approach we had developed among the Hualapai. Since then, we have helped to implement several projects. The effectiveness of our model with a new group is as yet unknown, but at this stage each member of the team has established her or his respect for each other and affirmed what each does best. The team includes two former and one current student of Yamamoto's, and both Watahomigie and Yamamoto have worked closely with the program.

5

Collaborative Educational Ethnography: Problems and Profits

Margaret A. Gibson

"We need studies of where the kids are going and how well the schools are preparing them for jobs, not just more studies of our culture." So said one of a group of Punjabi Sikh community leaders in 1979 when I discussed with them the possibility of launching a research project designed to improve educational opportunities for Punjabi children in their town. The local school district already had suggested such a study. The group agreed that if a study were to take place it ought to have community involvement. The community thus helped define a project and expressed a desire to collaborate in its implementation. From the inception of the Punjabi Education Project in "Valleyside," California, the Punjabi community not only participated, but made possible a substantial measure of success for the project.[1] Collaboration, however, also brought pitfalls.

Collaboration between anthropologists and those affected directly by ethnographic research has been advocated by researchers, change agents, and funding agencies as an effective means of generating better research and better change strategies (Cazden 1983; Erickson 1979; Hymes 1980a, 1980b; Schensul and Borrero 1982). Less evident in the literature are accounts that detail difficulties and merits of the collaborative process.[2] Yet, as Rosalie Wax's (1971) "Warnings and Advice" makes clear, it is useful to know what problems a researcher encounters, their impact on the research, and how they might have been avoided.

This chapter describes collaborative research involving a South Asian immigrant community, a local educational agency, a community-based organization, and an educational anthropologist. It starts with an overview of the project's history and a synopsis of research results as a context for the ensuing discussion of problems and profits of collaborative ethnographic research. The chapter concludes with some thoughts on the process of influencing educational change through collaborative research and a summary of "lessons learned."

EVOLUTION OF THE PROJECT

The community that hosted the research is a prosperous agricultural town in California's Central Valley. The town and surrounding county have experienced a rapid influx of population in recent years, including a substantial number of Asian Indians. Between 1965 and 1980 the number of Indians residing in the area increased more than tenfold, to approximately 6,000. The large majority are Jat Sikhs from the state of Punjab in northwest India. A few Hindu and Moslem families also have settled in the area. They, too, are Punjabis; Punjabi is their mother tongue, Punjab their homeland.

At the time of fieldwork (1980-1982) Punjabi children made up 13 percent of the student population attending schools in the Valleyside Unified School District.[3] The rate of increase during the 1970s exceeded 1 percent of the total student population per year.[4]

The impetus for the project was the school district's need for information about the Punjabi community and the problems faced by Punjabi youngsters attending Valleyside schools. Minimum competency tests, first administered by the district in 1978 and required for high school graduation, indicated a serious disparity between the academic achievement of Punjabis, as a group, and other students, including the Mexican American minority and the white majority. The latter group I call "Valleysiders." More than twice as many Valleysiders as Punjabis were "passing" the competency tests as junior high students (see Table 5.1).

District officials and Punjabi community leaders also were deeply concerned by mounting tensions between Valleysiders and Punjabis, in school settings and in the community. "There has been some really nasty backlash against the 'East Indians' in recent months," one school administrator reported during the project's planning stage: "Nasty poems circulating about them, people refusing to sit next to them." Another expressed concern that a "full-blown race riot" might occur if the situation continued to fester. A Sikh community leader noted that "the sense of hate is growing." Partial explanation, he believed, stemmed from the fact that "whites don't understand Punjabi culture." A widespread, negative reaction among Valleysiders to the district's newly implemented Punjabi-English bilingual education program was symptomatic of the larger issues.

TABLE 5.1
Competency Test Results: Students Whose First Scores Were Above Passing, By Ethnic Group, With National Comparison

Passing (Scaled Scores)	Samples of Students in Grades 7-8			
	National Sample of 8th Graders % Above	Valleysiders (N=88) % Above	Mexican Americans (N=92) % Above	Punjabis (N=126) % Above
Reading=135	71.0	76.7	52.2	34.1
Writing=130	76.0	73.9	56.6	32.5
Math=155	39.0	40.9	21.7	10.3

Both basic and applied research concerns stimulated my interest in the Punjabi Education Project. Social scientists working in the field of minority education have devoted comparatively little attention to immigrant groups, yet such research is needed to solve problems faced in school by immigrants and to advance theories of why minority students perform as they do. Previous studies have suggested that many of the difficulties encountered by immigrants in school are largely temporary in nature and that immigrant students can be predicted to do well in school once initial barriers are overcome (Blakely 1983; Gibson 1976, 1983b; Ogbu 1978, 1983). All preliminary data from Valleyside suggested that Punjabi immigrants were encountering serious difficulties in school, academic as well as social. I wanted to investigate the nature of the barriers encountered, to learn which students were affected by them, and to determine how the problems might be eliminated or reduced.

Valleyside's Punjabi population had come to my attention while I was working at a federally funded Bilingual Education Service Center. Some community members and teachers had suggested to center staff that the Valleyside School District was not moving as expeditiously as it might to address problems faced by Punjabi immigrants. The center, in accordance with its mission, offered to provide technical assistance and in-service training for teachers. District administrators, unsure of the specific nature of the problems and increasingly concerned by the polarization of the community over bilingual education, were reluctant to accept outside assistance.

The center's ability to respond to the needs of the district and community was questionable without first conducting research on the local situation. Accordingly, I proposed a research project on the cultural backgrounds of the major ethnic groups served by the district. Although school officials endorsed the study, the project was not funded.

Over the following year conditions worsened. Increasing numbers of Valleysider parents transferred their children to private elementary schools. Some white parents, I was told, did not want their children attending school with Punjabis or taught by Punjabi teachers. At Valleyside High, the one high school in the district, ethnic tensions appeared to be mounting.

During this period the school district became embroiled in an Office for Civil Rights (OCR) suit related to the Punjabi-English bilingual education program. The suit was instituted by an irate Valleysider parent who opposed bilingual education. The parent's major concern was that the bilingual curriculum, as it was then constituted, disrupted regular classes, causing educational loss for majority-group students, including his daughters. "The wants of the Punjabi minority have come first," Mr. Smith charged, "and the whole student body is being allowed to suffer to take care of a few." As he saw it, school policy was a clear example of reverse discrimination. He rallied support from other concerned Valleysider parents and launched a "Committee for the Protection of Standard Education." When he demanded explanation from Valleyside administrators, they cited laws and regulations requiring special services for language minority students. Mr. Smith then took his case to state and federal officials, arguing against bilingual education, but, to gain a full hearing, also suggesting that the district was out of compliance with government regulations.

The case, which dragged on for two years, brought increased attention to the needs of the Punjabi population. The district's negotiated plan with OCR called for more Punjabi teachers, more hours of ESL (English as a Second Language), and, at the elementary level, expanded instruction in Punjabi. Ironically, a case brought by an opponent of bilingual education and special services for language minority children resulted in the federal government requiring more services for these students, including instruction in the Punjabi language.

Within this climate of increasing tension and continuing influx of Punjabi immigrants, the school superintendent encouraged me to redesign and resubmit the home-school-community linkages research proposal. Key school officials pledged district assistance in the project's implementation. "You have my complete support and cooperation for such a study as well as the unlimited support of my school staff," the high school principal wrote in a letter of endorsement. This support proved essential to the project's ultimate success. A two-year grant from the National Institute of Education was received in April 1980. The Punjabi Education Project was officially launched that August. "Nothing like this has ever happened to our community," one Punjabi educator remarked upon learning of the award.

We decided to focus attention on the high school in Valleyside because it was representative of the larger community. We also wanted to investigate what students expected to do following high school and their views on the relationship between schooling and adult success. Educational opportunity and school success, of course, can be measured, described, and interpreted in a variety of ways. Our approach combined qualitative and quantitative measures and attempted to set a comprehensive picture of school performance within a larger sociocultural context.

Research samples included all 44 Punjabi students enrolled as seniors in September 1980 and an equal number of Valleysider seniors, selected by random sample. Interviews with these students, their parents, and more than 75 teachers and administrators form the heart of the project's data base. Members of the research team also were able to participate in and to observe school and community affairs over a two-year period. In addition, we collected student and teacher questionnaires, student themes, and school performance data, the latter for over 600 students—Punjabi, Valleysider, and Mexican American—in grades 9 through 12.

A primary project objective was to provide district personnel with detailed information on the school experiences and performance of Punjabi youngsters, including analysis of educational problems. Although we recognized that scholarly description alone would not bring about educational improvement (see Hymes 1972), we considered such description a necessary base upon which to plan for change. The study was not formulated as a change effort. It may be characterized more appropriately as a basic research project designed to generate locally useful information while addressing issues of wider concern.

Theoretical interests shaped the project from its inception. The major research question addressed by the study was: Why are some minority groups, or subgroups, more hampered than others by cultural discontinuities and by social and structural barriers embedded within school and society? The project provided an opportunity to explore in-depth the nature of the barriers faced in school by one group of immigrants, their perceptions of these barriers, and their strategies for dealing with them. It also allowed a chance to evaluate the relative merits, first, of the "cultural continuities/discontinuities" explanation for school performance (see, for example, Cazden 1982; Erickson 1984; Erickson and Mohatt 1982; Gibson 1982; Ogbu 1982; Philips 1972) and, second, of the "success theory" explanation, which focuses attention on a group's beliefs about the value of formal education (see Ogbu 1974, 1978, 1985).[5]

SUMMARY OF RESULTS

The project revealed sharply different patterns of school performance for those Punjabi students who entered American schools by first or second grade and those who came to the United States after fourth grade without prior experience in English-medium schools.[6] Over half of the 232 Punjabi students attending Valleyside High in 1980 had arrived in this country within the previous five years. Only 30 percent had entered American schools before third grade. Only 12 percent were second generation. It was the newer arrivals, for the most part, who had had difficulty passing the competency tests. The large majority of those who had failed as junior high students were limited- and non-English-speakers. As their English skills improved, so did their test scores.

Punjabi students raised in the United States had far less difficulty in school than new arrivals and many did comparatively well in high school. American-educated Punjabi girls, for example, took as many college preparatory classes in math, science, and English as their Valleysider classmates, male or female. The boys, on average, took even more.

We also found that Punjabi students spent more time on homework, missed fewer classes, and the boys received significantly higher grades than Valleysider peers. The girls' grades were similar to those of "mainstream" classmates. Moreover, no matter how recently arrived, almost all Punjabi students fulfilled Valleyside High graduation requirements and received their diplomas. Three-quarters continued directly to college, generally the local community college.

At school, Punjabi students relied on strategies similar to those pursued by their parents in farming--hard work, initiative, respect for authority, and a sense that they must make the most of their opportunities, in spite of difficulties. Parents impressed upon children from an early age the importance of individual effort. When a child did poorly in school, parents usually blamed the child. "It is not the fault of the school. What can they do?" one father commented. Punjabis believe that those who wish to learn will learn. They are not naive about the problems their children face. They simply brook no excuses for poor performance.[7]

Parents stressed that an American education and American credentials would open doors to employment, doors which, for the most part, had been closed to the parents. "We have to waste our life in the fields," parents explained. An American education, they believed, would enable their children to "work easily on their own" and "better their life." Valleyside educators commended Punjabi young people for their "sense of purpose" and "direction."

School success for all too many Punjabi students, however, was more apparent than real. Although armed with a high school diploma, large numbers of Punjabi students-- particularly newer arrivals--finished school with only a mediocre education. Almost 90 percent of those who emigrated from India after fourth grade continued to be weak in English through high school. Following school policy, students weak in English met math, science, and English graduation requirements through special ESL classes in which the instructional level and content was, at best, equivalent to that of the upper elementary grades. (Punjabi students themselves reported that high school ESL classes were "too easy"; several said they were less demanding than English classes in India.) For some limited-English-speakers, as many as one-third of all high school credits came from ESL classes, the remainder from a combination of general education and vocational classes. Some Punjabi students and their families were unaware that high marks received in ESL must be interpreted differently from marks received in more advanced academic and vocational courses. Others realized they would graduate from 12th grade without proper preparation for college. English-language competency seemed to divide Punjabi students into two widely disparate groups, one doing somewhat better than the majority norm, and the other doing much worse. Among fluent-English-speaking

Punjabi students over half took *at least* six "college preparatory" classes in English, science, and math—roughly two years in each. The large majority of limited-English-speakers graduated with no high school level instruction in any of these subjects. Many of the latter were passed "up and out" as part of a remedial track. Armed with good grades and a high school diploma, they proceeded to junior college, where much the same pattern repeated itself.

The instructional program at Valleyside High was designed to permit limited- and non-English-speaking students to complete high school in the same number of semesters as their American age-mates. A consequence of this policy was that many Punjabi students, especially those whose schooling began in India, entered the job market without competitive skills. The project also revealed a need for change in many other aspects of the ESL program, from placement, testing, and counseling to teacher training, materials, and curriculum design.

Punjabi students were handicapped also by the nature of minority-majority social relations on campus. All Punjabi students, including those born and educated in Valleyside, were troubled by a climate of prejudice that permeated their high school experience. Limited-English-speakers, particularly recent arrivals, were reluctant to speak in class or to practice English with non-Punjabi classmates for fear of ridicule. Many students felt constantly on guard and uncomfortable when mixing socially with Valleysiders. Name calling, food throwing, and pushing in line were recurrent annoyances. More serious but less frequent incidents cited by Punjabi seniors included Valleysiders sticking them with hat pins and spitting on them. Boys who wore their hair long and in turbans, in keeping with religious convictions, were teased continually. Several reported having their turbans snatched away, a serious offense in the eyes of the Sikh community. A far graver offense occurred shortly after fieldwork began when a Punjabi girl's long braids were set on fire as she walked to class.

Part of the problem stemmed from the prevalent Valleysider view of American culture. By perceiving their own way of life as "the American way," Valleysiders assumed a superior status, in what has been described as a standard practice among Americans (Royce 1982:3-4). Members of the majority group assign the *national* identity to themselves and an *ethnic* identity to culturally distinctive minority groups.

Punjabis see the process of Americanization quite differently. Most Punjabi youngsters not only wanted to learn English but were very attracted to many aspects of the mainstream culture. They were adapting and would have adapted all the more readily had their identity not been challenged in the process. From their perspective, Punjabi students were prevented from mixing freely and easily outside their group because many Valleysiders made them feel unwelcome and uncomfortable. As Punjabis saw it, prejudice was a *primary cause* of their social separation and a major barrier to their acquisition of English.

In addition to the analysis of barriers impeding educational opportunities for Punjabi youths, the project addressed specifically the mediocre academic performance of many mainstream youngsters.[8] Valleysider students manifested apathy by absenteeism, discipline problems, and an overall lack of serious academic effort. Teacher expectations, particularly for slow-track students, were low. Many students, including those in the top half of the senior class, readily admitted that classwork and homework took second place to extracurricular activities, part-time jobs, and teenage social activities.

One Valleysider senior expressed regret that his parents had not insisted on a more serious orientation toward academic work. "You gotta build a study habit before you start [high school], about seventh or eighth grade." This young man frequently cut class. "I go fishing a lot," he explained. He also cut to avoid tests. "I will go the next day and study that night.... Like we have [senior] follies now...and it was 12 o'clock when I got home last night." He said his mother was understanding and wrote an excuse.

In describing himself and his relationship with his parents the student noted that he had worked after school and in the summer since eighth grade. "I can do things on my own. I go out hunting by myself and I am pretty responsible, so [my parents] look at that.... They know it. They trust me." This emphasis on preparation for life on one's own was a prevalent theme in Valleysider interviews. When Valleysider youngsters found it difficult to divide their time between schoolwork and other activities, schoolwork frequently gave way.

THE PROCESS OF COLLABORATIVE RESEARCH

The project was collaborative in the dictionary sense of people working together in a scientific undertaking. It involved an educational anthropologist working with school and community people for the common purpose of improving educational opportunities for young people in the community hosting the research. It also involved collaboration with two institutions—a school district and a community-based organization—and collaboration among a team of researchers. The project included "some degree of mutual sharing of control," characteristic of the exchange model advocated by Hessler, New, and May (1979:337), although not all collaborators shared equal power or control.

Others use the terms "cooperative" (Hymes 1980a), "interactive" (Light and Kleiber 1981), and "participatory" (Herda and Malloy 1982) to describe research conducted jointly with those being studied. Common to all is the aim of making the research more responsive to local needs and interests, as well as to the needs and interests of researchers and the agencies funding research. The present case offers opportunity to explore varying degrees and types of collaboration, together with analysis of the advantages and disadvantages of the particular approach followed.

Local Participation

The Valleyside Punjabi community had been the subject of a number of other studies, including several dealing with education (see Khush 1965; La Brack 1980; Ramakrishna 1979; Shankar 1971; Wenzel 1966). None of these studies, however, focused on the sociocultural context of education and its effect upon students' responses to, and success in, school. The earlier studies, moreover, were viewed by members of the Punjabi community as rather worthless. "People get their degrees, but what do we get?" observed one man who had facilitated the work of several researchers.

Through our collaborative approach, we hoped to make our work more responsive to our host community. The research team included two Punjabi Sikhs--one senior, one junior. Local Punjabi educators assisted with many aspects of the project, from initial design through report presentation. Punjabi community leaders pledged support to the project and devoted formal and informal meeting time to discussion of its progress. The Sikh Temple of Valleyside, the largest of three *gurdwaras* in the area, formally endorsed the project and facilitated the researchers in various ways. Withdrawal of that support would have imperiled the project.

During the project's planning stage, one influential Punjabi pointedly inquired, "Why study us? The problem is the whites. They have the power and they don't have to change. We need studies of them by us." These concerns were reflected in the project design. We agreed that equal attention should be focused on Valleysiders. Previous studies in Valleyside had failed to attend to minority-majority relations or to examine the nature of conflict between the two cultural systems. We believed, moreover, that a comparative approach would contribute to our understanding of the Punjabi case.

The mode of local participation in the research varied according to individuals' areas of expertise and resources. Students, parents, and teachers contributed their insights through formal and informal interviews and responses to questionnaires. We took care to explain the study in order to maximize interest and cooperation. Visits with parents and students early in the fieldwork enabled us to benefit from their perspectives before setting our interview schedules in final form.

Selecting our sample of families for intensive interviewing and eliciting their cooperation presented some difficulties. Many hours were devoted to locating families and to explaining how and why they had been chosen. Migrant Education staff introduced us to Punjabi families with children in their final year at Valleyside High, and the high school faculty helped us contact the Valleysider families in our sample. The value of the project seemed apparent to most. Every Punjabi family, and all but three Valleysider families, agreed to having their children in the study and to being interviewed themselves. Although time consuming, development of cooperative relationships with parents was effort well spent.

The parent interviews proved to be the richest fruit of our collaborative endeavors. Transcribed verbatim, they became the heart of the project's data base. They lent themselves to a number of important intra- and intergroup comparisons, for example, oldtimers and new arrivals, rich and poor, male and female students, good students and those with problems.

Although the initial cooperation of the Punjabi parents was obtained easily, interviewing them proved more difficult than interviewing Valleysiders. Unlike the majority community, Valleyside's Punjabi community is close-knit. Almost all families in our sample were known to Punjabi Migrant Education staff members who made initial home visits with us. Most Punjabis, furthermore, saw immediate value in the project's stated objectives. However, Punjabi parents found the semistructured format of our interview schedule unfamiliar and awkward. Most participated fully in the interviews, but many had difficulty seeing the relevance of some questions; others worried about the correctness of their answers. In some cases the tape recorder was turned off to allow parents to discuss question and response with the interviewer. In a few cases, in accordance with parents' wishes, we relied only on notes made during and following the interviews.

The Valleysider sample had a different character. It proved difficult to find high school faculty or staff who knew the families even casually. In quite a few cases we made the initial contact by phone, followed by a home visit. A second major problem was our inability to clarify the potential value of the study for Valleysider youths. It was, after all, the Punjabi Education Project, and our letterhead bore the title of the Indo-American Education Association collaborating in the research. Our raison d'etre at the local level, according to our handouts, was the improvement of educational opportunities for Punjabi young people.

Home visits with Valleysider parents, together with initial interviews with Valleysider teachers, caused us to broaden our research objectives. Like Mr. Smith and other members of his Committee for the Protection of Standard Education, some of the Valleysiders whom we approached were less than sympathetic to yet another project designed to help minority children. What about their own children, they inquired, many of whom had also experienced academic and social problems at school? Where was the reciprocity? Why wasn't a federally funded project, using their tax dollars, aimed at improving schooling for majority as well as minority students?

Many Valleysiders recognized that it was in the larger community's interest to help relieve problems arising from the rapid influx of Asian immigrants. But how would this project do so, they asked? In retrospect, it is apparent that our research objectives and project title needed to embrace *all* segments of the Valleyside community. As fieldwork moved forward, we became more explicit about our concern for the educational needs of all students. Since interview schedules reflected broader concerns, Valleysider interest in the project heightened as the study progressed. Many Valleysider parents found our questions a welcome occasion to share views on community relations as well as on education. The typical parent interview continued for two to three hours. By asking questions of research team members, some Valleysiders also found opportunity to learn about the Punjabi community in their midst. Valleysider interviews thus took on an unexpected educational function.

The Research Team

Team research need not be collaborative in the sense of researchers themselves being representatives of the community studied. In the present case, however, the presence of a Punjabi coinvestigator proved critical to the project's success. The coinvestigator previously had approached the Bilingual Education Service Center where I worked to request assistance in addressing the educational problems of Punjabi immigrants. When I sought his counsel regarding this project, he expressed his desire to be involved directly and fully, not as a consultant, but as a research partner. Given his background in educational research and evaluation, his experience in working with teenagers in multiethnic settings, and his deep commitment to promoting Punjabi interests, he was a logical choice.

The coinvestigator, a *kesadhari* ("long-haired" or "bearded") Sikh of considerable status, and an imposing and dignified figure in tie and turban, took the lead in gaining support for the project among Sikh community leaders in Valleyside. Although not a Valleyside resident, he was very much an insider within the larger statewide Punjabi Sikh community. His background and position helped convey a sense that "this study is going to be different." Because the project did not originate with Valleyside Sikhs, it is unlikely that we could otherwise have gained such strong and continuing support within their community. In addition to the two investigators (I served as principal investigator and project director), the research team included two research assistants. The first, a young Sikh woman recently arrived in Valleyside from Britain, had worked previously with a cross-cultural mental health research project. She was comfortable with cultural analysis and with the need for strict confidentiality. She spoke conversational Punjabi like a proper Doabian--most Valleyside Punjabis originate from the Doaba area of Punjab--and through marriage was well connected within the Valleyside community. The second, a recent graduate of an East Coast college, had heard of the project from one of her professors. She convinced us by telephone to hire her on a trial basis, and she soon made herself indispensable. By their youthful appearance and personalities, both research assistants were able to mix easily with students and at times were mistaken as students by high school faculty.

The project benefited immeasurably from the multiple perspectives and talents of team members. Our team was mixed by age, sex, ethnic identity, and educational background. In the case of the Punjabis, it included both an insider and an outsider to Valleyside. Although the investigators took the lead in research design and problem solving, the full team was involved in framing research questions, designing instruments, and collecting and analyzing data.

The Punjabi assistant played a critical insider role. Several of her relatives-by-marriage attended Valleyside High. She served as a broker for the research, enhancing the project's credibility among Punjabi students, especially the girls. From her we learned what was going on among high school students and also what their parents had to say about it. Not only she but members of her extended family became the project's principal informants. Through her, and her networks, we also gained insight into the Punjabi female perspective.

Our approach to the "classic anthropological question" of whether one has to be "an A to study A's, or a B to study B's" (Cassell 1978:45) was to have both study both, i.e., all members of our research team interviewed both Punjabis and Valleysiders. This proved important politically and substantively. Having several people with quite distinct perspectives elicit information on the same topic increased the validity of the responses and provided additional range and depth to the interviews. Team members simply noticed different kinds of things in the same local scene. The team, moreover, assured the ready availability of others with whom one could check ideas and impressions. A single researcher could never have collected the same quality or quantity of data.

The team approach, although essential to the project's success, was not without its problems (see also Cassell 1978; Pelto and Pelto 1978; and Wax 1971 on the vicissitudes of team research). The research was largely anthropological in design, but only the principal investigator was trained in anthropology. Throughout fieldwork the investigators spent endless hours in planning sessions that frequently bogged down in issues related to theory and method.[9] Our need to reach consensus conflicted with the equally pressing need to push forward with research tasks. Our commitment to full collaboration consumed valuable hours subtracted from fieldwork. Difficulties that arose were complicated by the fact that I was working full time on the project, the coinvestigator only half time, and we both commuted to Valleyside from separate cities.

As project director I also found much of my time consumed in supervising others and in administering the project. Hours devoted to assuring the success of the comparative interviews were well spent. Time invested in encouraging and training team members to take field notes in the style of an anthropologist was less productive and a drain on all concerned, largely because the others were not guided in their note taking by an ethnographic perspective. I often felt that it would have been easier to conduct the fieldwork on my own rather than, as Rosalie Wax has expressed, to "beat my brains out trying to instruct others in how to perform research..." (1971:362).

Note taking was an ongoing and critical problem. When team members made notes of observations, insights, and informal conversations, I often found them wanting. When they failed to make notes, I knew that the information would be lost. Consequently, I devoted considerable time to interviewing team members about their work. This proved useful, but made deep inroads into time I had scheduled for personal observation and informal interviewing.

The fact that parent and student interviews were recorded and later transcribed was fundamental to the project's success. Systematic, comparative analysis of the interviews would have been impossible without the verbatim record of what our informants said. All members of the research team were good interviewers and all understood the purposes underlying the various sets of questions on the schedule. The patterns that emerged in the analysis would have been lost had we relied only on notes taken during and after the interviews. The direct quotations by parents and students, together with care in selection of families, increased the final report's credibility with the host community. The report not only represented local perspectives, it spoke in local voices.

Three Valleyside Punjabis and one Valleysider were hired to assist with parent interviews. In response to my urging, the Punjabis agreed to interview relatives or families well known to them. This turned out to be a mistake. It proved difficult for them to conduct semi-structured tape-recorded interviews with those whom they knew personally (see Cassell 1978:44 for a similar observation). Relatives and friends felt free to complain about the length of interviews and saw little purpose in providing information that they believed was known already to the interviewer. One of the three removed himself from the project after a cousin criticized his motives.

Members of the research team encountered no similar problems. Punjabi hospitality required that we be offered every courtesy. Valleysider courtesy and cooperation also were notable. Many of the most productive interviews were conducted by the coinvestigator. Both Punjabi and Valleysider interviews yielded remarkably strong patterns of response.

The magnitude and complexity of tasks to be accomplished in the fieldwork resulted in a serious delay in completion. Our original schedule called for 10 months in the field and 10 months for analysis and report writing. In fact, we shut down our field office only four months before our funding ended.

Over the next several months, the coinvestigator and I were unable to reach agreement on an approach to data analysis and report presentation. Since most of the analysis and write up had to be done on our own time and in different locations, we eventually--and with considerable reluctance--agreed to separate reports. This plan proved a serious error.

NIE was little interested in two reports covering similar ground but from different perspectives. Valleyside Punjabis felt strongly that a common report would have greater impact on the school district, and the district itself was dead set against the idea. The original grant proposal, endorsed by the district and community, mentioned only one report. It also called for review of the report by both school district and community members for clarification, elaboration, and to assure that no misunderstandings arose from our presentation.[10] Furthermore, it was the school superintendent's understanding, and clearly the intent of the proposal, that the report would be prepared in keeping with the anthropological framework and methodology laid out in the proposal.

The unfortunate outcome of the investigators' "agreement to disagree" with respect to report writing was that the school district would not approve the coinvestigator's report.[11] His response: "We're back to base zero, like two years ago, in terms of promoting change.... If the school district will not face and discuss the issues, then there is no hope for improvement." Not only did the district see the second report as out of concert with our original understandings, it also found the coinvestigator's presentation regarding prejudice in the schools unsubstantiated and biased. This unhappy state only bolstered the view of the coinvestigator and some others that those in power would not listen to minority perspectives and that nothing positive would come from the research. Better planning at the outset might have obviated this situation.

The Indo-American Education Association

To maximize the commitment and involvement of Punjabis in the research process, we elected to place the administration of the NIE grant within a Punjabi community organization. Such an arrangement, we assumed, would heighten the interest of Valleyside Punjabis and increase the likelihood that research findings would have local impact. We also believed the arrangement would contribute to the capacity of the organization to carry out similar community-based research in the future. We looked for an appropriate agency in Valleyside, but the only recommendations were to place the grant with one of the local *gurdwaras*. Fearing that such a relationship might align the project with one faction or another and jeopardize our ability to gain access to and support from various Valleyside Punjabi subgroups, we turned to a community service organization located in a nearby city, the Indo-American Education Association. The association's stated philosophy and mission complemented those of the project, and the coinvestigator was a founding member of the association and its current president. When he took the plan to his fellow directors for their consideration, the chief concern they expressed was whether Valleyside Punjabis would support the plan. In fact, they did. We discovered, however, that factionalism entered by the back door.

The anthropological literature is replete with studies of factions and factionalism (see, for example, Boissevain 1964; Firth 1957; Leaf 1972; Lewis 1954; Siegel and Beals 1960).[12] Different groups within small communities inevitably have conflicting interests and agendas that may interfere with cooperative endeavors. Anthropological discussions of research and development activities often note the dangers of becoming associated with one faction or another (see Edgerton and Langness 1974; Goodenough 1963; Wax 1971). Placing a research grant within a minority community organization away from the research site may avoid local politics but may elicit new and equally troublesome political problems.

In writing the project budget we included no compensation for association directors except for the coinvestigator's salary as a researcher. This was in keeping with board policy that all directors serve without pay. Only direct costs were included in the NIE budget, as the association had no approved indirect cost rate. Nor did anyone foresee how the project might create direct costs for the association. This proved to be an egregious error.

No sooner had the grant been received than association

members, including some directors, questioned the budget design. The coinvestigator was to be paid, so why not they? Although some board members were committed to research and recognized the project's utility in providing the association with experience in administering a research grant, others were more concerned with old agendas. In the past, all association activities had been service-oriented. They wanted the grant, in some small way, to further their immediate community service purposes.

Administration of the project quickly fell prey to Punjabi politics in the city where the association was located. The association's board split into two factions.[13] Each maintained separate membership rolls, collected annual dues, and insisted on its legal right to the organization name and control of the project budget. The dispute related to preexisting disagreements and jealousies among members of the organization, some of which, I was told, reached back to economic and social frictions in India. One camp, which I will call Group A, was headed by the coinvestigator. Group B was headed by the association's treasurer, who believed he had been unfairly prevented by Group A from exercising meaningful control over the project budget.

The coinvestigator, it turned out, was a controversial individual with many detractors among Punjabis in his home city. Group B members seized the occasion to discredit him. They demanded his resignation as a director, since he was receiving a salary. They also informed me that they could support the project only if the coinvestigator was removed from the research team.

Emotions grew hot. Insults delivered in rich Punjabi vernacular were exchanged at public meetings. Rumors were rife that we had given away large sums of money and that both investigators were drawing exhorbitant salaries. The treasurer wrote NIE that government funds were being misappropriated and that the coinvestigator had been removed from office (according to a vote by Group B members). One Punjabi academic described the problems as "a battle between the intellectuals and those who can't make it." Another Punjabi explained that Group B was "jealous" of the coinvestigator because of his education and status. Whatever the actual causes, factionalism placed a serious strain on the coinvestigator and encroached upon time for fieldwork. The entire project was endangered.

Group A was resolute in its support and determined that the research should go forward. To protect the research, I recommended that administration of the grant be transferred to a university. Several Group A directors devoted extraordinary effort and personal funds--a lawsuit ensued as part of the conflict--to keep the project within the community organization. They believed that a university transfer might encourage Group B to shift its attack to the field site, thereby making the research even more vulnerable. The coinvestigator insisted, moreover (and quite rightly),that any decision to remove the grant from the community organization had to involve those Valleyside Punjabis who had supported the project from the start. Several meetings were held. The full executive committee of the major Sikh temple in Valleyside affirmed anew its backing for the research and rejected removing the project from its community base. Community leaders in Valleyside also intervened to dampen the dispute between Groups A and B. This, in itself, may have helped forward on-site research. Although the lawsuit continued, Valleyside Punjabis remained neutral in the conflict. In spite of all the problems, the Indo-American Education Association furthered project goals in numerous respects. It facilitated entree to the Valleyside Punjabi community and helped demonstrate our commitment to community involvement. When the project became the center of controversy, Group A directors remained steadfast in their support. The collaborative arrangement with a nonprofit organization also permitted us to stretch our budget far beyond what would have been possible within a university setting, given usual rates for overhead and employee benefits.

It is much less obvious how the research served in any positive sense the interests of the association. Although placement of the grant outside of the research site helped maintain our neutrality in Valleyside Punjabi politics, we also should have considered more fully the ramifications of placing a relatively large research grant within a small service-oriented organization. We should have found some means of building indirect costs into our budget. At least this would have permitted board members to participate in the expenditure of some grant funds.

The School District

In the course of fieldwork and analysis, the importance of the school district as a collaborator became increasingly apparent. The district had the power and the responsibility to bring about educational change. Through its involvement in all phases of the research process the district helped to assure that project findings had local applicability.

District personnel viewed their role not as co-researchers but as providers of information and recipients of research findings. The superintendent requested that all district administrators facilitate the research, and the high school principal made a similar request of his staff. Educational personnel answered our incessant questions and always were available for consultation. They helped us gather massive amounts of data from school records. They arranged meetings with students during the academic day. In conjunction with the Valley County Employment and Training Office, they assigned Punjabi trainees to the project during two summers and for part of one school year. They encouraged Migrant Education staff to work with us during school hours.

High school teachers also cooperated in many ways. They permitted classroom observations, completed questionnaires, participated in semistructured interviews, and collected student essays on various topics. Some became more involved than others, initiating comment and assisting with analysis.

The one stipulation set down by the superintendent was that no students be interviewed unless their parents had signed a consent form. We worried at first that this would impede fieldwork seriously. How do you "hang around" a high school campus of 2,200 students but talk only to those 80-odd whose parents had consented? We focused attention on our senior sample, and no other students were interviewed formally. We sought out no others, but when offered comments, we listened. This approach worked well.

Many of the findings addressed the status of education at the secondary level in general, including the needs of majority as well as minority students. Completion of the final report, and with it the end of the formal research process, coincided, as it turned out, with the publication of a spate of reports and books calling for an upgrading of academic standards nationwide (see Howe 1984). A similar call for educational reform was occurring at the state level.

The Valleyside superintendent characterized the current ferment as healthy, stating that it was up to the district to bring about needed changes: local problems must be solved at the local level. Yet, as John Goodlad (1983) points out, most schools lack the necessary data base upon which to plan for change. Such a data base may well be the Punjabi Education Project's greatest contribution to its host community.

The research provided the district with extensive information about how the high school was functioning. Project findings, according to one local administrator, have enabled school officials to respond to new mandates and recommendations in ways that would have been unlikely had the district not participated in the research process. For example, the research caused district administrators to look at local graduation requirements in a new light. I suggested that the school system might be doing ESL students a disservice by lowering its standards and permitting them to graduate without taking high school English classes. (Several Punjabi informants had expressed similar views.) Beginning in 1987, all Valleyside High graduates will have to complete two years of regular high school English.

This new graduation requirement will have direct and immediate impact on limited-English-speaking students, particularly those newly arrived from India. It has major implications for instruction in the lower grades and at the high school level. Seymour Sarason states in *The Culture of the School and the Problem of Change* (1983:96) that "any attempt to introduce change into the school setting requires, among other things, changing the existing regularities in some way." Higher standards, I believe, can so adjust the "existing regularities" as to be a stimulus to educational reform.

PROJECT IMPACT

This project, although basic research in part, was also applied research in the sense that it stemmed from local problems and was oriented toward their solution (see Eddy and Partridge 1978). We wanted not only to understand how the system worked but also to make it work better. However, *describing* a problem is not the same as working together with school and community people to *solve* the problem. Courtney Cazden (1983) has pointed this out and also has noted that consciousness-raising alone is insufficient to bring about change (see also Erickson 1979).

It is exceedingly difficult to assess the full value of the Punjabi Education Project to its host community. The involvement of community and school people in all aspects of the research process clearly increased the validity of findings and the likelihood that findings would have local impact (see Hymes 1980b). Through the collaborative process we also gained a better understanding of the nature of acceptable interventions. Suggestions for change, made to the district, grew out of a local context. In spite of our wish to maximize the utility of findings to the host community, however, our research design included no adequate structures for diffusion or change.

Recent conversations with Valleyside educators have revealed a sense of rising expectations on the part of students, parents, and teachers. One local educator observed that high school classes, including slower-track classes, were becoming more demanding. Others noted changes relating to discipline and homework. Instead of worrying about lax standards, as some had in the past, high school faculty now expressed concern about "overloading" students, majority and minority alike. Their comments focused on the appropriate balance between academic endeavors and other activities. Given recent attention to raising academic standards, it is difficult to show any direct connection between the project and changes such as these. District officials have stated, however, that they have found the research useful in planning for change.

In other areas it is less obvious what changes have occurred. District personnel continue to grapple with special needs of limited-English-speakers. Concern about problems of prejudice remain, and school personnel remain unsure of appropriate remedies. It is in these areas of immediate concern to the Punjabi community that some mechanism for ongoing community involvement would have been most valuable.

We had hoped that the Indo-American Education Association, working together with the Valleyside Punjabis, might have facilitated a continuing process of change. Instead, the anthropologist was left trying to broker the situation with no formal role following the end of the grant period and submission of the final report. This approach, as noted by Borrero, Schensul, and Garcia (1982), has many problems. An alternative approach, which they recommend, is to train "individuals in local communities and in wider society institutions...to engage in a cooperative approach to problem-solving in which data play a central role" (p. 130).

In the present case, a nucleus of individuals could have been trained through active participation on a project advisory committee comprised of parents, teachers, administrators, and researchers. The committee, rather than the Indo-American Education Association, could have facilitated the change process. Our proposal called for such a committee, but other tasks always seemed to take precedence.

LESSONS LEARNED

In designing collaborative ethnographic research we need to distinguish among three types of collaboration between anthropologists and host communities: first, collaboration in the *development* of change strategies; second, collaboration with community institutions for the *administration* of research funds; and third, collaboration in the *research* itself.

The Punjabi Education Project was collaborative in the latter two senses. Were I to undertake this project again, I would focus more attention on the first, i.e., on strategies for change. A voluntary advisory committee ought to have been set up representing various segments of the community, including Punjabi community leaders (some selected by each of the Valleyside Sikh temples), district administrators, teachers (Punjabi and Valleysider), and Valleysider parents (selected with the advice of the PTA). The committee should have been involved in all aspects of the research process.

The Punjabis would have been especially well served by such a committee. Their children, as a group, have faced the gravest problems, and yet they have felt that the district was uninterested in their concerns and views. The committee could have generated dialogue between minority and majority parents, school personnel, and researchers and might have served as a vehicle for change. Given the existence of factions within the Valleyside Punjabi community, district administrators were unsure of whom to turn to for dialogue on problems relating to Punjabi students. This issue might have been resolved by having the Sikh temples appoint representatives to advocate their interests.

The district also was unsure how to diffuse project findings to teachers, given the length and complexity of the final report. Teachers on the committee could have assisted with this process. Teachers have recognized the need for change in many of the areas identified in the report (many of the ideas were their own), but, like Punjabi and Valleysider parents, they too felt largely powerless to alter the status quo. The sense of powerlessness was striking. The voluntary advisory committee could have provided one possible vehicle for significant action. The committee, moreover, would have relieved researchers of the full responsibility for keeping all parties informed about the project's progress and findings. Although there is no assurance that the committee would have continued in any formal sense after the research ended, at a minimum it would have produced a group of people knowledgeable about the research and as individuals able to continue their efforts to improve educational opportunities within their school district.

One caveat needs to be mentioned. We must maintain a balance between research designed to bring about educational improvement and research that helps us to understand why students perform as they do. I see a real danger in pursuing the former to the exclusion of the latter.

By far the most difficult aspect of the present project was its placement within the "community" association, the second type of collaboration. Nonetheless, the strategy had merit and was only partially a failure. It gave the minority community some power over the project and a sense that this differed from most academic endeavors. If a more appropriate institution had existed, it might have served as a mechanism for change after the formal research had ended (see Borrero, Schensul, and Garcia 1982).

I have recounted our difficulties not to discourage others from similar ventures, but rather, in the interest of all parties concerned, to urge great care in the choice of a community organization. Ideally, the organization should have experience in administering research, be unaligned and able to maintain its neutrality in the face of factionalism, and be able to work with various segments of the larger community in translating research into practice. In setting up a partnership with a community organization, the anthropologist needs to work directly with the organization's board to reach mutually acceptable understandings regarding roles, responsibilities, and the advantages of the relationship to all parties. If members of the research team are also directors of the community institution, it is important to consider how possible role conflicts would be resolved. If an appropriate community organization does not exist, it may be possible to create one (see Schensul and Borrero 1982).

Finally, I must comment on collaboration in the research itself. With respect to team research, let me underscore the need for care in choosing coresearchers. Both their commitment to the scientific process *and* their reputation within the host community are critical to the project's success.

When working with nonanthropologists the taping of interviews has special advantages. First, it is unrealistic to assume that nonanthropologists can be trained to take field notes in the style of an anthropologist. In addition to providing an alternative to relying solely on notes, taping allows team members to analyze one another's interviews. Analysis of unabridged interviews permits patterns to emerge that otherwise might be lost. Although time-consuming to transcribe and analyze, tape-recorded interviews provide a permanent record that can be reanalyzed in the future, perhaps for different purposes. The use of quotations in reports and publications also increases the impact and credibility of research findings.

In collaborative projects, the research proposal can serve as a kind of written agreement among all parties regarding research design and may be used to iron out areas of disagreement (see also Pelto and Pelto 1978). In the present case this proved critical with respect to the final report. If the project design specifically calls for an anthropological perspective, it may be best for anthropologists to draft the report and for the other team members to provide critical feedback throughout the report-writing process. With jointly authored reports it is advisable to discuss in advance how disagreements will be resolved regarding analysis, report composition, recommendations, and authorship of future publications.

A final word on project design. Educational anthropologists need to establish long-term relationships with school districts and to *document* the nature of these relationships. In so doing we will learn more about how to conduct research that is useful locally. We will also increase our credibility among school administrators, few of whom currently turn to anthropologists for help in solving local problems.

ACKNOWLEDGMENTS

Although written expressly for the present volume, this chapter first appeared in the *Anthropology and Education Quarterly* 16:124-148, 1985. It is reprinted here with minor changes by permission of the American Anthropological Association. I wish to thank John Ogbu, Jay Schensul, Jane Singh, John Singleton, and Harry Wolcott for insightful comments on earlier versions of this article. Their perspectives helped me stand back a bit from my own role in the collaborative process. I also acknowledge with gratitude the funding provided to the Punjabi Education Project by the National Institute of Education (Grant Number G80-0123).

NOTES

1. "Valleyside" is a pseudonym.

2. Linda Light and Nancy Kleiber's (1981) description of "interactive research" in a women's health collective is a notable exception.

3. I refer to the total Asian Indian population living in Valleyside, Sikh, Hindu, and Moslem alike, as "Punjabis," since all have their origins in Punjab. Punjabi is a regional identification. The term applies equally to natives of West Punjab, now part of Pakistan. In the present case, however, almost all immigrants have come to this country from East Punjab, or Indian Punjab.

4. According to school district reports, "East Indians" (the local term for Punjabis) accounted for 2.4 percent of the student enrollment in 1972, 8.4 percent in 1977-78, and 12.6 percent by 1980-81.

5. Elsewhere I discuss the applicability of these theories to immigrant groups (Gibson n.d.).

6. Full project findings are reported in the Final Report to the National Institute of Education (Gibson 1983a) and in a forthcoming volume titled *Accommodation without Assimilation: Punjabi Sikh Immigrants in an American High School and Community* (Gibson n.d.).

7. I explore Sikh parents' strategies for promoting school success more fully in an article comparing the Valleyside case with similar research carried out in London and Birmingham (Gibson and Bhachu 1986). British research on the educational performance of Punjabi immigrants reveals patterns notably similar to those of the present study (see Ballard and Vellins 1985; Bhachu 1985).

8. Elsewhere (Gibson 1987) I compare the high school performance patterns of the Punjabi minority and Valleysider majority, showing how the cultural background of each group bears directly on academic performance and social relations.

9. Pelto and Pelto (1978:227) suggest "agreements to disagree" as a strategy for avoiding "interminable debate" in interdisciplinary projects. We often found it difficult, however, even to agree to disagree.

10. The principal investigator's final report benefited greatly from critical readings by school personnel and by several Valleyside Punjabis representing both

traditional and more westernized segments of the community.

11. Pelto and Pelto (1978:227) suggest that "separate data analysis and separate publication can honestly reflect the alternatives of interpretation current in the research team." I support their view, but caution that there must be clear understandings among all parties concerned that more than one final report may be prepared.

12. Following Boissevain (1964:1276), I use the term faction to mean "a loosely ordered [and temporary] group in conflict with a similar group over a particular issue." By factionalism I mean "overt conflict within a group which leads to the increasing abandonment of cooperative activities" (Siegel and Beals 1960:399).

13. The factionalism that occurred within the Indo-American Education Association is similar to disputes in other overseas Sikh communities (see Desai 1963:45-55; de Lepervanche 1984:168-181).

PART TWO

Collaborative Research in the Third World

As Sol Tax was developing action anthropology among the Fox in Iowa, Allan Holmberg was implementing another distinctive intervention strategy--research and development anthropology--in highland Peru. Like Tax, Holmberg and his Peruvian colleagues wanted both to help and to learn from the people of Vicos. Holmberg believed that research and development were inseparable and that in the long run such an approach would "provide considerable payoff in terms of both a more rational policy and better science" (1958:12). The Cornell-Peru Project was intended to promote "a wide... sharing of...positive human values" (1958:13) and serve as a model for socioeconomic development in the Third World.

The Cornell-Peru Project did not become a predominant model for postwar development programs. Nevertheless, two decades after its end, the project is still the best known effort in applied anthropology. Vicos has been discussed often and passionately, yet it remains both mythic and enigmatic. Paul Doughty provides a valuable service to the field with his incisive review of the context, history, and significance of this most famous experiment in collaborative research.

In spite of the example set by the Cornell-Peru Project, the involvement of American anthropologists in collaborative research for social change in the Third World remains a rarity. The reasons for the relative absence of such efforts are to be found in the politics and development goals of the United States, development agencies, and host nations. American anthropologists working abroad are faced with constraints that are often absent at home, and approaches to action research developed in the United States are often inappropriate or impossible to implement in Third World communities. In spite of the many difficulties, successful examples of collaborative research are to be *found. The report by Murphy and his associates on the Mexican Urban Housing Project clearly demonstrates the benefits of collaboration in the planning and implementation of national policies as well as advancement of anthropological theory.*

Applied anthropologists overseas usually work for government agencies on projects of limited scope and duration. Hackenberg and Hackenberg have taken a very different approach over the past decade and a half in Davao City, Philippines. They have built a strong research presence through close collaboration with representatives of both the public and private sectors in the Philippines as well as with international development agencies. Although the specific projects and sectors with which the Hackenbergs have been involved have varied over the years, they have consistently pursued their dual goals of greater understanding of culture change processes and improvement of Philippine society.

In the projects discussed below, anthropologists have worked closely with representatives of their host communities to develop and implement significant programs of social change. While implementing these programs, they have remained committed to advancing anthropological understanding of the change process. These anthropologists have dedicated themselves to long-term involvement, recognizing that both theory building and significant social change require such commitment. Their work offers proof of Holmberg's belief that action research leads to improvements in both policy and science.

6

Against the Odds: Collaboration and Development at Vicos

Paul L. Doughty

From 1952 to 1966, Cornell University, in collaboration with the Peruvian government and the Quechua Indian community of Vicos, conducted a program in the Andean highlands known as the Cornell-Peru (or Vicos) Project. The project rented an archetypical Andean manor of 18,230 hectares with a resident serf population of 1,703 Quechua-speaking Indians. Designed to create a viable community freed of serfdom and ultimately in possession of the estate, this was the first formal attempt at holistic rural development and agrarian reform in Peru. The project achieved its goals when the community members purchased the hacienda, and thus their freedom, in June 1962 with monies they earned from selling potatoes in the national market.[1]

PATTERNS OF DEVELOPMENT

At the onset of the Cornell-Peru Project (CPP), Vicos was occasionally visited by the octogenarian parish priest, a mestizo holding negative attitudes about the human potential of the Quechua serfs. During a rare appearance at an Indian's funeral his acolyte shaded him with an umbrella as he prayed at the graveside, the bible in one hand and the other outstretched to receive a pitiful stream of coins dropped by the bereaved. When the coins ran out, the prayers stopped in midsentence. His interest was purely technical; the context of his actions meant little to him. Indeed, there was a certain inconvenience to serving impoverished serfs: no prestige and little profit. Moreover, the dirt and sweat that gathered under the old-fashioned "duster" worn to protect the priestly habit made his trip to the remote community barely tolerable even as an act of noblesse oblige.

This episode has often seemed a parable for the kind of development programs that typically flower and die in the Andes. In an era when foreign assistance channels millions of dollars through complex international bureaucracies and bilateral programs between the industrially rich nations and the Third World poor, direct-action, small-scale projects appear diminished in their effect or importance. The movement of large sums of money between governments is what the development "game" is about. The patterns of development emerging in contemporary models, brokered by technical consultants, pretentiously claim to be sophisticated and effective strategies, although it is doubtful that most benefit from past decades of experience in international assistance.

Personal involvement of specialists with the recipients of aid is usually indirect, filtered by secondary or tertiary employees through essentially unidirectional chains of command. Thus, the operational context of collaboration is between these employees as they pursue goals agreed upon by government agencies or private institutions. The participation of local recipient populations in assistance programs is largely limited to contributions of manual labor and acquiesence to the plans and decisions of outside techno-bureaucratic elites.

Another common attribute of development programs is the limited time span of their operations, most often confined to deadlines imposed by budgets and personnel contracts. Action is not driven by community or public needs so much as by impersonal bureaucratic forces beyond the control of even the agency personnel, since policy decisions rest elsewhere. Once the money stops and the contracted personnel go home, the "development" process quickly fades. Local initiative, work, and interest recede apace, for such programs are neither equipped, financed, nor prepared to continue on the course alone.

The shallow involvement of development agencies in pursuit of their oft-stated grandiose goals is further reflected in the fact that most of their activity is centered on the provision of infrastructure or technology per se and rarely with the social organization and cultural behavior that must sustain its use and function. However, dozens of cases worldwide (Spicer 1952; Roupp 1953; Bernard and Pelto 1986) demonstrate that maintaining a "hands-off" policy concerning social and cultural issues in development not only invites program failure but also uncontrolled and unanticipated consequences that often create serious new problems. This is so well documented it must be said that the introduction of infrastructure and technology without commensurate attention to the sociocultural forces that mold the context and repercussions of their use is irresponsible. Yet, this inept, indeed unethical, mode of development operations persists in full flower as infrastructural mansions rest vacant, besieged by the weeds of failure. Why this should continue is one of the never ending challenges to those who think that human beings can learn from past experience and consciously plan fair and effective improvements in society.

For this and other reasons, there have been many efforts to examine the outcomes of both contemporary and historic projects in the hope that some benefit from experience might be gained (Tendler 1975, 1982; Hewitt de Alcántara 1976; Hoben 1982; Morss et al. 1976; Morss and Morss 1982; Doughty, Burleigh, and Painter 1984). Only good case histories can assist in undertaking the processes and outcomes of social change programs. Case studies, however, have their limitations insofar as the interpretation of results differs with the developmental philosophy of the reader. Perhaps nowhere can this be seen more clearly than in the case of the Cornell-Peru Project at Vicos (Cochrane 1971; Morss et al. 1976:428ff; Mangin 1979; Stein 1985b; Babb 1985; Himes 1981; Lynch 1982). From the very first, this bold initiative by a group of anthropologists provoked widespread opposition as well as support in the United States and Peru in academia, in government circles, among development specialists, and, not the least, among traditional Peruvian elites.[2] For example:

> Vicos shows an absence of any real appreciation of what development work is all about. At Vicos the anthropologist apparently made all the major decisions. No competent administrator would himself deal with agricultural, legal, and educational matters since these are specialized subjects which require expert assessment and advice.... Vicos shows the kind of anthropologist who believes that he knows all he needs to know about development and who does not feel the need to cooperate with other disciplines except on a cursory basis (Cochrane 1971:18).

This characterization of CPP by a leading "development" anthropologist brings to the fore some of the fundamental problems that accompany all development projects: the issues surrounding collaborative enterprise. Although it will become abundantly clear that Cochrane's diatribe is without foundation (Doughty 1986b), the importance of collaboration to planned change can scarcely be overstated. The chronology of the Vicos community presented below indicates how some of the development characteristics and procedures noted were addressed by CPP and how these may affect the status of the community some 20 years after the close of the project.

More than three decades since it began, CPP still excites interest and controversy as a pioneering effort to apply the concepts and methods of anthropology. Is it a model to be emulated? What is its meaning today?

ANDEAN STRATEGIES OF CHANGE

Peruvian society in the 1950s has been well described by Holmberg (1960) as a rigid, stagnant ambience, tightly holding to its colonial values and institutions while resisting any substantive change. Yet, increasingly evident were fissures in the wall that defended the status quo: significant migratory streams of Andean peasants to the urban coast had developed; the economy was rapidly changing because of industry and fishing; and the political environment was ever volatile. Despite such portending conditions, the "Indian problem," rooted in racist attitudes of the mestizo and white elites, seemed beyond solution. Countless observers had identified the Quechua and Aymara peoples (well over 50 percent of Peruvians) as embodying the very essence of the nation's ills, keeping the country back from progress. Perhaps the most widely held opinion on this matter was that "the Indian" was incapable of change because of racial and ethnic deficits.

In the 1950s, many agencies delivering assistance relied upon a strategy of "community development" aimed at pulling "backward" populations "up" by offering new resources and opportunities, rather than altering structural or systemic conditions (Doughty 1986a). The CPP as an alternative development program challenged popular myths about Indians by establishing that the causes of Peru's lack of progress lay not with its Indian masses, but with a national socioeconomic system that exploited and benefited from their condition. There were powerful, dominant forces arrayed to thwart significant alterations in this system.

Allan Holmberg and his colleagues, Mario Vazquez and Carlos Monge M., felt that an official and scientific demonstration of the potential for peaceful, constructive change was required. Such a demonstration would modify racist attitudes and create an opportunity for wider programs by providing proof that Indians were capable human beings. Thus, it was important that the experiment be designed to deal with the core issues of the "Indian problem" in a feasible manner and within the capacity of Peruvians to undertake elsewhere. As anthropologists, they believed that the most fruitful strategy was a holistic one that addressed various levels of the question in an integrated fashion. Actions in one area would produce repercussions in others: functional relationships were not only theoretically interesting, but they could be used in planned ways (Holmberg 1969). It was Holmberg's idea to use a "research and development" approach, creating a cybernetic loop between theory, research findings, policy, and action. This approach plotted out the conditions and desired changes in concert with inputs from the community which would ultimately take charge (Holmberg 1955, 1958).

To break the cultural bonds of serfdom and restructure the hacienda social system required several operative conditions: a comprehensive perspective of theory and action; community interest; the ability to operate over a long period of time; and a collaborative effort on the part of the interested parties, including a willingness to make significant political and economic commitments to the project. Holmberg agreed with Homer Barnett's (1953:39-46) views about innovation, acknowledging that although changes would occur on an individual level, significant societal modifications would require an institutional and cooperative dimension. The "collaboration of effort," in Barnett's phrase, was to be the key to unlocking the required resources.

From the very start, although never boldly stated as such, Holmberg and his colleagues grasped the revolutionary implications of the project (Holmberg 1952c:239-240):

> Based on the prior studies largely by...Mario Vazquez, it was thought appropriate to renounce the free services provided to the hacienda by the employees. Instead of the free services native volunteers are contracted on salary to do key tasks. At the request of the native leaders no basic changes were made in the methods of work but they were made to see clearly, through prior consultation with the people, that all the profits proceeding from their work would be invested in their (the people's) interest in the hacienda, in works such as improvements in housing, schools, recreation, sanitary facilities and agricultural practices.... A complete program was outlined in 1952-3 for the devolution of the hacienda, in consultation with the native leaders, thus

establishing in this way, a series of realistic and concrete objectives in which we could work in collaboration with the people.

Having stated their goals so matter-of-factly, Holmberg and his colleagues proceeded to tackle a problem that today seems daunting, but to them was not, perhaps because of their idealistic enthusiasm buoyed by the "can do" spirit of the times. The foundation for their work rested upon a unique agreement, perhaps one of the first of its kind, between the university and the Peruvian government's Indian Institute of the Ministry of Labor and Indian Affairs. It was certainly well ahead of its time in establishing broad relationships and specifying particular actions (Anonymous 1952).

1. Cornell University and the Peruvian Indian Institute of the Ministry of Labor and Indian Affairs would work in the district of Marcará, Ancash in pursuit of their goals.
2. Cornell would finance its side of the program for at least a five-year period.
3. The project would apply anthropological ideas toward the solution of Peru's "Indian problem."
4. The project would be jointly operated by the two institutions, with permanent coordination provided by each.
5. A social scientist would head the program.
6. All studies would require prior approval of the Peruvian Indian Institute.
7. Participating foreigners would be officially assisted as needed (visas, importing of equipment).
8. Cornell would seek scholarships for Peruvians to work on the project and to study abroad in connection with the program.
9. Peruvian universities would be encouraged to participate.
10. Cornell would provide its knowledge and personnel to help in other areas of the country as requested.
11. The project would maintain an office in the Ministry of Labor and Indian Affairs for coordination purposes and to receive customs assistance and research sponsorship.
12. The institute would obtain a Presidential Resolution confirming all of these points of agreement.

Signed on November 30, 1951 and confirmed by Presidential Resolution five days later.

This program was to be launched in a place deliberately selected as one of the most conservative regions of the highlands, on a hacienda deemed by Peruvians to be one of the most archetypical and socially difficult.

THE COMMUNITY ENVIRONMENT

Hacienda Vicos occupies the hilly slopes of the famous Cordillera Blanca in the District of Marcará of the Department of Ancash, Peru. The extensive property ranges in altitude from about 10,000 feet to the *puna* grasslands over 14,500 feet at the foot of the glaciers and great snowpeaks over 20,000 feet high. The lowest portions of the district border the Santa River, which runs northward 150 miles through the beautiful intermountain valley known as the Callejón de Huaylas before splitting the mountains to plunge into the Pacific. The principal road in the valley spirals up from the coast to the department capital of Huaraz and thence through the Callejón de Huaylas, connecting the town of Marcará with other district and provincial capitals. The rough dirt road to Vicos winds up the hills from Marcará for 4 miles, passing by the hot mineral springs of Chancos. Eucalyptus groves and maguey plants border the road and the glacial stream that descends from the Cordillera. A more handsome and bucolic setting could hardly be envisioned (See Figure 6.1.)

Yet amidst this perpetual beauty, human society struggles with a long history of socioeconomic exploitation based on ethnicity and race. In 1952, the Spanish-speaking mestizos of Marcará constituted about 8 percent of the district's people; all the rest were classified as Indians, most of whom lived on Hacienda Vicos as serfs, with the remainder living in the "free" Peasant Communities[3] of Shumáy and Recuayhuanca and some other small estates. The mestizo townspeople controlled the political, economic, and other institutional spheres of life in the district in an absolute fashion,[4] which is best described as repressive. Indians were subject to physical and social abuse, deprivations, capricious jailings (Holmberg 1967), and were generally expected to serve and work for mestizos on demand, normally without pay except for some alcohol, coca leaf, or a token meal.

Peonage, ethnic discrimination, endemic starvation, ill health, the total absence of educational opportunity, and no effective protection under the law were the lot of all Vicosinos. The idea of "human rights" for Indians was considered by local mestizo landlords (as well as the ruling

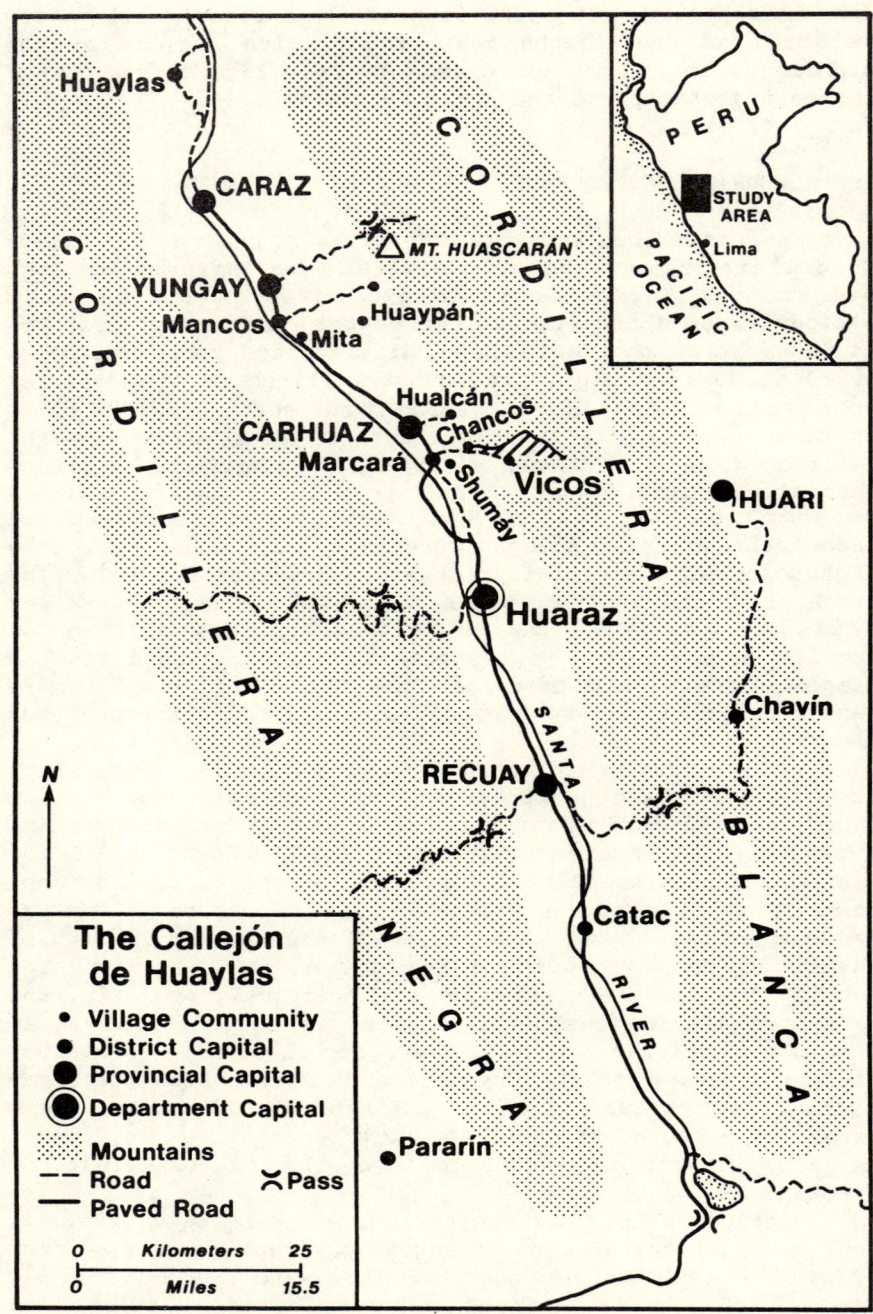

Figure 6.1 The Callejón de Huaylas.

class generally) to be a "communist" threat to their natural position of superiority. In this milieu CPP emerged as nothing less than revolutionary, despite current protestations that it was not.[5]

Pursuant to its formal agreements CPP set about its tasks and for the next 15 years dutifully held to the accords, as did the ministry. As would be expected, disagreements over policy and programs arose, but through almost constant consultation among the parties and personnel they were worked out. At times these were serious enough to produce real distress (Lynch 1981:28-9), especially with respect to the looseness of project organization and the difficulties provoked by low budgets. Despite these problems, the CPP moved toward its broad goals.

Initial research focused entirely upon the district of Marcara and the immediate area of Hacienda Vicos. Technical multidisciplinary studies by Peruvians and Americans initially covered agricultural practices, medical and health issues, nutrition, education, work, social structure and organization, religion, and demography, among other topics. Later project research continued these themes as well as land tenure, markets, credit and economy, legal factors, archeology and ethnohistory, personality, mythology, music, and politics. After 1960, at the behest of the ministry, a series of comparative studies were undertaken elsewhere in Peru on related matters (Andrews 1963; Doughty 1968; Hickman 1963; Bradfield 1963; Dobyns, Doughty, and Holmberg 1966). Using this broad range of research inputs, extensive consultations with the Vicosinos, specialists in the ministries of agriculture and education, and firsthand experience in operating the hacienda, the CPP intervened in the historic pattern of hacienda life and deliberately introduced a series of dramatic changes that continue to influence local events.

A CHRONOLOGY OF THE VICOS COMMUNITY
AND THE CORNELL-PERU PROJECT[6]

1470   The Callejón de Huaylas is conquered and absorbed into the Inca Empire.

1533   Moving toward Cuzco, the Spaniards under Pizarro take control of the Callejón de Huaylas, and Vicos becomes part of an extensive *encomienda*. Population declines dramatically because of disease; new settlements, including the village of Marcará, are established in the main valley after 1570; and the colonial regime stabilizes.

1593-94   Vicos is established as a hacienda with a serf population of 99 persons.

1611   Hacienda Vicos becomes the property of the provincial viceregal hospital in Huaraz, and its production is used to support the hospital.

1774   The population of Hacienda Vicos is counted at 301, a rate of increase per year of 0.6 percent over the past century and a half.

1825   After Peruvian independence from Spain, Vicos is transferred to the newly created Public Beneficent Society of Lima as a rental property. Manor operation continues to be based on peonage, remaining largely unchanged until 1952.

1850   The Vicos population is 513 with yearly growth of 0.7 percent over the 25-year period.

1876-85   In 1876, the national census records 682 persons at Vicos with a yearly growth rate of 1.2 percent. A major regional rebellion of Indian villagers in the Callejón de Huaylas largely bypasses Vicos in 1885. Manor renters increasingly exploit Vicos labor for off-farm work.

1912	In response to exploitive policies of the landlord, a delegation from Vicos makes a direct but futile request for expropriation of the estate to President Guillermo Billingshurst in Lima.
1925	Another Vicos delegation protesting the conditions on the manor is received by President Augusto B. Leguia.
1928-30	A plan to expropriate Vicos by the Leguia administration founders, and Vicos becomes a rental property of the Huaraz Public Beneficent Society, which now operates the regional hospital. The Chancos hot springs "resort" is leased independently from the Vicos hacienda.
1940	The Vicos population has increased to 1,570 and has a yearly growth of 1.3 percent.
1946	Another Vicos delegation goes to Lima to request government expropriation of the hacienda. The renter of Vicos is the Negociación Industrial Ancash, an agribusiness firm producing flax for export. Annual rent as set by sealed-bid "auction" is 14,500 *soles* ($600).
1948	Allan R. Holmberg and his San Marcos University students visit Vicos as part of a regional survey.
1949-50	San Marcos student Mario Vazquez conducts a baseline study of Hacienda Vicos and suggests steps to promote community change and development; thus, laying the foundation for CPP planning (Holmberg 1952a, 1952b; Vazquez 1952).
1951	In December, an agreement is signed between Cornell University and the Peruvian government establishing CPP for five years. The Carnegie Corporation provides research funding in the first of two grants that total $126,000. The project begins with Cornell University assuming the lease from the bankrupt agribusiness concern.
1951-52	The Vicos population stands at 1,703 with population growth at 1.1 percent yearly and a density of 65.7 persons per square kilometer of exploited land. In 1951 Hacienda Vicos produces no cash crop, and subsistence production yields less than 76 percent of the calculated minimum

caloric requirements per capita. No vehicular road to Vicos is open. The one-room school has 14 pupils; less than 1 percent of Vicosinos are literate. No medical service is available. Many Vicosinos do not know they are Peruvians, and few have ventured to the department capital, Huaraz, 50 kilometers away. Each of the 363 households is required to provide the hacienda with one laborer for three days per week in exchange for use of subsistence plots and a housesite. Less than half the adults earn the substandard $.20 daily wage, have a change of clothing, or own large farm animals. There is no residential nucleus around the plaza area. Community organization is entirely controlled by the hacienda administration; with patronal approval Vicos authorities (the *varayoc*) are only permitted to organize religious activities.

1951-56 CPP operates the manor, conducts research, and introduces changes in consultation with the people of Vicos: peonage is abolished, giving Vicosinos social freedom and the right to make employment choices as available; new agricultural practices and crops are introduced with the aid of the agricultural extension services (Stein 1971, 1972); CPP begins the political reorganization of the community; a complete primary school is constructed by the community and staffed by the Ministry of Education; biomedical studies are initiated and a public health program is begun. Peruvian agencies begin work at Vicos. CPP staff includes a field director and fluctuating numbers of U.S. and Peruvian student researchers (2-6 annually), a farm manager carried over from preproject days, and a school staff of 6-8 teachers after the primary school opens in 1953. In addition to work at Vicos, CPP conducts research throughout the adjacent region.

1956-62 The lease between Cornell and the Public Beneficent Society of Huaraz ends in 1956, and the Vicos community assumes the rent on a yearly basis. In 1956 the government issues a decree permitting the expropriation of Vicos, with the community to pay the value over six years. No price is fixed, however. A period of increasing community control of estate management ensues, including: public election of a community president, manager, and council;

expanding commercialization of the potato crop; a pioneering credit program operated by the Ministry of Agriculture extension program (SCIPA) is initiated and grows rapidly; the Ancash Program of the Ministry of Labor and Indian Affairs, with a staff of 4-6 persons at Vicos, coordinates all agency activities and becomes part of a national program, PNIPA.[7] The new program assumes much of the role of CPP in day-to-day management and extends work throughout the district of Marcará. In 1958, the government annuls the expropriation decree of 1956, opposed by the Public Beneficent Society of Huaraz, the owner of Vicos. CPP research continues as numerous students come and go.

1960 Police massacre serfs on the adjoining estate of Huapra who were trying to emulate Vicos, and a Vicos-Huapra peasant uprising is narrowly averted; Vicosino purchase or expropriation continues to be thwarted by the Beneficent Society and Peruvian Prime Minister Beltrán; the Huaraz Beneficent Society raises the sale price from 750,000 to 7 million *soles*; despite its sound financial standing, no loan capital is available to the community from banks. To promote the supervised credit program nationwide and in Bolivia, the Cooperative Extension Service (SCIPA), with USAID monies, makes a film of the successful program at Vicos, *Yo Trabajo en Vicos*. A delegation from Hacienda Huaypán in Yungay Province visits Vicos to request (and receive) a loan from the community so they can rent the estate on which they live as serfs.

1961 Visits to Vicos by U.S. Ambassador James Loeb, followed a month later by senator-to-be Edward Kennedy, enlist "official" U.S. embassy support of land reform for the first time. Loeb and Kennedy speak to President Prado and Prime Minister Beltrán regarding land reform and the expropriation of Vicos. The president reluctantly agrees to permit sale of the estate to the Vicosinos. Research shows that per capita nutrition levels in Vicos now exceed minimum requirements and equal national averages. Vicos population is now 2,102 with an annual rate of increase of 1.5 percent. Over 18 percent of Vicosinos are literate. Four houses are built in the plaza area. The farming enterprise continues successfully, and the community assumes greater management of its affairs. A delegation from the peasant community of Catac, Province of Recuay, visits Vicos to seek advice on potato production and their dispute with a neighboring hacienda. Problems erupt with the school because of teacher absenteeism and poor administration. The Vicos council closes the school, sends a delegation to the education ministry in Lima, and successfully negotiates a complete change of school personnel.

1962 Carlos Monge Medrano and Mario Vazquez push the government to conclude the sale of Vicos, which is accomplished on June 13, 1962. Vicosinos pay 500,000 *soles* down in cash from their farm enterprise profits (savings) to the Public Beneficent Society of Huaraz. Another half million is to be paid over three years, with the final million of the 2 million *sol* ($74,626) price provided by a government loan to be paid in installments over 20 years. The community buys a new 6-ton Ford "Deluxe 600" truck for shipping its potatoes to market. CBS and BBC television crews make widely circulated documentaries on the Vicos project.

1962-63 The Vicos community sells 182.9 metric tons of potatoes in the Lima market, making it one of the largest national suppliers. Additionally, 68 percent of Vicos families sell their own surpluses in regional markets. Since 1952, the number of Vicosinos with various occupational skills has increased by 68 percent; incomes exceed regional wage averages; family clothing possessions, often made in sewing classes, more than triple; ownership of basic household goods has similarly increased. Fifty-three percent of Vicos farmers participate in a community-financed agricultural credit program supervised by the extension service. An agreement between Vicos and the Agrarian University to establish a cattle program fails when university personnel do not follow through on the plan. Thirteen Peace Corps volunteers arrive to begin work under direction of the Ancash Program and the Vicos community.

1963-64 CPP activity is reduced; Vazquez leaves Vicos in 1963 and no Cornell field director remains in Vicos after this; Peace Corps volunteers promote and obtain Vicos's rental of the adjacent Chancos thermal springs and acquisition of the land; Vicos incorporates the freed Chancos serfs into the community and uses the new land for corn production. Peace Corps volunteers are expelled due to a misunderstanding over their role, finances, and activities at the Chancos Springs resort development project and because of personal conflicts with Peruvian teachers and Ancash Program staff; two volunteers are subsequently invited back. A study shows that Vicos men register increases in anxiety symptoms over 1952 levels similar to other transitional Andean communities. In 1963 the Peasant Community of Pararin, Province of Recuay, requests and receives assistance in setting up a farm cooperative and borrows several sprayer pumps from Vicos until they can purchase their own. The ministerial inability to staff the clinic regularly keeps the population vulnerable to disease and a high death rate; nevertheless, improved living standards lead to increased population growth (Montalvo 1967). Cooperatively exploited community lands increase to 53 hectares; family fields cover 97 percent of economically useful land. Population density is 81 persons per square kilometer of useful land.

1964-66 The reforestation of Vicos uplands is begun in cooperation with the Peruvian Forestry Service and a half million eucalyptus trees are planted, a quantity later doubled. Two Peace Corps volunteers continue teaching in outlying sectional schools. The last CPP research is conducted by a Peruvian student, and the project ends officially in 1966 as the second agreement with the Ministry of Labor expires.

1966-67 A Vicosino is elected to Marcará District Municipal Council for the first time. The Peruvian-funded Ancash Program (and PNIPA) of the Ministry of Labor ends and is "replaced" by the Regional Program for Indian Area Development, funded by the Interamerican Development Bank's (IDB) office in Huaraz; new government programs such as *Cooperación Popular* begin road construction in Vicos and continue the forestation program.

1968	Having long incorporated the Chancos people and lands into the community, Vicos finally resolves its dispute with the Peace Corps. Meanwhile, Chancos Springs has been rented from the Huaraz Beneficent Society by two Vicosinos who operate the rustic resort for the next 12 years.
1968-69	Vicos pays the last 100,000 *sol* installment on the government mortgage loan. Universal land reform is decreed by the new Peruvian government in 1969, and serfdom is abolished nationally.
1969-70	A Ministry of Agriculture program to upgrade cattle in Vicos fails when the animals prove sterile and employees involved are convicted of defrauding the community. Former employees of the Ancash Program now employed by the Agrarian Reform and Interamerican Development Bank programs dabble in Vicos affairs. A regional potato blight sharply lowers production, causing severe economic problems in Vicos and throughout the region; potatoes from the region are embargoed from the Lima markets.
1970	The great earthquake on May 31 devastates the Callejon de Huaylas, but causes comparatively minor damage in Vicos where two are killed and former CPP project buildings, now little used, are ruined.[8] The Vicos community quickly replaces the church and school roofs and fixes warehouse buildings without relief assistance. The earthquake relief agencies supply unwanted tents and garments. Chancos Springs is badly damaged, but no rehabilitation funds are expended there. The Peruvian Agrarian Reform Administration cancels the rest of Vicos's mortgage because "enough" had been paid in light of new agrarian laws, and all such debts throughout the region are forgiven because of the disaster. In the final analysis Vicos paid a total of 1 million *soles* for the estate, about 30 percent more than its original assessed value.
1971	The Revolutionary Government of the Armed Forces classifies Vicos as an official "Peasant Community" and decrees that organizational changes conform with new laws. The Vicosinos resist imposition of the changes when Peasant Affairs Bureau officials (former local employees of the Ancash Program) criticize CPP and call Vicosinos

"backward and impossible to help"; the government employees' attempt to rig Vicos elections fails, but a new organization is imposed. The community starts construction of a new "civic center."

1972　The Vicos population is now 2,909 with an annual growth rate of 3.4 percent. Representatives of the earthquake redevelopment commission (ORDEZA) visit Vicos to promote regional programs, including the installation of electricity.

1973　With urging from former Ancash Program employees now with the Ministry of Agriculture, the community reassigns school land use from vocational gardening practice and school support functions to community feedlot use as part of projected dairy and feedlot development plans. Protesting teachers are expelled from the community and replaced while community support for the school diminishes. Subsequently, the ministry's dairy-cattle program turns out to be a fraud, causing great financial loss to Vicos; community leaders are discredited and morale is low. The ministry officials involved are sent to new posts in the jungle. Although the community attempts to establish its mineral rights claims, a Huaraz company begins mining operations on Vicos property after winning usufruct rights under the national mining code, and the community is urged to collaborate by the Energy and Mining Ministry. The community seeks ORDEZA support for urban development and to gain control of and develop Chancos Springs along lines (ironically) originally suggested by the Peace Corps volunteers.

1974　Despite its problems, the Vicos community continues regular council meetings first started under CPP aegis in 1956. The community works with the ministries of Education (school reorganization and new kindergarten), Health (clinic), Agriculture (fertilizer program, Forest Service, corn campaign), ORDEZA (urban planning, electricity), and SINAMOS (road construction, community organization, regional peasant leagues). Vicos committees on road construction and school parents meet with neighboring communities about joint work.

1975-80   An Air Force colonel representing ORDEZA declares that Chancos belongs to Vicos and that Vicos's ownership of the resort will be approved, but this fails to happen. Under ORDEZA sponsorship, the electrification plan is begun around the old plaza and CPP project area, and the road is finished to the high pastures. The Ministry of Education opens the first secondary school in Marcara District at Vicos, and a kindergarten built by the community is staffed. Work continues on the community center at Vicos's expense. Regular bus service from Vicos to Huaraz is established. Community attempts to control mining on its land founder as mineral rights are exploited by outsiders. Although a dispute with the mining company is settled, with the company agreeing to give 8 percent of its Vicos earnings to the community and maintain the road and bridges, poor relations with the mine continue. Regional embargoes of diseased potatoes and cattle limit income and development in Vicos and elsewhere.

1980-82   A Vicosino is elected to Marcará District Council in the first national municipal elections since 1966. "Urban" Vicos encompasses 40 houses in the vicinity of the plaza, where most have electricity and public lighting. Television sets are purchased by three families. A permanent secondary school is under construction with community and ORDENOR (formerly ORDEZA) funds. University of Ancash (Huaraz) engineering students, with community agreement, begin a continuing study and project to promote the urbanization of Vicos. The mining conflicts continue. Students and faculty of Garcilaso de la Vega University (Lima) conduct a study of post-CPP Vicos.

1982   The Vicos population is reported to be 4,820 by the national census, increasing at an annual rate of 6.4 percent over the last decade. Vicos primary schools have over 500 students, and 78 attend high school in Vicos. Vicos community officers register complaints about mining operations and again seek to gain control. The migration of Vicosinos to Huaraz and coastal cities grows. The community begins to harvest and sell its eucalyptus trees, planted under the reforestation programs in the 1960s. A new clinic built by the community is staffed by a Vicosino from the Ministry of Health.

1983-84   The severe decline of national and regional economies is felt in Vicos as remittances from migrants slacken and crop prices remain low; in new municipal elections, the district of Marcará elects the former Ancash Program administrator as mayor; the Vicosino is reelected to the district council. Vicos migrants in Lima and Huaral (on the coast) organize "regional associations" with about 100 participants. The Marcará district government takes control of Chancos Springs over Vicos's objections and establishes a toll on the road to Chancos. Community attempts to lay claim to mining rights erupt in violence as police wound several Vicosinos in clashes at the mine; newspapers erroneously fix blame on the "Sendero Luminoso" movement.

1986   In municipal elections, the 1800 men and women voters in Vicos form the largest block in Carhuaz Province. Three Vicosinos run as candidates for provincial council posts, and a Vicosino is elected mayor of Marcará district.

DIMENSIONS OF CHANGE

This chronology highlights patterns that place the CPP effort in the perspective of both time and place. There were three distinct periods in the project's history: the *initial phase* of research and basic innovation from 1952 to 1956; the *consolidation period* from 1956 to 1962, ending with the sale of the estate to the community; and a *concluding phase* from 1963 to 1966, as the project retired from Vicos.

CPP sought to restructure the hacienda into a viable community that could fend for itself and enhance its situation in the region and nation without CPP participation. Holmberg saw this in terms of providing the Vicosinos with a key to a "wider sharing of human values": through CPP intervention, Vicosinos would come to enjoy greater access to power, wealth, skill, enlightenment, well-being, respect, affection, and rectitude. In addition to constituting an analytical model for a holistic view of changes in the lives of individuals and the community, these value areas also formed a basis for evaluating the end results of the CPP effort (Lasswell and Holmberg 1966; Dobyns, Doughty, and Lasswell 1971; Dobyns et al. 1966, 1967).

From the onset, one of the special concerns of the project was human rights. Vicosinos were denigrated as persons because they were Indians, serfs, poor, illiterate, and "ignorant." CPP introduced changes that affected each of these classifications directly by abolishing peonage, encouraging cultural pride, increasing incomes and skills, and offering educational opportunity and a wider social experience. The impact of such changes is felt in two broad areas, individual and institutional, and one may evaluate results in both in the chronology above.

With respect to the individual, the enforced tranquility of the hacienda society, which offered few options to anyone, gave way to an openness that was new to Vicos culture. A result of this freedom was an increase in travel by Vicosinos (Alers et al. 1965). With the innovation of cash incomes, both families and individuals acquired many new material items and invested heavily in clothing and other items. Choices offer opportunity for personal initiative, talent, and mobility, and the people of Vicos rapidly began to differentiate themselves in a variety of ways. Economic class differences had existed prior to the project and amplified as the society became more open.

CPP did not promote change at a personal level per se, such as trying to get people to dress differently or brush their teeth twice a day, although the schools did encourage such things among pupils. On the other hand, attempts to open up new areas for talent and interest development reached large numbers of persons. The result is particularly notable among the youth of today whose appearance, level of confidence in dealing with the "larger world," work experience, and goals differ dramatically from the Vicosinos I first met in 1960.

Nevertheless, while some have complained that Vicosinos remain "paternalistic" (Fonseca 1985:153), others have criticized the role of CPP in fostering "sexist" patterns as the result of "capitalistic" development policy (Babb 1985:162ff). Babb feels that women were better off in their status vis-a-vis men as serfs, lamenting that they have "lost" such critical economic roles as the right to glean the hacienda's fields because of improved potato production (Doughty 1971:111). It is certainly true that everyone was repressed under the hacienda system. But asserting that women suffered "deprivation" by not gleaning, ignores the fact that the people were spending more time with their own fields and animals and had vastly improved their diets under the CPP program. They did not *have* to engage in the denigrating act of gleaning. By 1960, families took their pigs to scavenge the fields instead. Women continued to play a major role in agriculture in the community cooperative in all manner of tasks from planting to grading potatoes and, on their own lands, in a full range of customary tasks. They also increased their roles as traders and brokers in the regional markets, thereby enhancing their status vis-a-vis men--a fact Babb conveniently ignores.

There is no doubt that Vicosinos have benefited differentially as a result of the CPP program. Women in Vicos were specifically the objects of several programs over the years, precisely because Vicos was then, and remains today, an androcentric culture in a patrilineal society, unlike the bilateral Hispanic kinship system of the nation.[9] Families were very reluctant to send their daughters to school throughout the first decade, and after years of patient coaxing by two generations of teachers, only in the past 10 years has female attendance reached one-third of the school population.[10] Nevertheless, the first Vicos woman graduated from high school in Huaraz in 1975 and later studied to be an accountant. She lived with her parents in Vicos where, although crippled by polio, she became a successful local broker, buying and selling farm animals.[11] Other young women are now attending the new high school in Vicos and presumably will play larger roles in their community than their mothers.

The changes in Vicos with respect to growing travel and migration are notable. Atypically for the region, Vicos has retained much of its population, although it seems inevitable that out-migration will eventually approximate patterns of other villages in the region. The impact of CPP in its initial years provoked such hope that it produced a halo effect (Vazquez 1963:93-102; Alers 1965:339-441) in attracting former residents back to Vicos, exactly opposite the national trend.

The increased ability of Vicosinos to travel beyond their region has brought its own consequences. The growing familiarity of Vicosinos with their country and exposure to new ideas and experiences has inevitably stimulated further changes. Following Barnett (1953:46-61), CPP saw this as a necessary mechanism in the social change process. Thus, people were encouraged to travel when they could to provincial markets and the capital, Lima.

There is no doubt, however, that the culture shock of such experiences can be disorienting, as Erasmus (1961:3-8) has amply demonstrated. The exposure of many Vicosinos to the "outside world" not only provided a great sense of expectation, but also a glimmer of how great was the gulf between their lives and the power and wealth of others. The effect can be destructive, as Stein (1985b) points out in recounting the problem of alcoholism as it overtook three Vicos participants in an AID-sponsored farm exchange program in 1963.[12] Although their situation was an exceptional one, it was perhaps a signal for what was occurring in Vicos as changes brought insecurity and demands upon individuals unaccustomed to such stress (Alers 1971:128-131). In retrospect, it seems clear enough that CPP should have anticipated and acted to ease this stress, although just how it might have done so with available resources and in the total absence of mental health clinics is certainly questionable. It is worth noting that stress and discomfort characterized the hacienda system (Holmberg 1967) enough to lead Vicosinos to become active participants in the project.

Finally, it is impossible to promote change in such a society so that it resolves all problems to the satisfaction of everyone. Many critics of CPP appear to fault the project for not being infallible or suitably anticipating issues that concern us today. CPP achieved no such perfection, but what it did was open the society to alternatives and choices previously denied it by serfdom and discrimination. Community members have indeed proceeded to differentiate themselves along class lines and as individual men and women in the context of Peruvian society. What Vicosinos have done or will do with their opportunities and potential was beyond the capacity of this or any project to determine, then or now.

THE COMMUNITY CONTEXT

The pattern of change introduced into the community was, by nature of the agreement, the interests of the times, and the goals sought, designed to integrate the people as effective participants in the region and nation. In the context of Peru, it may be debatable today whether or not that was a meritorious goal, if ethnic discreteness is seen in a positive light for its sake alone. Since the end of the project, Vicos has gained more in these terms than any commensurate community in the Callejón de Huaylas: electricity, a secondary school, a clinic staffed by a trained Vicosino, a soccer field, and a kindergarten. The assistance it still receives from the Ministry of Agriculture (unusual for any village in the region!) has been a mixed blessing at best, an experience shared by other beneficiaries of that agency. The early CPP encouragement of education and literacy as keys to political empowerment resulted in 1966 in the election of a Vicosino to a position on the Marcará District Council. This occurred because enough Vicosinos could meet literacy requirements for sufferage (at that time) and understood the political system (Vazquez 1967). Henceforth, the Vicos community, although still demeaned by local mestizos as populated by "dumb Indians," established itself as a political force.

On these counts Vicos proved, with some contretemps, that it has been able to manage its affairs with various state institutions and is willing to fight for its rights in that arena, as the unfortunate embroilment over mining rights shows. Viewed in historic perspective, Vicos has always been willing to engage in strong action, as seen in the various attempts to change the hacienda regimen (Barnett 1960), a pattern their willingness to discharge school teachers and Peace Corps volunteers follows. Some of these efforts have been "won," others, such as the dairy fraud and the dispute over the mine, have been "lost." The Vicosinos, however, are not alone in these problems.

The neighboring Peasant Community of Shumáy, adjacent to the town of Marcará, and another Peasant Community named Mita, farther down the valley, also suffered setbacks at the hands of incompetent agricultural planners between 1975 and 1980. In these cases the Ministry of Agriculture and ORDEZA, with about $140,000 in USAID and Peruvian funds, established swine-improvement projects and pork-processing plants to be operated by each community. In both instances, by failing to incorporate community members in any real decision making, but simply employing them as workers, the "expert" development consultants created havoc within each community organization and its leadership, while making vast expenditures on infrastructure. Although these two communities had long been recognized as official "Peasant Communities," both had had leadership problems and serious disputes for many years. Not surprisingly, both projects were moribund by 1980.[13]

The town of Marcará, long known throughout the valley as extremely conservative and poorly organized, showed little aptitude for pursuing its own amelioration. In fact, its traditional lack of "progress" was one of the factors that provoked such jealousy of the Vicosinos, who as "brute Indians" hardly merited the attentions of the CPP. Consequently, over the 26 years I have known the district, it recorded little change. After the 1980 elections, however, when a new municipal government came to office, headed by a former assistant administrator of the Ancash Program at Vicos working in cooperation with a new parish priest from Italy, the District of Marcará finally began to show signs of constructive change, with urban service improvements and plans to redevelop the decrepit Chancos Springs resort.

On the other hand, the huge infrastructural investments for an ill-fated trout farm on the bank of the Santa River at Marcará made by the earthquake redevelopment organization with USAID monies were never completed, leaving behind several hundred meters of concrete canals, sluice gates, and pools, at a reputed cost of $210,000. The fish-farm project never incorporated any local input aside from wage labor. It was, like the pig farm, a classic end result of "trickle-down development"--expensive and fruitless. Together with the aborted swine project at Shumáy, USAID and the Peruvian government spent well over $280,000 in Marcará and produced no positive socioeconomic impact whatever in one of the poorest, most undeveloped parts of the Callejón de Huaylas!

Elsewhere in the region, the former hacienda community of Huaypán in Yungay Province, which sought assistance in the form of advice and noninterest loans from the Vicos community in 1960, has encountered numerous difficulties in organization and development. Although it became an independent community, it has not achieved any of the institutional services or advantages that Vicos enjoys nor has it coaxed development attention from the regional development authority, now known as CORDEANCASH.[14] Indeed, in a survey of the region while evaluating the impact of

Food for Peace programs (Public Law 480), I did not encounter any comparable Indian community that approached the development status of Vicos (Doughty, Burleigh, and Painter 1984).

It seems clear that the 10-year program at Vicos (1952-1962) leading up to the community purchasing its lands, rested heavily upon extensive collaboration between the three major institutional players comprising CPP: Cornell's anthropology department, the Peruvian government and its ministries, and the people of Vicos. This is amply demonstrated in the preceding chronology and highlighted by the financial support provided by each.[15] For Cornell there were two grants from the Carnegie Corporation totaling $126,000 that were used to pay its staff, U.S. and Peruvian student scholarships, and related research expenses. Peruvian government funds, estimated at $210,000, went almost entirely to salaries. The Vicos people paid for most of the cost with thousands of man-days of labor. Each Vicos family provided one worker to the community as needed, about 122 days a year but often much less. Given local wages, the community input was worth about $375,000. With all expenditures, CPP cost about $711,000 over the decade of development operation, or roughly $355 per capita ($35 per annum). This was not only vastly less expensive per capita, but far more effective than the "big money" approach so popular with development bureaucracies.[16] Indeed, the Vicos project enjoyed the additional advantage of *achieving* its more far-reaching goals.

The critical differences between these juxtaposed projects can be summarized not only by their results, but by their methods and goals. The collaboration of effort, underwritten by investments of capital and work from each party, played a major role in giving continuity to the project throughout the period. Less than 18 percent of the cost of CPP came from outside Peru, and virtually all of that was spent in staff functions that centered on the research and policy formation that was the core of Holmberg's "research and development" approach. CPP intended to develop the human potential of Vicos and, thus, concern was with the social and cultural processes of the community. Infrastructure per se was secondary, contrary to the Marcará, Shumáy, and Mita cases.

Outlined in the original agreement, the success of the project was totally dependent upon its ability to integrate the normal, budgeted work of several ministries at one spot--Vicos. The net effect of this has been to place the community and its people in the flow of national events in a more advantageous position than they were in 1952. Despite many changes brought on by political turmoil, earthquake, and vacillating public policy, two decades after the official end of the project, Vicos continues to operate along the lines established under CPP guidance. The outline of results presented here indicates that Vicos has remained a viable community. On the other hand, the reluctance of international development leaders and national interest groups to learn from or accept such experience in any constructive manner is also well established (Himes 1981; Hoben 1982). Despite the rash of postproject evaluations it seems unlikely that the Vicos program, like other "pilot" development efforts, will be used as the model its founders intended. In final summation, the beneficiaries were the active participants and collaborators in the project: the Vicosinos, researchers, and staff.

NOTES

1. Despite long familiarity with Vicos, my association with the Cornell-Peru Project was spent mostly in research elsewhere in the region or the nation. I was, however, closely involved with events there from 1960 to 1964, subsequently returning on numerous short visits, the most recent in 1984. I owe many personal and intellectual debts to those who have been so supportive for so long. Particular mention should be made of the assistance and contributions of Polly French Doughty, Mario C. Vazquez V., and Henry R. Dobyns, as well as those of the late Celso Leon of Vicos, whose leadership, work, and comprehension were key factors in the project's success.

2. A systematic review of critiques of the Cornell-Peru Project is presented in Doughty (1986b).

3. These are officially chartered corporate entities that prior to 1969 were called "Indigenous Communities" or "Indian Communities"; they are legally recognized because they can prove colonial title to their lands. Vicos was never entitled to this status since it had always been a hacienda.

4. The social structure and lifeways of Marcara are thoroughly detailed by Humberto Ghersi (1959, 1960, 1961). Joan Snyder studied Recuayhuanca (1960). William Stein (1961) researched life in the neighboring Indian hamlet of Hualcán and has frequently written his

reflections on the experience (1985a, 1985b). These studies were carried out under CPP sponsorship from 1951 to 1953. In addition to the many works on Vicos itself, these provided CPP with a detailed picture of the Marcará area and the social processes affecting Vicos.

5. In 1960, the CPP staff painted portions of the United Nations' Universal Declaration of Human Rights (to which Peru is a signatory) on the walls of the community center (Dobyns, Doughty, and Lasswell 1971: frontispiece). Local mestizo visitors and officials objected to these as "inspired by communism," a phrase by which they condemned CPP. Today Marxist analysts see Vicos as "penetrated by capitalism" because of CPP, while others view it as a product of "creeping socialism," which created an "island in a capitalist sea" (Aramburú 1978:16-17). Still others complain that the project was not "revolutionary" because Vicosinos did not have to "fight" for their rights (Himes 1981: 52-3). Peaceful change, however radical, is thus seen as unacceptable from almost any ideological viewpoint.

6. This chronology is derived in the main from published sources on Vicos, principally the annual reports in *Perú Indígena*, Dobyns and Vazquez (1964), and Dobyns, Doughty, and Lasswell (1971). Further data come from field research at Vicos and in the Callejón de Huaylas by the author in 1970, 1971, 1978, 1980, 1982, 1983, and 1984.

7. *Plan Nacional de Integración de la Población Aborigen* (PNIPA) supplanted the Peruvian Indian Institute in the Ministry of Labor and Indian Affairs. Although national in scope, with operations in several other highland departments, it was a rather stiff bureaucracy, described in a pun by one of its administrators as going "*ni pa' delante, ni pa' atrás*" (neither forward nor backward). The three principal programs were in Vicos, Puno, and Cuzco at Kuyo Chico, Cuzco (Nuñez del Prado 1973).

8. The report of heavy quake damage in Vicos by Morss et al. (1976:421) is mistaken.

9. Vazquez and Holmberg (1966) describe the Vicos patrilineage systems of *castas*. The introduction of schools in Vicos produced a change in names. In

contrast to the Peruvian Hispanic tradition, children only carried one last name, that of the father's *casta*. In 1952 there were 52 *castas* in Vicos. Vicosinos did not use or recognize the maternal last name because a child did not belong to the mother's lineage. With the introduction of schools, the law required that Vicosino children begin using the maternal last name with the paternal name. I do not know whether this produced any further changes in Vicos kinship patterns, however.

10. The well-founded fears of the Indian women regarding abuse by mestizo men are documented in CPP records (Stein 1985a:268-275). Since many of the teachers were and are mestizo men, the reaction of Vicos families is understandable.

11. She died prematurely of heart disease in 1982.

12. Alcoholism was not seen as a problem in the early years of the project, although heavy drinking always accompanied festive events. It seems likely that anxieties created by rapid change converted culturally controlled behaviors into counterproductive ones (Mangin 1957). I doubt that the trip to the United States was the sole cause of their problems, since all three were heavy drinkers before that excursion.

13. Today, the large concrete pigsties serve as monuments to the failure and, as the community members quickly point out, "the pigs lived better than we did." In addition, contrary to Fonseca's (1985:153-4) glowing but inaccurate description of a peasant "movement" there, Mita has enjoyed little success in the projects it has attempted from 1963 to the present. By 1984 its best land was rented to the adjacent agricultural experiment station, and numerous debilitating internal conflicts continued. The Shumáy pig farm was rented to a Canadian forestry project in 1984.

14. This organism was originally set up as the earthquake rehabilitation and development agency called by its acronym, CRYRZA, with other subsequent name changes to ORDEZA and ORDENOR noted in the chronology.

15. There has been much comment and critique about the cost of development at Vicos. It has become an accepted "fact" that development there was very expensive (see Himes 1981:176-9; Morss et al. 1976:428) and that

Cornell spent vast amounts through its grants. This is not so, as shown here. Previous project costs have only been premised on the Carnegie grants (Doughty 1986b). The estimates cited are based on my generous reconstructions of Peruvian personnel, labor, and material costs at Vicos over CPP's first decade.

16. In an early evaluation of CPP it was judged to be underfunded (Adams and Cumberland 1960). In the comparative cases cited, the Peruvian government and USAID expended approximately $350,000 in material and other costs over about two years in Marcará, Shumáy, and Mita, with a combined population of just over 1600 persons, at a cost of $218 per capita ($109 per year). By comparison, the *least* expensive assistance programs in Peru today are those subsidized through use of Public Law 480 foods. They average between $28 and $89 per capita yearly costs, but yield questionable development results (Doughty, Burleigh, and Painter 1984:44, 175-270).

7

The Mexican Urban Housing Project: A Collaboration Between la Área Técnica y la Área Social

*Arthur D. Murphy, Ignacio Cabrera Fernández,
Henry A. Selby, and Ignacio Ruiz Love*

INTRODUCTION

This chapter chronicles the involvement of a group of anthropologists from universities in the United States with a federal development agency in Mexico--the *Instituto Nacional para el Desarrollo de la Comunidad y de la Vivienda Popular* ("The National Institute for Community Development"), INDECO[1] for short. For some time the association was confined to activities in Oaxaca, Mexico, where the anthropologists were located. This period proved, however, to be a preparation for a more far-reaching collaboration beginning in 1976, when a team of researchers from INDECO's national office came to Oaxaca to carry out the pilot study for an information-gathering project that eventually involved over 10 Mexican cities. Although this account follows the experiences of the anthropologists, our primary aim is to demonstrate how two groups of professionals, one practicing and another academic, came together, without prior design and with highly differing goals, to work toward a melding of goals and approaches.

The first group was comprised of Mexican administrators, architects, engineers, and social scientists who were working with INDECO. As members of an action-oriented federal agency, these individuals were primarily geared to deliver services and provide basic housing to the urban poor of Mexico insofar as the limited resources of their agency permitted. This group tended to be global in its perspective, accustomed to dealing with problems on a citywide or even nationwide scale.

The second group consisted of North American anthropologists with a more restricted point of view. They were "purists" whose research in Mexico had been in an esoteric subdiscipline of anthropology, and they were constrained by the traditional anthropological focus on local-level activities in single communities or neighborhoods. In the taxonomy of Arensberg (1947), their interests were in abstract rather than applied anthropology (Eddy and Partridge 1978).

We here recount how these two groups ultimately joined applied and abstract scientific concerns in a manner we hope will be instructive to others contemplating similar joint studies. This is not to say the venture was entirely successful (it has certainly had its failures and shortcomings) or that the participants have always been happy with each other (they have not; of the original participants, some no longer maintain contact because of conflicts left unresolved). It can be said, however, that a working relationship that began over 10 years ago has evolved and prospered and shows every indication of continuing for some time to come.[2]

THE SETTING

During the Echeverría administration (1970-76), INDECO was given the mission of helping alter the undesirable housing conditions suffered by many Mexicans because of rapid urban growth. Living conditions among the working poor were becoming a recognized problem that needed to be dealt with in a creative and forceful fashion. The national director of INDECO was given wide latitude in the development of housing programs for the urban poor who had jobs but did not earn enough to enter the formal housing market.[3]

To carry out its mission, INDECO's director pursued two administrative directions. First, he surrounded himself with young, aggressive individuals dedicated to developing as many innovative housing solutions as possible. An important aspect of his recruitment was bringing into the agency individuals from a variety of disciplines and political doctrines. Unlike other development agencies, which depended heavily on technicians, INDECO had a strong contingent of social scientists and social workers who were more than token representatives for the political left. Many of the programs subsequently carried out by the Mexican government were the result of brainstorming sessions held by this diverse group in Mexico City, whose ideas were passed on to the state directors of INDECO for implementation as they saw fit.

This decentralization of decision making regarding actual implementation of programs was the second key aspect of the administrative experiment at INDECO. Unlike other federal agencies, the state directors of INDECO had a great deal of leeway in the implementation of central office policy. That is, state offices were encouraged, even expected, to adjust the original conception of program ideas to suit local conditions. Further, state directors were encouraged to align themselves with local private and government sectors to increase their effectiveness.

These two aspects of the national administrative structure were critical to the incorporation of the academic anthropologists into INDECO's work. The emphasis on experimentation and the use of social science theory to develop new and innovative projects meant that—unlike the situation often pertaining in the United States—the anthropologists never had to justify their discipline or "prove" they could contribute to project planning (Nahmad 1977; Lomnitz 1979). Moreover, the national office's emphasis on local variation and autonomy within INDECO made it possible for the anthropologists to begin work with the agency at the level of analysis for which their discipline had prepared them and with which they were most comfortable—the neighborhood or community.

The incorporation of the anthropologists into INDECO and the relationships that have remained, despite the termination of that agency in 1982, have gone through four stages: the get-acquainted period, the period during which the relationship developed, the period of close cooperation, and the current period of productive coexistence.

PHASES OF THE RELATIONSHIP

Getting Acquainted

The anthropologists' first contact with INDECO came while they were carrying out an NSF research grant concerned with the decision-making process of migrants to the city of Oaxaca (Murphy 1973; Stepick 1974; Selby and Hendrix 1976). While their research was abstract, even at this early point the specter of applied, action-oriented anthropology reared its head. One day in early 1972, while reviewing preliminary results, the project director admonished the others to think of possible interpretations an administrator could make.

Of the three anthropologists, two were located in the city and the third was doing baseline work in a rural village. The choice of locations turned out to be fortuitous in setting the course of their future involvement with INDECO.

At that time, INDECO-OAXACA, in the context of the then national policy of providing services for the poor, was carrying out a project to deliver medical, water, and sanitation services to some of the poorer *colonias* ("neighborhoods") of Oaxaca (Higgins 1974). Providing health care involved the establishment of a basic health clinic to be manned by recent medical school graduates fulfilling their required year of social service. With respect to water and sanitation, INDECO wished to create an organizational structure through which the agency could provide materials at cost, while the *colonos* ("neighborhood residents") furnished the labor for installation.

During this time, the director of INDECO-OAXACA became acquainted with one of the anthropologists, who was working in one of INDECO's target neighborhoods. The director was open to suggestions for making his project more effective. Specifically, he wanted to know how to get the *colonos* to make more extensive use of the medical services and organize committees to manage the installation of water and sewerage. The anthropologist was able to provide useful information and advice on both counts.

As a result of this initial contact, the director decided an anthropologist could help advance the goals of his agency. He asked the anthropologists if one of them would be interested in returning to Oaxaca in the future to undertake a study of a site-and-services community that INDECO was developing for moderate- and low-income households. The site-and-services idea had come to Mexico through international agencies searching for a method to provide cost-recoverable housing to the poor in developing nations (see Bamberger, Sanyal, and Valverde 1982; Bamberger, Gonzalez-Polio, and Sae-Hau 1982; Payne 1984). INDECO-MEXICO adopted the concept, and in Oaxaca it was developed and modified to meet the conditions of the area. Several communities were planned or under construction, and INDECO-OAXACA's director felt that if one of the anthropologists could study the natural history of the development of a community, he could help INDECO modify its development plan so that future projects would be carried out with some notion of what could be expected from the people and what requests would be unreasonable.

Developing a Relationship

This project marked a new phase in the relationship between the North American anthropologists and the National Institute for Community Development. The courtship between the anthropologists and INDECO's state office in Oaxaca lasted four years and, like the period of courtship between two individuals, was critical in the development of an ongoing cooperative relationship. Because of the decentralized nature of INDECO, the anthropologists had an opportunity to learn how to make contacts and work with an official government agency at the local level--a level compatible with the traditional focus of study in the discipline.

Direct contacts in this phase were sporadic. Letters were exchanged with INDECO-OAXACA staff with whom the anthropologists had made acquaintance, and reports and papers were circulated. The anthropologists visited Oaxaca on several occasions and through readings and discussions familiarized themselves with the operation of the institute, with the data it had available, and perhaps most importantly, with the constraints under which it operated.

During the summer of 1975 two of the anthropologists, somewhat self-consciously and apprehensively, made their first foray into the world of government consultation. They went to Oaxaca intent on spending two weeks in the site-and-services community INDECO wanted studied. By getting firsthand experience in the *colonia*, they wished to see if it would be possible to do interesting "abstract" anthropology in an applied context.

Before actually moving into the *colonia*, San Antonio del Atoyac, the anthropologists talked with professionals at INDECO-OAXACA involved with the project (mostly young architects and engineers) to find out what they saw as the *colonia's* positive and negative aspects. In general, the INDECO staff felt the *colonia's* merits were in its planning. It was a well-designed community where everything had a place and a purpose. They felt the agency's commitment to allow people to build freely within broad limits was a strong point. On the negative side, they felt San Antonio lacked social organization and community spirit. In addition, they saw the residents' complaints over the cost of water and sewerage installation as an indication that, "like most people of this class," the *colonos* simply wished to extract a free ride from the government. They were also disturbed by the fact that their orderly design was being negated because numerous households were setting up tiny stores (*tienditas*) in their homes.

The anthropologists' time in the *colonia* was filled with all the professional activities common to anthropologists when entering a new field site--walking around, talking with people, gathering information on household size and family structure, and asking questions about people's attitudes toward INDECO and San Antonio del Atoyac (see Agar 1980). By the end of their stay, the anthropologists had become enthusiastic about the possibilities of their research and were able to provide INDECO with insights into the *colonia* and the people's attitudes toward INDECO, particularly with respect to the agency's concerns.

The matter of additional costs for installation of water, sewers, paved roads, and sidewalks could not be altered in any material sense. INDECO had not included these items in the original price of the lots, and their costs had to be recovered through direct charges. The residents' objections to paying "more" for these items came primarily from confusion over the meaning of the word *fraccionamiento*, the term INDECO had used in promoting this and other housing projects.

The word, translatable as "subdivision," carries a fairly consistent and specific meaning in Mexico. *Fraccionamientos* are places where, because of government building codes and the class of people who normally inhabit them, all the infrastructure for modern urban life is provided. In Oaxaca advertising for *fraccionamientos* commonly stresses the fact that "*todos los servicios*" are being provided by the developer (see Logan 1984). The anthropologists pointed out that many residents--regardless of the specifics of the contract they signed--thought they were purchasing a lot with full services. They were unprepared for an assessment of another several thousand pesos. INDECO had heard this argument before--from the residents of the *colonia*. However, hearing it again from two "outside experts" gave it credibility. The result was that in Oaxaca, INDECO refrained from using the offending word in subsequent advertising.

The second issue had to do with INDECO's attitude toward the *tiendas*, or shops, that had sprung up in the *colonia* shortly after its birth. Because the planners at INDECO valued orderliness--houses and stores in separate locations--they felt the residents were ruining their well-developed design. Notices went up that all shops were to be relocated to a small "market" in the center of the *colonia*. Although INDECO had never actually closed a shop, the threat created a great deal of tension in the community.

The anthropologists convinced the director that small-scale home enterprises were a natural and important part of this type of neighborhood. First, for families who could do so, opening a small store at home represented a significant step toward raising their economic position. A store run out of one room of a house can be managed by a woman with small children at home, whereas one in a separate location cannot. Second, the *colonos*, who were mostly strangers when San

Antonio was created, were forming in these *tiendas* the ties necessary to develop the social organization INDECO wanted. It was true that each *tienda* tended to represent a faction in the community, and INDECO had difficulties getting all groups to work together. However, some cohesive groups were better than the anarchy and malaise that would exist without these meeting places. Besides, it was futile to attempt to stamp them out.

Presented with these arguments, INDECO stopped regulating the stores in its developments. Today, the market INDECO feared would remain empty is full, and the small shops open and close with the regularity familiar to anyone who has spent time in a working-class neighborhood of Latin America.

This experience was critical in the development of the anthropologists' relationship with INDECO for two reasons. First, it further demonstrated that anthropologists could learn a good deal about a community in a short time and could use this knowledge to address issues of concern to INDECO. Second, and perhaps more important, it taught the anthropologists something about planners and developers as well as about themselves. The anthropologists, like many of their colleagues, held the stereotypic view that action-oriented technicians and social planners tended toward narrow-mindedness and generally did not listen to the advice of social scientists. They learned that quite the opposite was true. The anthropologists found they were dealing with professionals eager for suggestions that would help them provide housing for the poor at the most reasonable cost. As for themselves, the anthropologists discovered they were able to make reasonable recommendations on the basis of their theoretical models and ethnographic work. They found they could discuss problems with architects, engineers, and social workers in a professional manner and that those discussions could lead to some improvement in the living conditions of *colonia* residents.

The Period of Close Cooperation

Community Research. The period of close on-site cooperation between the anthropologists and INDECO began when one of the anthropologists arrived in Oaxaca to begin a community study combining abstract with applied anthropology. The research project involved a formal study of the concept of development (*desarrollo*) to determine if differences in the semantic domain of the word could account for some of the problems INDECO and its clients were having with one another. However, as an outsider the anthropologist quickly found himself in a peculiar position.

INDECO personnel expected him to smooth over the agency's problems with residents. For some at INDECO, the role of the social scientist was that of a state servant who helps break down social and cultural barriers to the benevolent actions of the state. At a more parochial level, the site supervisor wanted assistance in advancing the project so he could move up and out of the *colonia* as quickly as possible.

For their part, the citizens of the *colonia* felt that because of his ties to the INDECO hierarchy, the anthropologist should act as a go-between for them. If they had a problem they felt they could not address to INDECO directly, they asked the anthropologist to do it for them. This structural position made it possible for the anthropologist to learn most of the minor complaints against INDECO. However, his being classified as an "official" by *colonia* residents made it difficult to get them to discuss their more fundamental concerns. Only after demonstrating his agreement with their dissatisfaction with activities of the site manager and his willingness to present their case to the administration did people begin to discuss their deeper hopes and disappointments with the anthropologist. With this community-level breakthrough the anthropologist began to act more and more as a conduit for information and opinions between the community and INDECO.

During this time, INDECO-OAXACA's director requested evaluations of the *colonia* and of the development model being used. The dialogue carried on between the anthropologist and the professional development agents of INDECO in the early months resulted in a growing appreciation by the anthropologists of the constraints—physical, structural, and political—within which INDECO was working. At the same time, INDECO planners grew to appreciate the aid anthropology could provide in making small adjustments in the program that would smooth the transition for people moving into a new housing project (Murphy 1980; Stepick and Murphy 1980).

As the months passed, a close friendship developed between the director of INDECO-OAXACA and the anthropologists. The director became their key informant on INDECO-OAXACA and its operations, INDECO at the national level, and the general attitudes of the Mexican government toward the poor. As often happens with key informants, he entered into fictive kinship relationships with the anthropologists and continues to be supportive whenever they are in the area. The anthropologists, for their part, became

part of his *equipo*--that group of advisors around every rising Mexican entrepreneur/politician (Grindle 1977).
The relationship was mutually beneficial. For the director, it enabled him to use the anthropologists as outside experts. He was also able to add a degree of academic respectability to the projects under his direction. For the anthropologists, the association was a broadening experience. They began to look beyond their closely defined interests and perceive the possibilities of research at a level other than the neighborhood or village. Discussions with INDECO personnel led them to consider the relationship between the city's power structure and the citizens living in public *colonias*. Further, as the anthropologists began to move away from a concentration on INDECO in Oaxaca to other agencies at the state and national levels, their connection with the state director stood them in good stead. As members of his group, they were able to make contact with influential people in other agencies within the bureaucracy. They were, in essence, able to tap the informal exchange network that exists among members of any stratified system.
It was the anthropologists' membership in this network that made possible the second phase of the period of close cooperation, which began in March 1977 with the arrival of a team of architects, engineers, and social scientists (mainly sociologists and social workers) from the national office of INDECO. This group had come to test a method for determining the housing and infrastructural needs of the urban poor. The data gathered were to be used in creating a zoning code and development plan for each city studied.

National-Level Collaboration. In December 1976, with the inauguration of a new president, several changes were made in Mexico's governmental structure. A new cabinet--the *Secretaría de Asentimientos Humanos y Obras Públicas* ("Secretariat of Human Settlement and Public Works," commonly known as SAHOP)--was formed to coordinate all public works activities. INDECO was folded into this new cabinet. With the formation of a new government, a period of instability and flux was inevitable while politicians and administrators grappled with the problems of getting organized and establishing their goals for the next six-year term. Despite the initial disorganization within SAHOP, certain well-placed individuals felt that one thing the new cabinet would need was information on the actual material living conditions of the poor.
On their recommendation, an advisor to the new minister of SAHOP approached INDECO administrators, who agreed to undertake a study of housing conditions. They knew that aside from the inherent interest of the assignment, an

ongoing project in this period of flux would give INDECO positive visibility in the government and the nation. The team chosen to carry out the project was centered around the administrative leaders of the planning section of INDECO's main office in Mexico City.

The study, as originally envisioned, was based on a sampling method developed by the Center for Urban Planning at the Massachusetts Institute of Technology (MIT) (Baldwin 1974; Caminos, Turner, and Steffian 1969; Bazant S. et al. 1978). The original design was developed as an architectural method for determining the location and extent of poverty in urban areas. It was based on the assumption that homogeneity in the built environment implied homogeneity of social class. The method relied on aerial photographs to locate homogeneous neighborhoods and to identify each neighborhood's characteristics. Direct socioeconomic data were to be gathered only from a few "select" cases in each block.

When the study design was presented to the team that would carry it out, differences in approach and perspective arose between the architects and engineers, known as *técnicos*, and the social scientists. The social scientists were convinced that more variation existed within neighborhoods than was assumed by the project design. They wished to modify the program of research to uncover that variation and the links between socioeconomic status and types of houses, their size, construction materials used, and available infrastructure. The social scientists were more concerned with the political economy of service delivery and housing conditions than with the conditions themselves.

The *técnicos* were more pragmatic. They wanted to know where services and housing were inadequate and then develop a plan for improving them. As professionals trained in the tradition of the MIT method, they could accept the basic premises of the design plan and were prepared to move ahead with it.

The two segments within the INDECO team ultimately decided their differences could not be resolved in Mexico City, but had to be worked out in the field as the project went along. The study would start with the original research design and be modified during the pilot stage to satisfy the concerns of both segments of the team.

The Mexico City team arrived in Oaxaca[4] with a tentative project design and a desire to get to know a provincial city in a way that few social scientists, architects, or engineers from Mexico City ever do. In the beginning there was a great deal of distrust between the

Mexico City team and INDECO personnel at the state office. Project members felt that people in the state office were uninterested in what they were doing and could add little to their study. For their part, state office employees (as well as the foreign anthropologist in residence) were suspicious of anyone from Mexico City. The two groups were brought together by the director of INDECO-OAXACA at an official party neither could avoid attending. After a good deal of political, theoretical, and methodological sparring, the anthropologist and the local INDECO staff were incorporated into the development and implementation of the study, which in time became known as *Tipología de Vivienda* (Cabrera 1979), or the "Mexican Urban Housing Study."

Initial problems encountered in sampling were critical in dissipating distrust between the North American anthropologist and the Mexican team. The original plan was that the city would be stratified for sampling on the basis of aerial photographs. Fortunately, adequate photos did not exist for Oaxaca, and it was decided that miniteams of a social scientist and a *técnico* would map the entire city. Thus began an intensive period of close cooperation between the technicians and the social scientists. Each team walked together over a designated area, noting the conditions of the houses, talking to various people (mostly shop owners, bar keepers, and local officials), and comparing notes about what they saw and what they felt was occurring in the area.

Two houses in each neighborhood were designated as "typical," and the architect asked permission to draw a site plan of the house, lot, and any outbuildings, noting the construction materials used. The social scientists interviewed any available members of the household, getting information on income, occupations, family size, length of residence in the city, and so on. It was a unique combination of architectural methodology and open-ended, intensive interviews--a combination that often resulted in the architect aiding in the interviews and the social scientist helping measure and evaluate the structures. The *técnicos* and social scientists learned a great deal from one another. The social scientists gained firsthand knowledge of the physical constraints in providing services and housing. The technicians became aware of the magnitude of material deprivation that existed in urban Mexico and the socio-economic causes of the problems facing INDECO as it attempted to provide housing solutions to the poor.

Even so, during this period the differences between the technical and social science portions of the team intensified. Both groups had come to agree on the importance of learning what services people felt they needed as well as the actual conditions of housing and services. Differences between *técnicos* and social scientists emerged in their attitudes toward the use of space, the proper approach to preparing housing programs and urban master plans, and, therefore, the ultimate nature of the study.

The architects and engineers saw the primary purpose of the study as providing data for the development of a "rational" design plan for housing and services for the greatest number of people at the lowest cost. They tended to be interested in normative housing styles so they could develop one or two "culturally adequate" house types for all the households of a given category. The social scientists tended to be more libertarian in their view of space. While they acknowledged that reasons of safety or sanitation might dictate that individuals use certain building materials or install sewers, they were much less concerned with notions of efficiency. Instead, they were propelled by a fascination with the human and cultural variation found in cities. The social scientists began to agitate for expansion of the project to include a survey questionnaire that would tap the entire range of socioeconomic variation. They insisted that far too little was known about general living conditions in the cities of Mexico in the first place and that INDECO's constituency was much too heterogeneous to be adequately served by a handful of house designs.

This led to many long discussions about what the ultimate purpose of the research project should be and how that purpose could be fulfilled while satisfying both the *técnicos*' basic requirements for information and the social scientists' insistence that any housing master plan for the cities of Mexico take account of population variation. The convergence of these points of view was a socioeconomic survey including a series of questions dealing with housing conditions and available services.

The project ultimately developed in two directions. One was the technical aspect, with the architects and engineers making maps and drawings of each city studied, showing availability of services (i.e., water, sewers, and electricity), the location of each neighborhood, and its dominant style of construction. The social scientists developed and administered a questionnaire designed to relate socioeconomic status and occupation to living conditions.[5]

With the termination of the Oaxaca phase of the study, the anthropologists returned to their academic positions in the United States. From this point forward, their participation consisted primarily of periodic visits to consult with the Mexican team and in the analysis and interpretation of the data (Murphy 1979; Murphy and Selby 1979; Hackenberg, Murphy, and Selby 1984; Selby et al. 1981; Selby and Murphy 1982; Hendricks and Murphy 1981; Kim 1982). The remaining fieldwork was carried out under the direction of INDECO-MEXICO. Ultimately, data were gathered on over 10 Mexican cities (Cabrera 1979; Castaneda 1981; INDECO 1980; Lorenzen 1986). This phase lasted until 1980, when one of the *técnicos* left INDECO to pursue graduate studies in the United States (Cabrera 1982). The collaboration then entered its current phase of productive coexistence.

Productive Coexistence

The relationship between the North American anthropologists and several of the Mexican planners and social scientists has moved into a less intense but more long-term relationship. It is no longer based on the daily contacts that marked the Oaxaca phase of the study. Rather, it is based on the realization that as each attempts to learn about Mexican society and provide services for it, low-level contacts can be mutually beneficial. We have much to offer each other both as colleagues and as friends. The luxury of time to digest data and think out the long-term consequences of a housing or development project are denied the *técnico,* who is often faced with unexpected social movements (such as invasions) requiring an immediate response. It is the role of the academic to provide the reports and long-term projections. At the same time, the North American anthropologists cannot be aware of all the political, social, and technical changes affecting housing and development in Mexico. It is the role of their Mexican colleagues to temper their projections and statements concerning urban society with the insights only a good native informant can give. This dialectical process, which has resulted in several publications and new research projects, has kept us in close contact and has the potential for continuing for some time.

PRINCIPLES FOR COLLABORATION

In analyzing our collaboration and the relationships that made a close linkage possible between North American anthropologists and Mexican professionals directing development in their country, we identified three features of particular importance to success: (1) key administrators in the change agency who recognized the utility of social science in general and anthropology in particular; (2)

community-level entry into collaborative work for the anthropologists; and (3) the lack of binding institutional relationships. An understanding of these features could prove helpful to others interested in undertaking similar collaborative research.

Key Administrative Informants

Other anthropologists, in discussing their successful entry into applied work, have mentioned the importance of key administrators who saw local-level, on-the-ground ethnography as worthwhile (e.g., Liebow 1967; Agar 1980). In our case, two individuals were instrumental. What they shared with other administrators who have brought anthropology into their agencies was an understanding of the link between microlevel activity and macrolevel policy. That is, the best-laid plans of a change agent can be thwarted by a mother who insists on maintaining a store in her house where she can care for her children.

The director of INDECO's Oaxaca office brought the anthropologists into his personal advisory team. As they worked together, he showed them how they could have an impact on policy that affected the people among whom they did their "abstract" research. Further, he served as the anthropologists' guide into the larger world of national policy, helping them learn a culture and style of operation at a level they were unfamiliar with, just as any key informant helps an anthropologist in a village or community learn how to operate in an appropriate manner. Finally, it was he who first saw the implications of joining the approach of the anthropologists, who specialized in acquiring a detailed understanding of social processes and social systems, with the work of the researchers from INDECO's national office. Faced with general uncertainty and suspicion all around, he quite literally forced a reluctant anthropologist to make contact with the group from Mexico City and at least undertake a dialogue with them.

The second important individual was the director of planning at INDECO-MEXICO. He formed the core of the research team in Mexico City, led it through its early stages, and saw it to maturity. In selecting individuals to carry out the study, he was guided by the spirit of the first national director of INDECO and chose energetic, enthusiastic young architects, engineers, and social scientists, whose job was to take a vague project concept and form a study method that could be broadly applied within the Mexican context. Finally, he welcomed the anthropologists and their point of view into the process and ultimately made possible their collaboration at the national level. As an architect of great experience in the Mexican publc sector, he was well aware of the validity of the social scientists' contention that flexibility is often the key to success in community housing projects.

These two individuals encouraged strong collegial ties between the anthropologists and the engineers, architects, and social scientists who were beginning their careers in the Mexican system working on the Mexican Urban Housing Survey. As these young professionals have moved through the system, they have maintained their ties with the anthropologists and have made several trips to the United States to participate in conferences, continue their studies, and proffer aid to the anthropologists in their academic pursuits.

Local-Level Entry

For the anthropologists it was important to enter into the field of applied anthropology through local-level research. Anthropology's forte is providing insights into the everyday human condition. Anthropological theory rests on the analysis of linkages between various aspects of on-the-ground human activity. When change agents contact anthropologists, it is to gain this kind of knowledge. Thus, basic research can serve (as it did in this case) as the foundation for collaboration. The anthropologist should remember, however, that time is required to discover areas of mutual interest and to develop the trust necessary for collaboration between social scientists and *los técnicos*. This is especially true with individuals from another nation or culture.

In this case the formation of ties between the Mexicans and North Americans was aided by the fact that none of the individuals responsible for the study displayed the strong anti-American feelings often seen among middle- and upper-level bureaucrats and functionaries in Mexico. The confidence of the Mexicans and the naivete of the anthropologists as they tried to grapple with problems bearing national implications made possible many lively and stimulating debates. The free nature of these discussions concerning the theoretical and practical implications of their work was important to the anthropologists. Through them they began to understand and respect the enormity of the task facing Mexico and its public servants. The nation faces the need to feed, clothe, and house a population that, to a large extent, is relegated to the marginal segments of the world economic system. Mexican change agents must deal with the seemingly impossible task of providing services for an ever-growing population with a continually shrinking resource base.

Institutional Links

A further factor in the success of this collaboration was the lack of direct formal links between the anthropologists and INDECO or between INDECO and an institution in the United States. Although the anthropologists acted as consultants to INDECO, none were ever paid employees of INDECO or any other Mexican agency. This gave the collaborators several advantages.

First, INDECO administrators and directors were happy to make use of the services of anthropologists they did not have to support. When needed, academicians could be brought in as outside experts at little expense, and they could be ignored at even less. They were not part of INDECO's overhead and therefore did not have to be used to justify their existence. Further, the absence of institutional ties during the period of the large survey project meant to Mexican team members that they would not be required, because of a structural relationship, to accept what they might consider improper interpretations of the Mexican situation by foreigners.

Far from making the anthropologists more reticent to voice their opinions, their independence enhanced their willingness to be forceful in their arguments, even if they were sometimes critical of a position taken by INDECO or particular members of the organization. They did not have to fear being dismissed, and INDECO could not place any direct pressure on them to change their position on any issue.

In the context of the Mexican system, where agencies are created and disbanded with each new presidential administration, this lack of dependence on institutional links had the additional advantage of not being subject to termination with each new administration. Without the weight of a formal declaration of cooperation, the collaborative association could, like members of a change agent's *equipo*, move from one agency to another and in and out of government as the politics of the moment dictated.

SUMMARY AND CONCLUSIONS

The authors have developed, over the past 10 years, strong linkages between private- and public-sector professionals in Mexico and anthropologists in the United

States. These linkages, which seem destined to continue and to produce further research on the process of social and economic change in a rapidly developing nation, are the result of specific actions taken by individuals interested in developing and maintaining their connections.

The anthropologists did, if you will, an ethnography of INDECO to learn about its needs and constraints. This enabled them to make realistic proposals to the agency when asked to do so. It also enabled them to develop strong ties within INDECO and other governmental agencies that transcended the single-job approach often present in applied anthropology.

The Mexicans, for their part, were sensitive to the implications of the embryonic relationship. They, more quickly than the anthropologists, realized that the latter could contribute to the study they were undertaking. In addition, they took into account the desire of the anthropologists to carry out academically acceptable research that would lead to career advancement. The Mexican social scientists and *técnicos* stimulated consideration of many of the practical and theoretical issues that have sustained the academicians since the early 1980s. It was the technical group that opened their eyes to housing and the built environment as important symbolic and cultural features in the urban setting. And Mexican social scientists forced the anthropologists to move out of the neighborhood and focus attention on the links between life in the *colonia* and macrolevel economic and political activity. Thus, a symbiotic relationship developed between the anthropologists and the planners, as each group made an effort to meet certain needs of the other.

Our final advice to other anthropologists wishing to establish linkages with agencies and institutions involved in social processes would be this: develop a strong sense of the place of anthropology in the study of humanity. It is important to remember that "doing anthropology in applied contexts should never take the anthropologist out of anthropology" (Hill 1985:80). The goal is to achieve a context in which abstract and applied concerns interact to improve people's lives at the same time that anthropological theory is advanced.

ACKNOWLEDGMENTS

When four individuals write about a collaboration with a long history, the list of people and institutions which should be acknowledged is likewise long. The authors would like to express their sincere thanks to Arq. José María Gutiérrez, Ing. José Luís Aceves, Dr. William Glade, Arq. Romeo Olivárez, Rebeca Contreras, Enrique de la Mora, Gerardo Díaz Infante, Diane Luque, Mario Orozco, Rosa María Salgado, Alberto Robles, Elena Solís, Blanca Susan Venegas, Alex Stepick, Myung-Hye Kim, Virginia Murphy, and Jeanie Fitzpatrick. In addition, we would like to thank Aida Castañeda, Laura Finsten, and Steve Kowalewski, who read and commented on an early version of the manuscript. Financial support during the period covered in this paper was provided by the *Instituto Nacional para el Desarrollo de la Comunidad y de la Vivienda Popular*, the Fulbright-Hays program, the Institute for Latin American Studies at the University of Texas at Austin, the University of Georgia Research Foundation, and the Baylor University Research Committee.

NOTES

1. The acronym INDECO-MEXICO will be used to designate the national office of the *Instituto Nacional para el Desarrollo de la Comunidad y de la Vivienda Popular*, and INDECO-OAXACA will be used for the state office, when a necessary distinction is not clear from the context.

2. As we first envisioned this chapter, it would consist of the text of a paper written by Murphy and Selby (1982) for the annual meeting of the Society for Applied Anthropology, where they presented the unchallenged view of this collaboration from their perspective. It was to be followed with a series of comments and criticisms by members from the Mexican group. Some felt the original paper was basically faithful to the history of the project (if a bit selective in the information included and overblown in its assertions of the virtues of anthropologists and their craft). Others objected much more strenuously to the content. We thought it would be good to place in print the types of discussions (sometimes heated) that have been an ongoing part of this collaboration.

In the end, however, we decided to rewrite the paper and present an entirely new document; for it is even more in the spirit of our collaboration that we attempt finally to provide a coherent point of view. In this way others may benefit from a synthesis of our discussion without having to sort through the details of agreement and disagreement.

3. FOVI, a subsidized housing fund administered by Mexican banks, states that a household must earn nearly five times the local minimum wage before it can enter into the formal housing and loan market.

4. The decision to use Oaxaca as the pilot study was made because the local director of INDECO was well known to the team leaders in Mexico City and had the reputation of being a mover who would get things done and be willing to provide significant assistance to this kind of study. Oaxaca was INDECO's model state office and an ideal place to carry out a pilot study.

5. For most of the cities studied, the maps and data base resulting from this project remain the most current available.

8

Saving the City: University Research, Political Action, and the Squatter Problem in Davao City, Philippines

*Robert A. Hackenberg
and Beverly H. Hackenberg*

AN OLD PROBLEM AND A NEW SOLUTION: SQUATTERS AND SITE-AND-SERVICES PROJECTS

Third World urbanization is not a new field for the applied social scientist. Rapid urban growth, resulting from both high fertility and rural-to-urban migration, has been the norm for four decades. The consequences at the level of the city include deficiencies in infrastructure, services, investment, and planning. These in turn result in insufficient employment, low incomes, and inadequate purchasing power for an increasing majority of urban inhabitants. The problems of the city and of its recently arrived households clash at the interface between them: the squatter settlement.

But all this can be gleaned from standard works such as those of Breese (1966, 1969) or McGee (1967). What is new is the attempt to institutionalize a solution to the squatter problem and to implement it cross-nationally. The site-and-services model of low-cost multidimensional development for the benefit of the urban poor is a product of the last decade. Laquian's (1975) discussion commemorated its arrival and identifies it with sponsorship by a single global agency: the International Bank for Reconstruction and Development (IBRD), or the World Bank.

Applied anthropologists are no strangers to the squatter settlements of the Third World (Lloyd 1980; Perlmann 1976). But they have seldom participated in large-scale efforts to upgrade them and to eliminate the hazards to health and economic or personal security inflicted on their occupants. One reason for this is that the World Bank and other international agencies have seldom called upon their services. On the rare occasions when the input of anthropologists has been invited, short-term consultancies of several months have been the mode of employment. Since the design, implementation, and assessment of the impact of urban projects extends across a number of years, such consultancies do not provide a real opportunity for adequate participation in either research or development. For these reasons, the present case history may prove to be one of a kind. It describes the involvement of a team of applied anthropologists with (1) a city with a massive squatter problem; (2) the evolving notion that the site-and-services model offered the only practical solution to this problem; (3) the entry of the World Bank as the sponsoring agency; and (4) the design, construction, and operation of a substantial intervention project. The story unfolds over a decade and a half during which the anthropologists (not the World Bank) provide the continuity.

The occasion for our long-term involvement was the operation of a field station (Hackenberg and Hackenberg 1981) with a multiphasic research program incorporating both rural and urban studies on a wide range of issues. While the squatter settlement issue was only one of these, it received more of our attention over a longer span of years than any of the others. And it was the one to which circumstances determined that we keep returning. In the process we learned more than we had anticipated about the city, the World Bank, applied anthropology, and ourselves.

We have centered this discussion around a theme: the steps through which research begun by expatriate scientists can evolve into an intervention program that the community institutionalizes as its own. We intend to document this sequence of events to highlight both that which was deliberate and anticipated on our part and that which was either coincidental (unplanned and fortuitous) or completely external to our scope of operations and, therefore, beyond our control. The sequence begins on a stage provided by the local community and unfolds at last in the national and international arena of what has come to be called, once again, "political economy."

We have confronted the story, and the nature of our personal involvement in it, with what we believe to be candor and objectivity. Above all, we have sought to avoid that tendency toward retrospective rationalization that converts a haphazard series of accidental events into a logical sequence and then smugly concludes that "we planned it that way." In so doing, we permit the reader to judge how much control, or lack of it, characterizes the anthropologist's role under circumstances that, we believe, came close to being ideal.

We believe that intervention projects, if they survive, have an implicit life cycle that undergoes the following steps:

1. An *initiative phase* during which the most important activity is research: defining the problem, describing it, and choosing among alternative solutions.
2. A *consolidation phase*, in which the technical, financial, personnel, and organizational resources must be identified and assembled. Project design occurs at this point.
3. An *institutionalization phase* in which a group structure must integrate these resources and effectively apply them to the problem. Project construction may then take place.
4. A final phase termed *maintenance of continuity*; it refers to the need for the institution to generate its own adaptive strategy for dealing with changes in the internal (project) and external (community) environments. Project operation may then proceed indefinitely.

Before reverting to this sequence of steps, which will occupy the major portion of the narrative, we must introduce Davao City, the arena within which it begins.

DAVAO: A CITY ENDANGERED BY EXPANDING SQUATTER SETTLEMENTS

Davao City, with a population of 795,000 (1985 estimate) located in eastern Mindanao on Davao Gulf, is the second largest urban center in the Philippines, separated by 900 kilometers from Manila. The regional capital, it serves as the primary administrative, industrial, and commercial location for its immediate hinterland, a five-province area with 3.3 million persons. It is also the metropolis for the 11 million occupants of Mindanao. To serve its hinterland effectively, it must experience substantial and continuous economic growth and must also become an efficient source and distribution point for institutional services.

As a growth center for the Southern Philippines, Davao has experienced population expansion at the rate of 5 percent or more per year since the end of World War II. This expansion has permitted the urban economy to diversify and evolve to accommodate the requirements of homestead agriculture, a variety of agribusiness enterprises, timber production, and mining ventures. But it has placed an immense strain upon the physical resources of the community. And the city suffers in other ways. Among these is the absence of indigenous research and development talent. Because of the ties of all enterprises and government agencies to the primate city, most educated Davaoeños have closer ties to Manila, and know more about it, than they do to their own residential community. Therein lies the opportunity for the expatriate scientist.

The knowledge that Davao residents possess concerning their city is inversely proportional to their socioeconomic status. The professional, managerial, and technical classes reside in newly constructed luxury residences within subdivided coconut plantations at some distance from the densely settled central city; they are driven to and from their work, school, or market in closed and refrigerated vehicles, and socialize at the four international-class hotels or the even more exclusive Davao Beach Club. This tendency was reinforced during the 1970s by the introduction and expansion of the production of "world-market" commodities such as bananas and sugar. Expatriate personnel, mostly from the U.S. and Central America, were rotated in and out of Davao on two-year tours of duty. The native middle class sought to duplicate as many aspects of this segregated life style as they could afford; for example, a fringe of middle-income subdivisions appeared in remote locations at the edge of the city. As successive elements of community leadership departed the urban core, their knowledge of it diminished and their interest in it declined.

In place of knowledge concerning the community, its people and its problems, there were self-serving misconceptions in the minds of middle- and upper-income households and political decision makers that were most often directed at the lower-class residents who are the sources of the most visible problems: housing and health. These are the customary, one might say global, moralistic perceptions of the poor as people who are unmotivated and uninterested in investing the efforts needed to improve their status.

In Davao, as in most cities in the less developed countries (LDCs), there was a complicating factor that tended to crosscut discussion and polarize class positions. It was the squatter issue. Due to the total lack of prior provision for incoming migrants, they were forced to fall back on their own ingenuity to provide for their housing needs. They did this by organizing for the seizure of undeveloped sites that were strategically situated with respect to income opportunities. First choices for squatter invasion tended to be government property. The invaders, who were also new voters, could frequently obtain the patronage of a local politician to prevent government action against them in return for their support.

Later, organized seizures were aimed at undeveloped private property, which, if within the central city, often represented choice business locations held for speculative purposes by upper-class landlords. Because of the leapfrog pattern of urban expansion characterizing the history of Davao (Hackenberg and Hackenberg 1971; Hackenberg 1983), sites of this second type were quite numerous. Philippine law recognizes "squatter's rights"; thus, the claim of one who has occupied and "improved" a property has merit against the claim of another who has title to the land but neither occupies nor improves it. Even when their claims were flimsy, it was common for squatter associations to tie up for years in the courts eviction actions by the holders of valid title to the land they had seized (Hackenberg and Hackenberg 1970).

The landowners and the squatters had opposed each other for a decade or more before our arrival in Davao, and this central issue had colored discussion of every other problem on which the total community might have come together. The prominence of the squatter situation was intensified by two additional complications: (1) the squatter and low-income neighborhoods, which were largely congruent, comprised 60 to 70 percent of the community's population and land area; and (2) it followed from this that their residents became a majority of the electorate, leading to the unshakable conviction on the part of the middle- and upper-income groups that city government was a corrupt instrument in the hands of the squatters and their lawyers (who were frequently holders of political office).

The University of Colorado research team that arrived in Davao for its first year-long field trip in 1969 consisted of the authors and Francisco Claver, a Filipino who completed his dissertation research (Claver 1973) during that interval. We were oblivious to the urban scene. To anthropologists in the 1960s, the agrarian problem was the *only* problem. Geertz (1963) had sensitized us to the race between rice production and population in Java. We were seeking the escape from involution among the homesteading households who had migrated to the agricultural frontier in Mindanao (Hackenberg 1971).

During the next decade, that escape was achieved through application of Green Revolution rice technology throughout Southeast Asia's lowlands. Rural Mindanao prospered, but land reserves were soon exhausted. Migration from elsewhere in the Philippines continued, but the city rather than the countryside became the target. Since the migrant equates city size with opportunity, Davao was the destination of first choice. We did not know it at the time, but a new pattern of nonindustrialized urbanization was evolving in Southeast Asia (Hackenberg 1980). This pattern utilizes few formal-sector workers because the major trade items continue to be unprocessed plantation and forest products. We soon observed that urban growth without industrialization creates the "marginal subsistence urbanite" (Hackenberg and Hackenberg 1971). By the mid-1970s, the acceleration of this process, embodied in the metastasizing squatter problem, seemed to threaten the vitality of the city.

The narrative to follow will unfold through the four developmental stages described in the previous section. No project reaches completion in the same environment in which it was begun. Unforeseen changes in the community context produce unexpected consequences. In Davao City, much of what happened was unintended, and much of what was intended did not happen. The key unforeseen event during the decade of the 1970s was the seizure of power on September 21, 1972 by Ferdinand Marcos, establishing a dictatorship that extended his administration to February 26, 1986, the day on which he was transported to the United States. This change in political status colors much of the discussion to follow. We have permitted it to do so because, as we perceive it, a totalitarian government provides the normative environment encountered by the applied anthropologist throughout most of the Third World in the 1980s. It has become ubiquitous.

STAGE I: THE INITIATIVE PHASE

In 1969, when first undertaking a comparative rural-urban study of factors associated with population growth in Mindanao, with support from the National Institutes of Health, we did not perceive ourselves as "social engineers" intent upon reconstructing the community. Our interests were those of detached social scientists. We had chosen a very recently settled region with plentiful economic resources, adequate household income, and explosive levels of fertility and rural-to-urban migration. With population requiring a mere 12.5 years to double in Davao City, and only 1.5 times that in the countryside, we hoped to conduct time-series studies that would explain adaptation of social and economic institutions to demographic stresses.

Our study included two rural locations in Davao del Sur (a high- and low-income municipality) and an urban squatter settlement at the south edge of the city (Talomo Beach). Our office in Davao City consisted of a rented room in the Mindanao Development Center (MDC), a Jesuit enterprise concerned with rural communities and their problems. MDC's director, a rural sociologist, was also a member of the board of Davao Development Foundation (DDF), a civic action enterprise founded by a group of prominent local businessmen who owned, among other things, the local power plant and the plywood factory, Davao's two largest industrial enterprises.

DDF, a tax-exempt nonprofit welfare organization, was actually begun as a tax shelter for a coconut plantation recently acquired by one of the board members at Mandug, about 12 kilometers from town. But to maintain its tax-exempt status, it needed to undertake some social development work. When told of Beverly Hackenberg's squatter research at Talomo, DDF members requested, in mid-1970, that she undertake a second squatter survey in an area near the plywood factory populated largely by company employees. Since no funds were provided, she recruited a class of theology students from the Jesuit college (Ateneo de Davao) to conduct the survey of Lanang District. She was assisted in this by the president of the college, who was also a board member of DDF.

Several DDF board members, who were descendants of the 19th century Spanish *hacendero* class, knew of efforts by industrialists in Brazil and Venezuela to develop worker-occupied housing. They were motivated in part by the desire to introduce these "Latino" solutions for Southeast Asian problems and in part by the even stronger desire to show the superiority of the private sector over the government in its capacity to solve social problems, even though these were the government's responsibility. The mayor of Davao at this time, a member of the nouveau riche timber-concession millionaires, was not socially acceptable, and his devotion to nightclubbing made him anathema to the stiff-necked Hispano elite, who were members of the Christian Family Movement, a Catholic reformist group with Jesuit sponsorship.

Our drift toward close identification with the Jesuit-Hispano "conservative" upper class took place before we were clearly aware of it. As with all such linkages, it proved in later years to be both an asset and a liability. However, despite the methods-textbook advice to stay nonaligned, our experience in both Southeast Asia and Latin America confirms that, at least in these regions, you are better off "belonging to" (in their terms) one or another of the stronger factions than to none at all. It is impossible to operate within these patron-client systems unless you have strong sponsorship. Nor does this type of identification exclude you from access to members of the opposing faction. As we shall see.

Mandug was a remote rural site with primitive community facilities linked to the city by a near-impassable dirt road, where "DDF Village" was to be constructed. The DDF board of directors, based on Latin American preconceptions, was certain that the Lanang squatters would accept resettlement from their in-town, employment-adjacent locations to Mandug. The incentives were title to homesites and full ownership of any improvements built upon them. And there would be amenities--electricity and a domestic water supply. The Lanang survey proved the DDF assumption completely incorrect.

The Lanang survey (Hackenberg and Hackenberg 1970) acquainted the DDF board members, for the first time, with the thought processes and life-style priorities of their neighbors "on the other side of the tracks." Their first concern was not land title but *location*. Lanang was close to work and located on a main street with heavy traffic. This permitted many housewives to operate street-side businesses as supplementary income sources. Electricity would be useful, but their next most important need, as they saw it, was for an elementary school within their village to provide both free primary education and a public meeting hall.

Both access to income and education would be sacrificed by the move to DDF Village. Title to their homesites, which conveyed residential security, was a recognized advantage. But the squatter association, with its phalanx of attorneys, had successfully resisted eviction for a decade. Lower-court decisions went against them, but there were always higher courts, and each appeal took several years to adjudicate. There was a low level of anxiety in Lanang in 1970. It would soon be heightened by subsequent events.

The Lanang experience convinced the DDF board of both the need for research and the level of their own ignorance concerning the community. They offered us both a challenge and an opportunity. The challenge was to develop a similar data base, with information on household composition, employment, housing, and income sources, for the whole of Davao City. The opportunity was to conduct the research within the framework of a Philippine institution, Davao Research and Planning Foundation, Inc. (DRPF), which was established in parallel with DDF in 1971. It also extended the tax advantages provided to the sponsors by the original foundation.

With this encouragement, we obtained a second National Institutes of Health grant for the first Davao City survey, which was based on 1,000 households. The study, completed the following year (Hackenberg 1974), disclosed two principles of socioeconomic structure that guided our subsequent policy recommendations: (1) the areas occupied primarily by squatter households receive higher levels of income, and a larger proportion of total support, from informal-sector employment (vending, stallkeeping, petty trade in prepared foods and handicrafts, buy-and-sell business) than from wage work in all forms of commerce and industry; and (2) this type of employment is dependent upon access to a large volume of prospective customers, which requires that the informal-sector household have a place of residence near the center of the city from which its commerce can be conducted.

The first Davao City survey demonstrated that the continued residence of all squatter households adjacent to the central business district, and not just those in Lanang, was essential for their continued self-support. This required sponsors to change both their evaluation of the squatter problem in Davao and their prescription for its solution. Like other business and professional leaders, the DDF/DRPF board advocated an early demise for the ramshackle and deteriorated neighborhoods that surrounded the central business district and extended along the seashore both north and south. All planning exercises produced by the city government envisioned conversion of this area to coastal boulevards, government and private office complexes, park areas, recreational uses, and upper-income housing.

A high priority on the agenda of both government and private civic groups was the removal of the offending low-income households, the majority of which were illegal occupants of squatter settlements. The most offensive of these was the notorious Piapi slum, a dense concentration of 5,000 households occupying the foreshore area adjacent to the city government complex. Piapi is located on a tidal flat, with access to neither water nor sewer facilities. Its central location, furthermore, means that it is the most densely populated residential area in the entire city, with the largest proportion of its support drawn from the informal sector. Since the nature of its site did not permit substantial autoconstruction, many shelters were built on stilts or platforms above the mud. Piapi epitomized the squatter problem in its extreme form.

Removal, of course, could not be implemented without relocation. All plans for displacement of Piapi residents, and those from adjacent neighborhoods, involved resettlement at distances of 15-20 kilometers from the central city, i.e., at distances farther out than Mandug and DDF Village! The immediate reason for this was the perennial one: land values. The size of the site required and the limited budget available for its purchase obligated planners to go far from town to find an affordable site. Needless to say, such a site was completely unsuitable for survival by informal-sector employment.

On the basis of the conclusions reached in the first Davao City survey, the DDF/DRPF board members choked a few times, swallowed hard, and began to issue press releases and hold civic group meetings (to which government officials were invited) advocating *improvement of squatter settlements* as an alternative to removal to remote locations. Because we were "their" research unit, they were committed to accept our findings and did so after a total of about four hours of seminar presentations in the conference room of Davao Light and Power Company. Our analysis, issued in a monograph entitled *A Developing City in a Dual Economy: Economic and Demographic Trends in Davao City, 1972*, became very well known in Philippine professional circles as "The Hackenberg Report."

Inadvertently, we had given our sponsors a useful instrument with which to (1) advance themselves as unlikely, but nonetheless sincere and powerful, champions of the lower class; and, at the same time, (2) belabor the city government as the champion of special interests and wealthy promoters aiming to profit from redeveloping the area adjacent to the central business district. The mayor, through the city architect, issued a counterproposal featuring a sanitized and fully redesigned contemporary core city with an outer ring of "satellite communities" to which the residents of Piapi and their neighbors would be banished. The church and most professional groups lined up with DDF/DRPF; so did the smaller businessmen who made up the Kiwanis and Lions Clubs, at which we were favorite guest speakers for the entire year. The large landowner-business interests, especially those of non-Hispanic origin, lined up with the mayor. We had reached a standoff.

On September 21, 1972, President Ferdinand Marcos proclaimed martial law and seized dictatorial powers, including control of local governments, for the ensuing 14 years. In Davao City, the world turned upside down. The mayor and city government, who belonged to the opposition Liberal party, were completely neutralized by the total power now in the hands of the president's Nacionalista party. Since the operating premise of the dictatorship was cooptation, an early effort was made to assimilate non-government power bases, which, if uncontrolled, might create difficulties. One of those was represented by the private-sector Hispano business leaders sponsoring our foundations. Within months the president of DDF/DRPF, who was also the owner of Davao Light and Power Company, was appointed Presidential Regional Officer for Development (PROD) in southwest Mindanao (Region XI) and also Director of the Mindanao Development Authority. For a time we assumed that we had become "insiders." We later learned that we, together with other civic action groups, had been effectively neutralized. The initiative phase was over.

STAGE II: CONSOLIDATION PHASE

Circumstances surrounding the seizure of power by Marcos have been misrepresented by U.S. government sources to make it appear that the dictatorship was justified by threats to the established order from leftist radicals. Longtime observers, less likely to interpret the scene from the standpoint of the "communist versus free world" polarity that colors all official American analysis, noted that much of the disorder was generated by Marcos and his henchmen to justify seizure of power and continuity in office beyond 1973, the year his second term would come to an end. A third term was prohibited by the constitution!

Regardless of the circumstances, the first year following the creation of the new regime witnessed (1) general repression of all forms of opposition, both political and criminal, both overt and covert, together with suppression of criticism by students, journalists, and special interest groups of all sorts; and (2) a flowering of technocrat-inspired development programs initiated by the central government. The response of the private sector and the church was initially positive because it seemed probable that a favorable climate for business expansion would be accompanied by a schedule of reforms aimed at alleviating both rural and urban poverty.

As a result, Davao City business and professional leaders, including those within DDF/DRPF, joined in accepting the rationalization that "government-imposed discipline" was a much-needed antidote to an "excess of popular democracy" that had threatened to become anarchy or worse (communism) since 1970. Indeed, foreign multinationals sought Philippine business partners for joint ventures, and overseas banks promoted mergers with local financial institutions. Land reform and production programs for smallholder agriculture were proclaimed, together with an agenda of forced-draft industrialization projects. New commitments of foreign development assistance poured in from all multilateral lenders. The United Nations Development Program (UNDP) established a branch office in Davao City. The World Bank and the Asian Development Bank established their high profile presence in Manila.

During the 1960s, Davao was underserved by agencies of central and local government. The gap was filled by private-sector organizations. In the early years of the dictatorship the balance was dramatically reversed. All power and prerogatives for meeting local needs began to flow toward Manila. As they did so, privately supported activities were sequentially replaced by public counterparts. By the end of the decade, the public was overserved by a labyrinth of redundant government agencies, many under the supervision of the first lady, Mayor of Metro Manila and Minister of Human Settlements, Imelda R. Marcos. The private-sector organizations were virtually eliminated as the cooptation process advanced.

For DRPF, the changed political and economic climate required that we also revise our strategy for urban redevelopment in Davao City. Prior to martial law, the ballot in the hands of squatter association members represented potential political control since they were a majority of voters in city elections. Our strategy was simply to offer them the option of improving their residential locations as an alternative to the unpopular resettlement scheme advanced by the mayor's office. With DDF/DRPF cooperation some substantive accomplishments had already taken place. At Lanang, the city had agreed to accept the expense of operating an elementary school if the local people provided the building. The foundation (actually, the board member who operated the plywood factory) supplied the construction materials and the Lanang Homeseekers Association produced the labor. At our insistence, electric service was provided to both the Lanang and Piapi squatter settlements by Davao Light and Power Company.

With the coming of the dictatorship, the security of the squatter community, which rested upon its potential voting strength, came to an end. Local government was superceded by a series of directives, known as Presidential Decrees (PDs) or Letters of Instruction (LOIs), emanating from Manila. For several years, these edicts appeared to counter our message concerning squatter area redevelopment, primarily because the technocrats making policy for Marcos reflected the obsolete "garden-city" mentality of the urban planners of an earlier decade. In the Manila metropolitan area they established remote resettlement sites like Carmona and Sapang Palay, primarily to remove "unsightly" central city slums to make way for networks of freeways, boulevards, shopping malls, and numerous new public buildings.

In Davao, Manila's lead was eagerly followed with the full support of the mayor, who was seeking to improve his position with Marcos. He proposed an Action Coordinating Team (ACT) to develop a "rehabilitation plan" under the leadership of the city engineer. However, the executive officer for the plan was the most widely feared "muscle man" in city government, known throughout the community by the descriptive label of "Idi Amin."

The plan, reduced to essentials, consisted of dumping 8,129 households (perhaps 50,000 people) on a plot of public land in the remote mountain town of Mintal, 15 kilometers from the city. The 64-hectare plot, when subdivided, would have yielded approximately 2,400 lots of 140 square meters. While the plan contained many references to coordinated action by a plethora of agencies intended to provide community organization, vocational training, initiation of "home industries," and "emergency" medical care, no special appropriations were provided to those expected to assume this substantial additional burden. The only concrete commitment was a reference to "rations" to be extended to "indigent households" for a period of one week to one month.

In the early months of martial law, our foundations still believed in the potential for civic action based on careful research to deal with this sort of authoritarian incursion. To broaden the base of protest, DDF/DRPF sponsored the formation of the Coordinating Council of Davao (CCOD)--a loose federation of 40 or more civic clubs, professional associations, and business groups. We then launched an assault on the Action Coordinating Team. Our strategy was two-fold. First, DRPF assayed the availability of legal housing with a survey of all "house-and-lot" packages offered by private builders in and near the city. Our survey, which included all 59 subdivisions registered in that year, disclosed that only one, DDF Village, operated by the Davao Development Foundation, offered terms within reach of even middle-income households. The obvious implication was that squatting was essential to survival for most households.

We then took the second step: estimating the volume of the squatter problem. Using data from the city's own survey, we concluded that more than 17,400 households (104,000 people) were squatting. Therefore, the ACT scheme, if implemented, would solve less than one-half of the *existing* problem. And it made no allowance for the fact that the backlog of unmet demand would continue to grow at the estimated rate of 10,000 units every five years. We were supported in this conclusion by the only other research institution in Davao: the Mindanao Regional Office of the United Nations Development Program.

Armed with these arguments, CCOD held a series of open meetings to voice its opposition to squatter removal. Its membership included most of the influential citizens. Since only the Manila newspapers had been subordinated to the control of the Ministry of Information, the local press gave us limited support. Our greatest weakness was that we had no alternative to resettlement other than a defense of the status quo: let the squatters remain in place or you will destroy the fabric of the urban economy that depends on the informal sector. And this, in turn, requires that you permit the stallkeepers and small businessmen to remain where the traffic upon which they depend is located.

This appears to be a counsel of inaction, but it was somewhat more sophisticated. In the early 1970s, we were mesmerized by the writing of John Turner (1967) and his dogma that, left to themselves, squatter settlements would evolve into presentable residential communities through self-organization for improvement. One of our doctoral students, Kerry Feldman (1973, 1975), sought to test this proposition in his dissertation study, completed on the eve of martial law in 1972. The Turner doctrine was also embraced by William Mangin (1970) and Aprodicio Laquian (1971), two social scientists most familiar with squatting as an urban growth process in developing countries.

The ACT plan was never implemented. First, it required the expenditure of two million pesos to achieve the minimum goals of site preparation and transportation. Second, the administration in Manila refused to release the land on which resettlement was to occur. Third, and certainly least important, we had generated a substantial protest through the CCOD which succeeded in casting some doubt on the wisdom of the plan. It also established a permanent adversary relationship between DDF/DRPF and the city engineer, the city architect, and the infamous "Idi Amin."

So long as our only option to resettlement *without* housing (the ACT plan) was resettlement *with* housing (as in DDF Village located at Mandug, 12 kilometers from the city) we could do little more than oppose government policy. Our DDF houses, like those of the subdividers, were priced above the reach of the lower-class households that comprised the poorest 40 percent of the community. We believed in the Turner doctrine, but did not know how it could be implemented. In the examples with which we were familiar (Lima, Mexico City) the process was self-generated and self-managing.

Our dilemma was resolved in late 1973 by the arrival of the World Bank in Davao. It was represented by Douglas Keare of the Development Economics Department. His task was to implement the Bank's urbanization sector working paper (IBRD 1972) by establishing site-and-services projects in selected major cities of the developing world. Their common feature was the provision of homesites on which former squatters could construct legal dwellings using self-help methods.

At the time of his visit, the Bank had plans for nine site-and-services projects in 1974, beginning with Dakar in Senegal. They included the Tondo/Dagat-dagatan settlement on the Manila waterfront--the most visible squatter problem in the Philippines. The capital city projects were described in the housing sector policy paper issued the following year (IBRD 1975). But to implement the policy at the national level, the inclusion of secondary cities was required.

Keare learned in Manila that DRPF possessed the only survey data outside the capital region that could provide a planning base for a site-and-services program. During his visit, which included a tour of the densely settled foreshore squatter settlements near the central city, the potential for extending the Tondo/Dagat-dagatan plan to Davao was instantly perceived. The visit evolved into a working relationship that would endure for the next decade.

The essence of the site-and-services philosophy (Laquian 1975) is to develop residential advantages for low-income households without displacement from the locations that contain their economic support. This is to be accomplished by a multipurpose program that includes: (1) security of tenure; (2) reblocking of lots into uniform homesites with access roads and footpaths; (3) leveling and drainage improvement; (4) provision of utilities, improved urban services, and basic sanitation facilities; (5) extension of loans and technical assistance to homeowners wishing to expand and improve existing shelter units; (6) development of commercial and industrial property within the residential area to increase income/employment opportunities; and (7) recovery of total costs on an amortization schedule of monthly payment by all beneficiary households.

The urgency of a program of this sort was underscored by our 1974 second-round citywide survey of Davao, supported by a grant to DRPF from Philippine Business for Social Progress (PBSP). Conditions among the urban poor worsened dramatically under the impact of a 40 percent annual inflation triggered by the first round of the oil crisis. Population growth, coupled with the search for additional income sources by middle-class households, placed the most severe strain upon the absorptive capacity of the informal sector by vastly expanding the number of households seeking to share in its activities. When the CCOD presented the preliminary findings in February 1975 they met with much wider receptivity than before. A summary of the 1972-1974 trends appears in Hackenberg (1977).

The year 1975 witnessed a number of critical events that both heightened and resolved conflicts over alternate urban development strategies. The "city beautiful," propagated by academically oriented planners, still held its magnetic appeal for influential members of the community, including the mayor, his staff, and the president of Ateneo de Davao University, the only credible source of higher education in the city. The university president was instrumental in persuading the Development Academy of the Philippines (DAP), a social science center created by the dictatorship to coopt and neutralize faculty members suspected of leftist political leanings, to undertake a planning project for the city, which the mayor funded with a contract for 870,000 pesos.

The DAP product was a glossy, full-color lithographed exercise in imagining urban utopia on the shores of Davao Gulf. Most of the existing unsightly (i.e., low-income) residential areas within the central city were to be converted to parks, boulevards, government office complexes, and commercial centers. Traffic arteries, connecting with a circumferential beltway, would move employees and shoppers smoothly from a differentiated set of satellite suburbs to the central-city locale of business and administrative activities. The suburbs themselves would serve either industrial, agricultural, or residential purposes; each was seen to contribute one essential element to the emerging model metropolis.

Because of the ideological climate of the early years of the dictatorship, it was necessary for DRPF to take the plan seriously. DAP was the darling of the first lady. It had produced other equally unrealistic schemes for a futuristic science fiction community, called "New City," to be built on reclaimed land in Manila Bay, and a huge seaport to be built on the Pacific shore of Luzon, opposite Manila (and squarely in the path of the worst typhoons in Asia, a fact explaining the avoidance of this site by the Spanish for four centuries). But in the first years of the *Bagong Lipunan* ("New Society"), development loans seemed to wash up every day with the tide, the caprices of Mrs. Marcos were commands, and everything seemed possible. In that environment, the DAP plan for Davao City appeared as plausible as the other schemes announced in each day's Manila press releases. The bills did not come due until the end of the decade.

The line was now clearly drawn between the official bureaucracy with its model city on one side and DRPF (endorsed by the World Bank) with its commitment to site-and-services development on the other. In a dictatorship it is not possible to enlist the support of the opposition party and put the issue to a vote; there is neither legitimate opposition nor election. Our previous strategy assumed that we were operating within the framework of a popular democracy. We sought to generate facts through research, bring them to the attention of a wide audience, and create support through molding public opinion to endorse our position. But the martial-law government did not play by the rules.

We needed to seek a position *within* the monolithic structure from which it could be manipulated. The World Bank experienced similar problems, but was in a better position to solve them. In 1974, with the commencement of the Tondo/Dagat-dagatan project in Manila, the Bank demanded that the government create an institution capable of managing it. It emerged as the National Housing Authority (NHA) in July 1975, under the direction of General Gaudencio Tobias. From its inception, NHA was committed to the rescue of squatter settlements in major Philippine cities. It was dedicated to site-and-services projects because its major source of funding (several hundreds of millions of dollars between 1974 and 1983) came from the World Bank.

The establishment of NHA created a polarity within the dictatorship. Over the next decade, it often opposed the much more powerful Ministry of Human Settlements headed by the Dragon Lady herself: Imelda Romualdez Marcos. At a meeting with NHA officials on October 9, 1975, DRPF made a presentation on behalf of a site-and-services project for Davao's largest and least secure squatter community: the Piapi foreshore settlement. The meeting gave DRPF the opportunity to (1) establish its research credentials with NHA; (2) associate itself with the World Bank's housing policy; (3) obtain the first NHA project outside Manila for Davao.

General Tobias invited DRPF to provide a site-and-services project proposal for Piapi. We presented it to the Development Economics Department in Washington in January 1976. We argued that the existence of baseline measures of housing, employment, and income in Davao made it possible for us to evaluate the impact of a Bank site-and-services project on urban poverty within the city. Only in Davao could the Bank test the hypothesis underlying the housing sector policy paper. In July, the Bank proposed a loan for upgrading squatter areas in regional cities, to include Davao, Cagayan de Oro, and Cebu. The NHA imposed its policy on the local city government, with which DRPF now enjoyed an uneasy partnership. The coordination of research, project design, political decision making, and financial support necessary for urban problem solving had been achieved.

STAGE III: INSTITUTIONALIZATION

The goals of social and cultural change cannot be reached by negotiation and contract. They differ from infrastructure projects in an important respect. The nature of the intervention is not episodic but continuous. The redesign of squatter settlements would require continuous interaction with beneficiary households over several years of construction and initiation of services. The communities to be upgraded by the World Bank's site-and-services programs would incur financial obligations to be repaid over 12 years. Intervention is thus projected across a 15-year interval.

To be successful the intervention must be institutionalized. This requires the creation of a new social structure blending attributes and elements of each of the parent institutions reaching agreement during the consolidation phase. These include (1) the political authority of the NHA; (2) the financing and technical assistance of the World Bank; (3) the longitudinal data base to be provided by DRPF; (4) local administration by an agency of the city government; and (5) approval of plans and procedures and compliance with agreements to be provided and enforced by the squatter organizations on behalf of member households.

The process of linking a project to a parent institution, which will insure its continuity and progressive redesign to make adaptive responses to internal change (project growth and/or aging) and external change (in the political and/or economic environment), is neither studied nor understood (Hackenberg and Hackenberg 1984). Yet it is the area of development programming where anthropologists may best make use of their training and expertise.

This complex issue is further complicated by the knowledge that each participant institution, engaged in shaping the new social structure, has its own (usually hidden) agenda. In retrospect these agendas, or self-determined goals, appear to have been the following, although representatives of each institution would probably disagree:

1. *The National Housing Authority* was engaged in a turf war with the Ministry of Human Settlements, which in 1977 announced its own New Society Site-and-Services Program under the patronage of the first lady. The NHA was handicapped in this struggle by the need to maintain good relations with the World Bank, its chief source of finance. The situation was further complicated by the open hostilities between the Bank, which defined site and services as limited self-improvement of existing squatter settlements, and the first lady, who favored wholesale replacement with multiunit high-rise structures with beautification, imitating Singapore and Hong Kong. Two examples of these conflicting views may be seen side by side on Manila's North Harbor shoreline where the Bank's Tondo Urban Redevelopment Project sits adjacent to the first lady's *Kapitbahayan* project at Dagat-dagatan.

2. *The World Bank* at times appears to be a hydra-headed monster with no central nervous system. Our contacts were with the Urban and Regional Development Division of the Development Economics Department. Its mission was chiefly to produce "concepts" for implementation by regional or sectoral components of the agency (which had much more clout since they were actually engaged in lending). The concept upon which we joined forces was a commitment to the need for evaluation of different project designs and an assessment of their impact in order to reach some insights concerning (1) comparative potential for growth and significant reduction of overall poverty indicators; and (2) cost-benefit aspects that would determine their potential for replication and cost recovery. Within the Bank, this view is associated with those who believe that the agency's mission is to design and construct projects. The "projects view" is opposed by the "sectoral view," preaching the traditional economist's idea that "factor distortions" account for development failures in the housing sector. They can be corrected by "getting prices right" for building materials, improving technology, adjusting wages for construction workers, or creating a mortgage market with a transfusion of capital. We have contrasted these positions fully elsewhere (Hackenberg 1985). In Davao, our fate was clearly linked with the "projects view."

3. *Municipal government* under the dictatorship was essentially redundant. Its mission was to carry out instructions from Manila. But the directives from multiple ministries were often in conflict. Local officials learned that if they failed to act on a particular PD or LOI, it would often be superceded, cancelled, or more often, simply forgotten. A classic example was the 1978 PD on "urban land reform" which threatened to confiscate all undeveloped private land in every chartered city for transfer to squatter households; no action on this was ever taken. In the case of urban redevelopment, people with no political leverage (urban squatters) occupied central-city property with a very high assessed valuation. It was to the potential advantage of city council members (who were also private businessmen) to seek to reserve that property for the type of development that would pay the highest return. Several high officials were also said to be seeking favor with the first lady, who shared DAP's vision of the future of Davao rather than the World Bank's. The city government saw advantage in dragging its feet or actively seeking to obstruct the site-and-services project. Certainly, no one saw any material benefits from its completion. And under the dictatorship, many sought to follow those at the top in seeking material benefits.

4. *Davao Research and Planning Foundation* also had its agenda. Its senior staff were faculty members at the University of Colorado. They expected to derive career benefits from research and publication. They sought professional advancement through demonstrating the potentials of a multipurpose field station (Hackenberg and Hackenberg 1981) and through a test of their hypothesis that longitudinal studies under conditions of rapid growth were the only appropriate instruments for describing processes of change (Hackenberg 1963, 1970). A related goal was to keep DRPF in operation for at least 12 years, during which the city could double in size and its socioeconomic adaptation, especially at the household level, could be documented.

DRPF patched financing together from a number of sponsors between 1970 and 1980: in the U.S., the National Institutes of Health, U.S Agency for International Development, the Ford and Rockefeller foundations, and the East-West Center contributed; in the Philippines, the Population Commission, the Population Center Foundation, the Banana Export Industry Foundation, and Philippine Business for Social Progress were major sources. But support was episodic and agency-centered rather than focused on DRPF's objectives. The foundation frequently bootlegged its projects by inserting them into research designed and funded for other purposes.

Our remaining task was to consolidate the arrangement with our World Bank associates for DRPF to conduct the impact assessment. Our goal was to build DRPF into the Piapi site-and-services loan project. This would insure the survival and continuity of our study of citywide adaptation to rapid growth for at least 5 and perhaps as many as 15 years. To achieve this, DRPF must participate in building the social structure intended to carry out the project. Our prediction of victory at this point failed to recognize the conflicting agendas within the other institutions involved: the World Bank and NHA.

The enthusiasm for monitoring and evaluation of site-and-services projects that originated in the Bank's Development Economics Department (the unit responsible for conceptualizing operations) was not shared by the Urban Projects Department (the unit responsible for implementing them). As the design of the project advanced, the latter department assumed total control. The economist representing Urban Projects believed that a well-designed project, completed on time and within budget, was its own justification. When DRPF opposed this view, he countered with the assertion that if further evaluation or impact assessment was necessary, it should be conducted by the NHA's own Research and Analysis Division (RAD). When we countered that RAD was staffed by totally inexperienced young persons with no baseline for comparative purposes, he blandly asserted that learning by doing was the core of the Bank's institution-building philosophy.

While this attitude precluded the incorporation of a DRPF research component in the Bank's regional cities loan for the Piapi site-and-services project in Davao, the resulting gloom was not complete. In June 1977, NHA prepared LOIs 555 and 557 for the president's signature, thus obtaining sweeping powers to order local city governments to establish, at their own expense, Slum Improvement and Resettlement (SIR) offices to develop slum upgrading and site-and-services projects. Davao City entered into a SIR agreement with NHA on June 22, committing it to prepare feasibility studies for projects to be located on both sides of the central business district: New Matina on the south and Piapi on the north.

The studies were initiated by a British engineering firm in August. The following month DRPF obtained indirect representation in the SIR office when David De Groot, a doctoral candidate in applied anthropology at Colorado, was invited to join the Davao SIR team, together with his wife

Barbara, an urban planner. With the exception of home leave to submit a dissertation (De Groot 1979), David and Barbara remained with NHA as consultants to the end of 1984. DRPF contributed the socioeconomic data on Davao and helped the De Groots plan a survey of the squatter slums, both of which were incorporated in the feasibility studies. DRPF was excluded from financial support from either the Bank or NHA, but remained a participant in all the action taking place.

But worse setbacks were in store. The Development Economics Department, which continued to favor research for evaluation, was also excluded from Bank financial support. To remain involved, DED applied to the International Development Research Centre (IDRC) for a grant to conduct a five-year (1975-1980) comparative study of site-and-services projects in Dakar (Senegal), Lusaka (Zambia), San Salvador (El Salvador), and Manila. IDRC, a Canadian agency, complied but stipulated that no expatriate personnel be employed. NHA interpreted this to mean that its own RAD unit could fulfill this function. The Bank's Urban Projects personnel then argued that if RAD could do the larger job in Manila, they could also do the smaller job in Davao. Ergo, no need for DRPF and its expatriate leadership!

We devised an alternative strategy. If we could not operate from within as participants, we could remain outside and act as observers. Our hand was strengthened unexpectedly from an unlikely quarter. Mayor Luis T. Santos, a formidable opponent in confrontations over squatter removal since 1970, now became our advocate. In a letter on December 28, 1978, he acknowledged the benefits of the site-and-services project and gave DRPF exclusive authorization to conduct a comprehensive evaluation in the name of Davao City. We expected that the letter would assist us in raising external financial support. And it was proof of our success at institutionalization in our own back yard!

The social structure built to conduct the Piapi/New Matina project in 1977-1978 was quite different from what DRPF had anticipated. We had expected to form an alliance with NHA and the Bank against the city officials. Instead, city hall became a pivot around which DRPF, the Bank, and NHA rotated in separate but often intersecting orbits. The link that connected us was the Davao SIR Office. While DRPF continued as a player at the table, we needed to raise outside funds in order to stay in the game.

STAGE IV: MAINTENANCE OF CONTINUITY

The title of this section actually refers to two issues of concern after 1979. Certainly the most important was the maintenance of the continuity of the project now taking shape in New Matina and Piapi. A second and less vital concern was the maintenance of the continuity of DRPF as the proper agency for evaluation and impact assessment. We will deal with them both, but in the reverse order of importance.

On the strength of city endorsement, Development Economics Department friends encouraged us to prepare a proposal for presentation to the Bank's research committee. The research would assess the effectiveness of the project in meeting the following issues: (1) the squatter problem; (2) quality of housing stock; (3) income and employment; (4) access to urban services; and (5) demand for new housing. Each of these issues would be studied over a suitable interval of time. However, the existence of the four previous Davao citywide surveys (1972, 1974, 1976, 1978) would permit clear establishment of trends within five years; i.e., by 1982 we would have acquired a decade of data on socioeconomic trends within the city.

However, the winds of change were already beginning to blow within the World Bank. At the same time our prospectus was circulating, another research proposal by the Development Economics Department, "Housing Demand and Housing Finance" (RP 67-246), was already in the process of receiving approval. This study, in which DRPF later participated, was part of the shift away from the "projects" perspective to the "sectoral" emphasis in Bank lending. Instead of targeting an economically depressed district or a category of households within the city for project development, this project sought to examine the demand for new or improved housing throughout an entire city so that the financial institutions might respond to it more effectively. Its target was not a spatial or socioeconomic component. It was the housing market.

The concepts of monitoring, evaluation, and impact assessment had gained us our access to World Bank personnel and resources in 1975. Six years later the concepts were still of central importance to DRPF. They represented an indispensable methodology for the observation of adaptive structural change, or, if you prefer, microevolution. For the Bank's Development Economics Department, concern with these issues was interconnected with the obsolescent "projects" perspective. It was to their advantage to "drink up and split" as discretely as possible. This was accomplished rather smoothly by both our Bank associates and their IDRC counterparts during 1981-83.

The four-country research program, comparing sites and services in Zambia, Senegal, El Salvador, and the Philippines, expired in 1980. Publications were prepared by the World Bank (Keare and Parris 1982) and IDRC (Yeung 1983; Laquian 1983). While substantial achievements are authentically documented in each of these volumes, they may be prematurely self-congratulatory since none of the projects had been fully operative for the entire five years prior to the cutoff date. Furthermore, as noted earlier, the World Bank-IDRC focus was limited in scope. The comparative studies concentrated on the *project*, but not on the *people* or the *problem*. Since 1983, neither agency has pursued the subject further.

It is quite possible, perhaps even probable, that the residents of the project following its full development differ substantially from the original occupants of the undeveloped squatter community, i.e., the project may selectively eliminate the lowest income stratum. It is also possible that while selected households within the project benefit from its completion, the status of the urban poor throughout the entire community continues to disintegrate. Answers to these questions fall outside the scope of the methods employed. It is issues of this sort that were to be addressed in the DRPF research on Piapi and New Matina.

The Bank's continuing interest in housing has veered sharply toward the sectoral approach. DRPF participated in the "Housing Demand and Housing Finance Research Project" of 1981-82 in a dual role: (1) we provided a tape of the 4,000 households interviewed in the 1978 citywide survey, containing data on housing quality, facilities, rental/amortization, and estimated sale price; (2) we also prepared a manuscript analyzing housing trends among the urban poor in Davao City from 1972 through 1979 ("Ecology of Poverty in Davao City, 1972-1979"). The tape file was used for the definitive publication from the project on estimating housing demand (Follain and Jimenez 1983). The manuscript was accepted without comment or further action. It failed to reflect current interests. Since then, the World Bank's East Asian and Pacific Regional Office has issued a monograph entitled *Housing Finance* (IBRD 1982). It also is concerned exclusively with adjusting the mechanism of the housing market on a national scale.

A final spark of hope concerning the possibility of Bank financing for DRPF was ignited in 1983 when a new loan agreement was completed with NHA to convey a fresh $60 million for the renewal of Philippine regional cities, including Davao. While the air at NHA was filled with talk about applying "the Davao model" to a number of other urban centers with this new support, the model itself remained elusive since neither a comprehensive description of the stages in its development nor an evaluation of its impact had been completed. Despite the continuous operation of NHA's RAD unit during the 1978-1983 interval, its operation had been confined to Manila.

Since funding for expatriate consultants was included in the new loan agreement, the Davao SIR staff invited DRPF to prepare a *planning study*, based on the accumulated Davao City experience, which would point the way toward its transfer to other regional cities. The concept received a supporting letter from Mayor Elias B. Lopez, and a proposal was forwarded to Manila on April 2, 1984. Its main features included (1) a description of the condition of the site-and-services households in 1984, compared with their status at time of entry into the project; and (2) a fifth citywide survey to determine residual demand for similar shelter arrangements elsewhere in Davao. The planning study would determine who had benefited from the Bank's intervention and how much. It would also measure the extent of project impact on the housing problem of the city as a whole.

Although the project found favor with General Tobias and his staff at NHA, it was never funded. Once again, adverse circumstances intervened. The Philippine economy had been suffering a rapid decline since 1980. The combined impact of accelerated foreign borrowing, declining prices for export commodities (sugar, copra, and timber), increased energy costs, and redistribution of assets to Marcos cronies raised the foreign debt to $27 billion over this interval. Reduced consumer purchasing power and lack of foreign exchange to pay for imported raw materials promoted an urban industrial collapse to match that of plantation agriculture in the provinces.

Since mid-1984, austerity has been the watchword. One of the first forms of expenditure to be terminated was the agenda for new development loans. Even where new projects were to be initiated, loan agreements had to be cancelled because the Philippine ministries could not produce the small amounts of required counterpart funds. The regional cities loan negotiated by the Bank in 1983 has been scaled back to funds already received. In the midst of the existing crisis, the Bank has sent several missions to meet with representatives of the Aquino government. New lending for urban development is under discussion, but there will be no fresh commitments until 1988 at the earliest. And they will be sectoral loans to the financial institutions that support the private housing industry.

This account has interwoven two stories: (1) that of the benefits provided to low-income squatters by the extension of site-and-services programs from Manila to Davao and other regional cities; and (2) that of the effort to complete a scientific study of the development process and its outcome. We will complete the narrative with an inventory of the substantive accomplishments. In keeping with the title of this section, these have been continuously maintained across the five-year interval and incorporate two different dimensions of improvement.

The first concept applied to squatter area development is slum upgrading of existing communities. It consists of jacking up the old houses and putting an improved foundation under them. Most squatter areas are deficient in sanitation, utilities, drainage, access roads, and spacing of structures. Upgrading remedies these deficiencies and returns the original residence to an improved site. The process involves considerable disruption, the elimination of advantages enjoyed previously by only a few, and significant indebtedness incurred by all. Homeowners are expected to expand and improve their residences with self-help, labor, technical assistance, and loans for construction materials. Although it creates a vastly improved quality of life, the upgrading concept often engenders substantial opposition.

In Davao, the Piapi district was the first to sustain upgrading. Organized resistance was expected from several squatter associations with a history of opposition extending back over a decade. It did not materialize, perhaps because the residents were intimidated by the authority of the dictatorship. And perhaps it was because of the fires. The first occurred in May 1978 and consumed 5 hectares. The last, in May 1980, destroyed 6.5 hectares. Altogether, more than 6,000 persons were rendered homeless and the entire upgrading area was effectively "cleared."

Mayor Santos saw the opportunity to turn the situation to his advantage. He had the SIR team locate households recorded in the July 1977 survey and issue each a permit to reoccupy a site in Piapi to be assigned following the resurvey and subdivision of the entire site. Meanwhile, they were issued supplies and housed in public buildings. When they were allowed to reenter Piapi, all were issued new construction materials, creating a much more attractive community than would have resulted from conventional upgrading alone.

When upgrading was completed, 10.3 hectares of the Piapi area had been improved and 1,183 lots were occupied by

1,600 households (almost 11,000 persons). The upgrading exercise in New Matina was less eventful. Since houses were newer and more substantial than in Piapi, the resurveyed community also provides the appearance of substantial quality. The site contains 8.3 hectares and 643 lots occupied by 900 households (almost 7,000 persons). At a cost of 22 million pesos ($2.75 million), 18,000 people have been given a healthy environment, a structurally sound residence with secure tenure, and the motivation to improve it and themselves as well. It is expected that the cost will be fully recovered.

The first phase of the Davao SIR project also includes a new community to be developed on site-and-services principles with do-it-yourself dwelling construction in New Matina. A total project area of 23.1 hectares has been developed into an industrial, commercial, and residential planned community. The sale of industrial and commercial real estate will help to subsidize the cost of the residential area, which now contains 1,350 homesites. It is expected that, when fully occupied, the new community will house 1,900 households with a population of 12,000. This will raise the total beneficiaries of the self-financing first stage development to 30,000 former squatters. This figure equals at least 25 percent of the estimated 1985 urban squatter population.

Because SIR is a part of both city government and, through NHA, national government as well, its prospects for maintaining continuity appear to be secure. However, as this is being written six months after the removal of the Marcos dictatorship, prospects for the short run are not good. The new government has a deficit of more than $2 billion in its operating budget. Salaries are not paid and appropriations for continuation of budgeted projects are frozen. In Davao, the director of SIR has resigned and a skeleton staff of four persons is all that remains.

While this is an unhappy state of affairs, the major improvements required for Piapi and New Matina to succeed are already in the ground. They are permanent. There is a network of social services that complements them: a health clinic and daycare facilities for mothers and children; adult vocational training programs to develop small business and cottage industries. It is in this area that budget cuts will be severe. Cost recovery during the present disastrous economic interval is also likely to be unsatisfactory. But it is improbable that resident households will be dispossessed for nonpayment. A move of this sort would win recruits wholesale for the insurgent forces that are already quite strong within low-income neighborhoods throughout the city (Hackenberg and Hackenberg 1986).

UNIVERSITY RESEARCH AND COMMUNITY ASSISTANCE

This narrative has skipped across a decade and a half of development experience in a major Third World city. It began with an externally supported university research project producing an unpopular set of conclusions that were introduced in a hostile community environment. It ended with internally funded implementation of the conclusions of that research by the community, no longer aided by its expatriate consultants and research support. From the conventional viewpoint of the applied anthropology textbook this would be an unqualified success story. We developed a project, assisted it toward institutional continuity, and then got out of the way.

That is what you are supposed to do. But we have introduced some contextual material to describe the interplay of institutions that played the major role in bringing about the changes which occurred. At times it appeared to both DRPF and to the government of Davao City that they were merely passive participants in the central drama which took place in Manila and Washington. Consider the following:

1. The seizure of power by Marcos in 1972 placed the squatters at a disadvantage by destroying their power base at the ballot box.

2. The central bureaucracy created by the dictatorship provided the occasion for ministries with national authority supported by PDs and LOIs, such as NHA, to dictate to regional cities and their squatter districts.

3. Equally important, it provided the opportunity for expatriate lenders, such as the World Bank, to negotiate bilaterally with a single ministry for a package of developments to be implemented at remote points without confronting the cacophony of individual municipal governments, each with its own agenda.

4. Since the source of many of these initiatives was the agenda of a remote subagency within the World Bank, the evolving programs were oblivious to the changing context of the Philippine economy or the changing needs of the community. They proved to be much more sensitive to turf wars and administrative changes within the Bank and within the Manila bureaucracy.

5. In the absence of research at the local community level on project impact and citywide socioeconomic trends,

and the interactions between the two, it remains difficult to perceive the implications of the Davao experience and its potentials for replication either within the city or elsewhere.

It is from this perspective that the failure of DRPF to fulfill its oversight mission may have unfortunate consequences. Critical questions remain unasked and therefore unanswered. Was the obvious living-standard improvement sustained by the Piapi district as a result of the project equal to or greater than the decline resulting from deteriorating national economic circumstances? Could the site-and-services project buffer its residents against "world system" uncertainties? Were the beneficiary households occupying the district at the end of the project the same as the target households described at the beginning? Or did the original residents perceive the gains in Piapi property values, sell out, and become squatters once again elsewhere? Was the number of squatter households improved by the project less than, equal to, or greater than the number of new squatter households formed within the city over the 1977-1985 interval?

A closer working relationship between the Bank, NHA, SIR, and DRPF would have provided the answers and incorporated them into future plans. But our relationship with NHA/SIR was sequential rather than simultaneous.

It has been a story of mixed success and frustration. The arms-length relationship is explained in part by our growing conviction, based on the experience of three decades in three countries, that economists are committed to a deductive approach to project design that is practically impervious to modification based on evidence from the field (Hackenberg 1985). This intellectual framework is so foreign to the applied anthropologist's inductive (often improvisational) style that representatives of the two disciplines find it hard to communicate. The economist asks our preference among growth models; the anthropologist replies by asking, "What's out there?" One is an idealist and the other a realist. Neither considers the other's question to be meaningful. But the project leader is always an economist!

We believe we have found a solution to this dilemma in "progressive project redesign"--a strategy in which research on both the development model and the environment in which it is introduced proceeds interactively over time. The design of the project is continuously modified to keep pace with its impact on its target and also with changes in the surrounding environment (Hackenberg and Hackenberg 1984). The implementation of this strategy requires monitoring of both the project and the community at fixed and frequent intervals. Furthermore, the funding of the monitoring and evaluation *should be* (but almost never is) independent of the project, and the continuation of the research should not depend on producing favorable reports.

DRPF was almost ideally situated to perform under this prescription. Our funding was diversified and did not depend on any single agency. Our commitment was to the community and to the advancement of development research (which we perceived would promote our own professional careers). Our interest was in maintaining a long-term multidimensional link with Davao City and not with a sponsor institution. We took such opportunities as we could to make evaluative judgments in terms of the city's advantage. It follows from this, of course, that the city itself, rather than the sponsoring agencies, should have supported DRPF's work. But in the Philippines during the years of the dictatorship, such independence on the part of local communities was not tolerated.

Not unexpectedly, the relationship that emerged between university-based research and community-based intervention in Davao City during the 1970s was only activated at those points where the agendas of the powerbroker agencies intersected and required it. Perhaps more candor on the part of other applied anthropologists concerning the intersecting agendas shaping both intervention successes and failures is indicated. Knowledge of these episodes might promote a more realistic assessment of what practitioners of our discipline can hope to accomplish, and under which circumstances. Attempts to perceive regularities and construct typologies of these factors and circumstances are, to the best of our knowledge, absent at this time.

PART THREE

Concluding Comments

9

Perspectives on Collaborative Research

Stephen L. Schensul

Anthropology has always been concerned with those peoples in our world who have limited access to social, economic, and political resources. Even before the turn of the century, the discipline was concerned about the clash between colonial powers and non-Western/nonindustrialized peoples, the suppression of ethnic enclaves by mainstream national cultures, and the domination of the lower classes by powerful elites. Anthropologists have lived among these peoples, identified with their needs, and been involved in efforts to make others understand their situations. These concerns have to some degree "marginated" anthropology along with those peoples who are the focus of its studies. Much of the literature in applied anthropology addresses ways both anthropologists and their field associates can become less marginated and more effectively integrated into productive socioeconomic and political systems.

This volume very clearly continues this tradition. We see anthropologists at work among urban shantytown dwellers in the Philippines, Indians in Arizona and Kansas, Puerto Ricans in Connecticut, Sikhs in California, and Quechua Indians in the Andes. The fact that we are involved with groups such as these, that we seek to understand their lives and their world in *their terms*, and that we have been associated with attempts to improve their quality of life, is one of the most significant elements in the anthropological tradition.

The anthropologists in this volume are associated with the subfield of "applied anthropology"--those investigators who direct their research to the improvement of the lives of the people they study. This objective has always stirred considerable controversy in our discipline. Basic researchers have charged applied anthropologists with losing the "objectivity" that comes with basic or "abstract" research (a term used by several of the volume's authors) or with acting as "social engineers" rather than investigators.

On the other hand, there is disagreement among the ranks of self-identified applied anthropologists. Those applied anthropologists who see themselves as advocating for political and ethnic empowerment and self-determination have criticized others for providing information to colonial governments and other oppressive institutions. In this way, they argue, such anthropologists only increase the effectiveness of external agents of control and oppression, thereby decreasing the potential of the local community to determine its own approaches to change.

The authors in this volume are well aware of these critiques. They attempt to address them by building on the experiences of post-World War II applied anthropologists to generate new models for the application of research to the solution of human problems. Action anthropology among the Fox Indians (Gearing, Netting, and Peattie 1960) developed the proposition that it was possible for the anthropologist to work directly for and within the community and not on behalf of external institutions. Vicos (for which Doughty provides a valuable update and analysis) showed us that anthropologists could play a central role *both* as researchers and as policy makers in conjunction with local communities.

With the rise of community organizations in the United States in the 1960s, many applied anthropologists began to use the action anthropology approach more directly from their bases in universities and community-oriented change programs. Through this more intimate relationship with program staff and community representatives, anthropologists began to share the research process with their nonresearch colleagues. This process, in which community and/or institutional participants worked with anthropologists to identify research questions, operationalize concepts, design methodologies, collect, analyze, and utilize data to generate policies and programs, can be viewed as "collaborative research."

Collaborative research, as it is described in this volume, has a number of advantages over other types of applied anthropology:

1. It brings together people of diverse skills and knowledge (see J. Schensul's notion of the "policy cluster" in this volume).
2. It "demystifies" the research process, allowing those who will utilize the results the opportunity

to understand and shape the data collection process.
3. It builds a research capability in the community and/or organization that can extend beyond and operate independent of the anthropologist.
4. It increases the likelihood that the results of the research will be used by nonresearchers.
5. It improves the quality of the research through access to the community or institution and to key bodies of knowledge.

The approach of these anthropologists, then, is to begin the applied research endeavor *in collaboration with* community and/or institutional participants. Most communities have a variety of potential collaborative sectors. Based on these articles and my own experiences, I would include the following categories:

1. Informal community leaders.
2. Formal community leaders (e.g., elected officials).
3. Leaders of community-based and community-run organizations (advocacy and service groups).
4. Local service and development institutions.
5. Regional public organizations.
6. National-level public ministries and development organizations.
7. International aid and development organizations.

In each article we see a concern for the local community and the use of participant observation in combination with quantitative approaches to understand small communities, villages, and neighborhoods. The focus on this unit of analysis continues the anthropological tradition of in-depth studies of relatively small populations.

The articles in this volume do, however, present considerable differences in the selection of collaborators and the utilizers of the research. Stull and his colleagues, and Watahomigie and Yamamoto worked directly for tribal councils (category 2 in the typology listed above) and later for tribal schools (category 3). Jean Schensul and associates worked with the Hispanic Health Council (category 3), the Connecticut State Health Department (category 5), and later with local hospitals and health care facilities (category 4). Murphy and colleagues worked with INDECO, a Mexican federal agency (category 6), and the State of Oaxaca's branch of this agency (category 5). Hackenberg and Hackenberg describe collaboration with the Davao Development

Foundation (category 3), the Davao Research and Planning Foundation (category 3), and the World Bank (category 7). The Cornell-Peru Project in Vicos, as a result of the freedom acquired as the *patron*, worked with informal community leaders (category 1) and then formed for the first time a number of democractic community organizations (category 2). Barger and Reza worked with a union of migrant workers on the local and national levels (category 3). Gibson reports working with a local community organization and a local school district (categories 3 and 4).

The work described in this volume displays three basic approaches to the collaborative process, any or all of which may be used at different times and for different reasons in a single project. One approach, characterized by the work with the Kickapoo, Hualapai, farmworkers, and Vicos, involves close collaboration with members of the target community and limited or no collaboration with external institutions. The second approach, as seen in the work in Davao City and Oaxaca, focuses on collaboration with developmental agencies external to the communities to be affected. A third type, reflected in the work in the Puerto Rican and Sikh communities, involves collaboration with agencies and leaders internal to the community and institutions external to the community but interested in working with it. Each approach brings with it both advantages and disadvantages which are well documented by the authors. Consistent in each description, however, is the focus on the local community as the source of data and directions for change.

The question might be raised as to which of the three is the better strategy from the point of view of short- and long-term structural change. To address this question we must examine the goals of collaborative research as reflected in the work of these authors and only then consider the advantages or disadvantages of the approach.

APPROACH I: COLLABORATION WITH THE TARGET COMMUNITY

The goal of this approach to collaborative research is to build the capability of the target community or population to utilize research as a tool in self-development, to advocate on their own behalf with external programs and institutions, and to develop their own research infrastructure.

Advantages

The community is not only the unit of study but the prime beneficiary of the research activity in this approach. Research skills are transferred directly to community leadership and residents. Grants and projects generated by the research come directly to community organizations (categories 2 and 3). The community and its representatives control data, utilization, and dissemination more directly. Research becomes integrated into self-determination initiatives.

Problems

All communities and population groups have factions vying for resources and control. Several of the authors describe ways in which anthropologists were drawn into these factional disputes. When anthropologists have to choose sides there is rarely a right decision. All the authors have described how institutions in the wider society have undercut self-determination efforts in local communities. When anthropologists work exclusively with community groups, they risk the undermining of the results of their work by oppressive or unknowledgeable outside authorities.

APPROACH II: COLLABORATION WITH OUTSIDE AGENCIES

The goal of collaborative research in this approach is to introduce the community/population perspective into national and regional development plans and programs. Anthropologists focused on local-level perspectives can provide developers with the community perspective and assist in building that perspective into the ongoing planning and intervention process.

Advantages

Outside institutions and agencies (private and public) on the regional, national, and international levels possess the political and economic power to "get things done." They have expertise, money, and political support. Externally designed programs usually lack an understanding of community dynamics and values, however. The integration of this knowledge with the other well-established resources can provide significant improvements in the life of poor communities.

Problems

The balance of power has, for poor communities, been in the hands of external agencies and institutions. Despite the best of intentions, many of these development agencies undermine local infrastructure and fail to take into account detrimental effects of their technical programs on diverse aspects of community life. While paying lip service to community involvement, programs must meet externally imposed deadlines and economic and political contingencies. Under these circumstances, the anthropologist's contribution, some have claimed, is to increase the capabilities of external agencies to manipulate local communities. Anthropologists working in this mode depend on the community to provide entry and information, but utilize the results to meet external agency needs. Often reluctantly, they are forced into the role of broker, required to speak on behalf of, rather than with, the community to their employer.

APPROACH III: INTERSECTORAL FACILITATION

The goal of collaborative research in this approach is to establish relationships with community groups and leaders on the one hand and external agencies on the other. The anthropologist seeks to expand the community's capability to conduct and utilize research and to expand the external agency's ability to work with local community leadership.

Advantages

This approach recognizes the multisectoral nature of development projects. It confronts directly the need for community groups to take a significant role in self-development while avoiding the tendency of external vested interests to undercut community change. It addresses as well the requirement that external agencies provide appropriate resources and technology that can be effectively utilized by community members. This dual approach can bring about more effective communication and collaboration between community members and development agency staff. The anthropologist avoids the need to speak "on behalf" of the community so that community members and external agency personnel can develop their own relationships.

Problems

Most poor communities have a significant history of negative relationships with external agencies such as local hospitals, the Bureau of Indian Affairs, or Mexican or Peruvian governmental agencies. Under these circumstances it may be extremely difficult for the anthropologist to work on "both sides of the fence." Incompatible demands, the need to take a position in a dispute, and a concern over the anthropologist's real loyalties may undermine this "systems" approach (see Barger and Reza in this volume) to problem solving.

DISCUSSION

Each of the authors has used these approaches in combination and at various times during the lengthy periods of relationship with the communities and institutions described in the case materials. Each is caught in a dilemma not easily solved. Over and over again they portray national and international forces undermining community improvements in basic needs—housing, education, and health status. Short of participating in revolutionary movements supporting broadscale systems change, what does anthropology have to offer that is useful in these situations?

The work of anthropologists concentrates on those people at greatest risk in national systems. Among the social sciences, anthropology is the one discipline committed to looking at the world from the "bottom up"—from the local community *to* the rest of the world. Earlier, anthropology was accused of treating local communities as if they existed in a vacuum. Now, most ethnographers carefully examine the impact of economic policies, political changes, the media, and other national and international influences on urban and village residents. In my view, we need a discipline "on the side of" those people who are most at risk. The fact that our efforts (as well as those of our community- and institutionally-based colleagues) are frequently undermined by dysfunctional national and international systems is part of a reality that our colleagues are even more aware of than are we. Our continued work on the "bottom end" provides a unique perspective in the social sciences and makes our own small contribution to "balancing the scales" in the effort to create more significant social change. Our contribution, then, involves continued work with these collaborators at the local level, enhancing social science theory while establishing and testing models for development in touch with local people and local needs.

Several authors in this volume cite the distinction between theoretical, basic, or abstract research on the one hand and applied or action research on the other. These authors seem to think of themselves as contributing only to "applied research." On the other hand, their community and institutional colleagues, as nonresearchers, are carrying out action and intervention programs which presumably contribute only to program development. If we accept their statements we must conclude that both the anthropologists and their colleagues have little to contribute to theory in anthropology.

I have argued elsewhere (S. Schensul 1985), that the real science of anthropology lies in applied research. The key to this argument lay in the validation and revalidation of theoretical models when those models were tested in association with programs of planned change. I would like to reiterate this view from a different perspective, one which I believe has considerable relevance for the collaborative research process.

Community leaders, planners, policy makers, and program implementors require an understanding of how a social system works and how it can be changed. A program plan, that is, a model of how things should be changed, differs little from a theoretical or abstract model that forms the basis for and the output of research. Once establishing this model (and program plan), both the applied researcher and program personnel are concerned about how it works. (In a natural science context, this step would be referred to as experimentation.) Then both the applied researcher and the program staff are interested in revising the theoretical model (program plan) so that it will describe (and work) better in the next place and time. In stark contrast, our presumed abstract anthropological researcher collects data, develops a theoretical model, and concludes the process with little or no ability to validate the resulting theory, since continual testing was not built into the research process.

This congruence between the anthropologist and the change agent is the basis of the collaborative research approach. The competent change agent must be a researcher generating theoretical/planning models and evaluating their impact. The anthropologist must be a change agent involved in the experimentation that leads to better scientific models. As the authors in this volume have effectively demonstrated, we must eliminate the false barriers of discipline versus discipline, applied versus abstract, researcher versus intervener. These case studies have provided us important examples of the ways community residents, program developers, and anthropologists can collaborate to achieve both a better understanding of our world and a better life for its people.

Bibliography

Adams, R.N., and C.C. Cumberland
  1960 United States University Cooperation in Latin America. Institute of Research on Overseas Programs. East Lansing: Michigan State University.
Agar, M.H.
  1980 The Professional Stranger: An Informal Introduction to Ethnography. New York: Academic Press.
Alers, J.O.
  1965 Population and Development in a Peruvian Community. Journal of Inter-American Studies 7:422-448.
  1971 Well Being. *In* Peasants, Power and Applied Social Change: Vicos As A Model. H.F. Dobyns, P.L. Doughty, and H. D. Lasswell, eds. Pp. 115-136. Beverly Hills, CA: Sage.
Alers, J.O., M.C. Vazquez, A.R. Holmberg, and H.F. Dobyns
  1965 Human Freedom and Geographic Mobility. Current Anthropology 6:336.
Alland, A., Jr.
  1967 Evolution and Human Behavior. New York: Natural History Press.
  1970 Adaptation in Cultural Evolution. New York: Columbia University Press.
  1972 Cultural Evolution. Social Biology 19:227-239.
  1975 Adaptation. Annual Review of Anthropology 4:59-73.
Alland, A., Jr., and B. McCay
  1973 The Concept of Adaptation in Biological and Cultural Evolution. *In* Handbook of Social and Cultural Anthropology. J. J. Honigmann, ed. Pp. 143-178. New York: Rand McNally.
Andrews, D.
  1963 Paucartambo, Pasco, Peru: An Indigenous Community and a Change Program. Ph.D. dissertation, Cornell University. Ann Arbor, MI: University Microfilms.

Anonymous
  1952 Convenio Celebrado con la Universidad de Cornell de los EE.UU. Perú Indígena 2(4):85-92.
Aramburú, C.
  1978 Aspectos del Desarrollo de la Antropologia en el Perú. In Estado de las Ciéncias Sociales en el Perú. B. Podesta, ed. Lima: Centro de Investigación de la Universidad del Pacifico.
Arensberg, C.M.
  1947 Prospect and Retrospect. Applied Anthropology 1:54-57.
  1978 Theoretical Contributions of Industrial Development Studies. In Applied Anthropology in America. E.M. Eddy and W.L. Partridge, eds. Pp. 49-78. New York: Columbia University Press.
Babb, F.E.
  1985 Women and Men in Vicos, Peru: A Case of Unequal Development. In Peruvian Contexts of Change. W. Stein, ed. Pp. 163-209. New Brunswick, NJ: Transaction Books.
Baldwin, J.M.
  1974 Guide for Survey Evaluation of Urban Dwelling Environments. Cambridge, MA: MIT Press.
Ballard, R., and S. Vellins
  1985 South Asian Entrants to British Universities: A Comparative Note. New Community 12:260-265.
Bamberger, M., E. Gonzalez Polio, and U. Sae Hau
  1982 Evaluation of Sites and Services Projects: The Evidence From El Salvador. World Bank Staff Working Paper No. 459. Washington, DC: World Bank.
Bamberger, M., B. Sanyal, and N. Valverde
  1982 Evaluation of Sites and Services Projects: The Experience from Lusaka, Zambia. World Bank Staff Working Paper No. 548. Washington, DC: World Bank.
Barger, W.K.
  1977 Culture Change and Psychosocial Adjustment. American Ethnologist 4:471-495.
  1982 Cultural Adaptation. Anthropology and Humanism Quarterly 7(2-3):17-21.
Barger, W.K., and A. Haas
  1983 Public Attitudes Toward Mexican American Farmworkers in the Midwest. La Red 63:2-4.
Barger, W.K., and E. Reza
  1984a Views of Midwestern Farmworkers Concerning the Farm Labor Movement. La Red 78:2-7.
  1984b Midwestern Farmworkers Support the Farm Labor Movement. Science for the People 16(5):11-15.

1985a Processes in Applied Sociocultural Change and the
    Farmworker Movement in the Midwest. Human Organization
    44:268-283.
  1985b Views of California Farmworkers Regarding the Farm
    Labor Movement. La Red 91:3-5.
Barnett, C.
  1960 Indian Protest Movements in the Callejón de Huaylas.
    Ph.D. dissertation, Cornell University. Ann Arbor, MI:
    University Microfilms.
Barnett, H.
  1953 Innovation: The Basis of Cultural Change. New York:
    McGraw Hill.
Barth, F.
  1956 Ecological Relationships of Ethnic Groups in Swat,
    North Pakistan. American Anthropologist 58:1079-1089.
Bazant S., J.E. Espinosa, R. Davila, and J. Cortes
  1978 Tipologia de Vivienda Urbana: Analisis Fisico de
    Contextos Urbano Habitacionales de la Poblacion de
    Bajos Ingresos en la Ciudad de Mexico. Mexico City:
    Editorial Diana.
Bee, R.L.
  1982 The Politics of American Indian Policy. Cambridge,
    MA: Schenkman.
Bernard, H.R., and P. Pelto, eds.
  1986 Technology and Social Change. Second Edition.
    Prospect Heights, IL: Waveland.
Bhachu, P.
  1985 Parental Educational Strategies: The Case of Punjabi
    Sikhs in Britain. Research Papers in Ethnic Relations
    No. 3. Coventry: University of Warwick Centre for
    Research in Ethnic Relations.
Blakely, M.M.
  1983 Southeast Asian Refugee Parents: An Inquiry Into
    Home-School Communication and Understanding.
    Anthropology and Education Quarterly 14:43-68.
Boissevain, J.
  1964 Factions, Parties, and Politics in a Maltese
    Village. American Anthropologist 66:1275-1287.
Borman, L.D.
  1979 Action Anthropology and the Self-Help/Mutual-Aid
    Movement. *In* Currents in Anthropology: Essays in Honor
    of Sol Tax. R. Hinshaw, ed. Pp. 487-511. The Hague:
    Mouton.
Borrero, M.G., J.J. Schensul, and R. Garcia
  1982 Research Based Training For Organizational Change.
    Urban Anthropology 11:129-153.

Bradfield, S.
    1963   Migration from Huaylas: A Study of Brothers. Ph.D.
    dissertation, Cornell University. Ann Arbor, MI:
    University Microfilms.
Breese, G.
    1966   Urbanization in Newly Developing Countries.
    Englewood Cliffs, NJ: Prentice-Hall.
    1969   The City in Newly Developing Countries. Englewood
    Cliffs, NJ: Prentice-Hall.
Burnaway, M.
    1976   Functions and Reproduction of Migrant Labor.
    American Journal of Sociology 81:1050-1087.
Cabrera, I.
    1979   La Vivienda de los No Asalariados en Oaxaca. CIDIV
    (November-December). Mexico City: INDECO
    1982   La Estructura Interna de Hermosillo, Mexico: Un
    Analisis Tridimensional (Social, Economico, y
    Politico). Master's thesis, University of Georgia.
Caminos, H., J.F.C. Turner, and J.A. Steffian
    1969   Urban Dwelling Environments: An Elementary Survey of
    Settlements for the Study of Design Determinants.
    Cambridge, MA: MIT Press.
Carlson, A.W.
    1976   Specialty Agriculture and Migrant Laborers in
    Northwestern Ohio. Journal of Geography 5:292-310.
Cassell, J.
    1978   A Fieldwork Manual for Studying Desegregated
    Schools. Washington, DC: National Institute of
    Education.
Castañeda, A.
    1981   Analisis Historico Economico de las Condiciones del
    Habitat en la Poblacion de Bajos Ingresos, Reynosa,
    Tams. Thesis, Facultad de Ciencias Politicas y
    Sociales, Universidad Nacional Autonoma de Mexico.
Castile, G.P.
    1974   Federal Indian Policy and the Sustained Enclave: An
    Anthropological Perspective. Human Organization 33:219-
    228.
Cazden, C.B.
    1982   Four Comments. *In* Children In and Out of School. P.
    Gilmore and A.A. Glatthorn, eds. Pp. 209-226.
    Washington, DC: Center for Applied Linguistics.
    1983   Can Ethnographic Research Go Beyond the Status Quo?
    Anthropology and Education Quarterly 14:33-41.
Chambers, E.
    1985   Applied Anthropology: A Practical Guide. Englewood
    Cliffs, NJ: Prentice-Hall.

Chavez, C.
  1976 California Farm Worker's Struggle. The Black Scholar 7:16-19.
Claver, F.
  1973 Sharing the Wealth and Power. Ph.D. dissertation, University of Colorado, Boulder. Ann Arbor, MI: University Microfilms.
Cleveland Plain Dealer
  1986 Farm Workers, Campbell Soup Agree to Contracts. February 20:14.
Cochrane, G.
  1971 Development Anthropology. New York: Oxford University Press.
Cochrane, G., ed.
  1976 What We Can Do For Each Other: An Interdisciplinary Approach to Development Anthropology. Amsterdam: B.R. Gruner.
Coles, R.
  1970 Uprooted Children: The Early Life of Migrant Farm Workers. Pittsburgh: University of Pittsburg Press.
Comadrona Program
  1985 Final Report. Manuscript, Hispanic Health Council.
Cook, T., and D. Campbell
  1979 Quasi-Experimentation: Design and Analysis Issues for Field Settings. Chicago: Rand McNally.
Coye, M.J.
  1985 The Health Effects of Agricultural Production: I. The Health of Agricultural Workers. Journal of Public Health Policy 6:348-370.
Craddock, B.R.
  1979 Farmworker Protective Laws. Austin, TX: Motivation Education and Training.
Dahrendorf, R.
  1964 Toward a Theory of Social Conflict. *In* Social Change. A. Etzioni and E. Etzioni, eds. Pp. 98-111. New York: Basic Books.
De Groot, D.
  1979 Initiating Urban Development: Slum Improvement and Resettlement in Davao City. Ph.D. dissertation, University of Colorado, Boulder. Ann Arbor, MI: University Microfilms.
Denelli-Hess, D.
  1986 Preliminary Analysis of Comadrona Data Base. Ph.D. exam question, Department of Anthropology, University of Connecticut, Storrs.

Denny, W.M.
　1979　Participant Citizenship in a Marginal Group: Union Mobilization of California Farmworkers. American Journal of Political Science 23:330-337.
Desai, R.
　1963　Indian Immigrants in Britain. London: Oxford University Press.
Dobyns, H.F., P.L. Doughty, and A.R. Holmberg
　1966　Measurement of Peace Corps Impact in the Peruvian Andes: Final Report. Washington, DC: Peace Corps.
Dobyns, H.F., P.L. Doughty, and H.D. Lasswell, eds.
　1971　Peasants, Power and Applied Social Change: Vicos as a Model. Beverly Hills, CA: Sage.
Dobyns, H.F., and R.C. Euler
　1976　The Walapai People. Phoenix: Indian Tribal Series.
Dobyns, H.F., A.R. Holmberg, M.E. Opler, and L. Sharp
　1966　Methods for Analyzing Cultural Change. Report to the Office of Technical Cooperation and Research, U.S. Agency for International Development. Ithaca, NY: Cornell University, Department of Anthropology, Comparative Studies of Cultural Change.
　1967　Strategic Intervention in the Cultural Change Process. Report to the Office of Technical Cooperation and Research, U.S. Agency for International Development. Ithaca, NY: Cornell University, Department of Anthropology, Comparative Studies in Cultural Change.
Dobyns, H.F., and M.C. Vazquez Varela
　1964　The Cornell Peru Project: Bibliography and Personnel. Ithaca, NY: Cornell University, Department of Anthropology. Cornell Peru Project Pamphlet No. 2.
Doughty, P.L.
　1971　Human Relations: Affection, Rectitude and Respect. *In* Peasants, Power and Applied Social Change: Vicos As A Model. H.F. Dobyns, P.L. Doughty, and H.D. Lasswell, eds. Pp. 115-136. Beverly Hills, CA: Sage.
　1986a Directed Change and the Hope for Peace: Peruvian Experiences. *In* Peace and War: Cross-Cultural Perspectives. R. Rubenstein and M. L. Foster, eds. Pp. 105-118. New Brunswick, NJ: Transaction Books.
　1986b Vicos: Success, Rejection and Rediscovery of a Classic Program. *In* Applied Anthropology in America. Second Edition. E.M. Eddy and W.L. Partridge, eds. Pp. 145-169. New York: Columbia University Press.
Doughty, P.L. (with M.F. Doughty)
　1968　Huaylas: An Andean District in Search of Progress. Ithaca, NY: Cornell University Press.

Doughty, P.L., E. Burleigh, and M. Painter
  1984 Peru: An Evaluation of P.L. 480 Title II Food Assistance. Washington, DC: Agency for International Development.
Dubos, R.
  1965 Man Adapting. New Haven: Yale University Press.
Eddy, E.M., and W.L. Partridge, eds.
  1978 Applied Anthropology in America. New York: Columbia University Press.
Edgerton, R.B., and L.L. Langness
  1974 Methods and Styles in the Study of Culture. San Francisco: Chandler and Sharp.
Efrat, B., and M. Mitchell
  1974 The Indian and the Social Scientist: Contemporary Contractual Arrangements on the Pacific Northwest Coast. Human Organization 33:405-407.
Erasmus, C.J.
  1961 Man Takes Control: Cultural Development and American Aid. Minneapolis: Minnesota University Press.
Erickson, F.
  1979 Mere Ethnography: Some Problems in its Use in Educational Practice. Anthropology and Education Quarterly 10:182-188.
  1984 School Literacy, Reasoning, and Civility: An Anthropologist's Perspective. Review of Educational Research 54:525-546.
Erickson, F., and G. Mohatt
  1982 Cultural Organization of Participation Structures in Two Classrooms of Indian Students. *In* Doing the Ethnography of Schooling: Educational Anthropology in Action. G. Spindler, ed. Pp. 136-174. New York: Holt, Rinehart and Winston.
Feldman, K.D.
  1973 Squatters and Squatting in Davao City, Philippines: The Dynamics of an Adaptive Institution in a Developing Country. Ph.D. dissertation, University of Colorado, Boulder. Ann Arbor, MI: University Microfilms.
  1975 Squatter Migration Dynamics in Davao City, Philippines. Urban Anthropology 4:123-144.
Firth, R.
  1957 Introduction: Factions in Indian and Overseas Indian Societies. British Journal of Sociology 8:291-295.
Folarin, A.
  1985 Lesson Plans: Kickapoo Language Instruction. Report submitted to the Administration and Board of the Kickapoo Nation School, Powhattan, KS, July.

Follain, J.R., and E. Jimenz
  1983 Demand for Housing Characteristics in Developing Countries. Working Paper No. 8314C-DSU. Washington,DC: World Bank.
Fonseca, C.
  1985 Peasant Differentiation in the Peruvian Andes. *In* Peruvian Context of Change. W.W. Stein, ed. Pp. 124-162. New Brunswick, NJ: Transaction Books.
Foster, G.
  1969 Applied Anthropology. Boston: Little, Brown.
Friedland, W.
  1969 Labor Waste in New York: Rural Exploitation and Migrant Workers. Transaction 6(4):48-53.
Friedland, W., and R.T. Thomas
  1974 Paradoxes of Agricultural Unionism in California. Society (May-June):54-62.
Gearing, F.
  1960 The Strategy of the Fox Project. *In* Documentary History of the Fox Project, 1948-1959: A Program in Action Anthropology. F. Gearing, R.McC. Netting and L.R. Peattie, eds. Pp. 294-300. Chicago: Department of Anthropology, University of Chicago.
Gearing, F., R. McC. Netting, and L.R. Peattie, eds.
  1960 Documentary History of the Fox Project, 1948-1959: A Program in Action Anthropology. Chicago: Department of Anthropology, University of Chicago.
Geertz, C.
  1963 Agricultural Involution: The Process of Ecological Change in Indonesia. Berkeley: University of California Press.
  1972 The Wet and the Dry: Traditional Irrigation in Bali and Morocco. Human Ecology 1:23-40.
Ghersi, H.
  1959 El Indígena y el Mestizo en la Comunidad de Marcará. Revista del Museo Nacional 28:118-188.
  1960 El Indígena y el Mestizo en la Comunidad de Marcará. Revista del Museo Nacional 29:48-128.
  1961 El Indígena y el Mestizo en la Comunidad de Marcará. Revista del Museo Nacional 30:95-176.
Gibson, M.A.
  1976 Ethnicity and Schooling: A Caribbean Case Study. Ph.D. dissertation, University of Pittsburgh. Ann Arbor, MI: University Microfilms.
  1982 Reputation and Respectability: How Competing Cultural Systems Affect Students' Performance in School. Anthropology and Education Quarterly 13:3-27.

1983a Home-School-Community Linkages: A Study of Educational Opportunity for Punjabi Youth. Report to the National Institute of Education, Washington, DC.
1983b Ethnicity and Schooling: West Indian Immigrants in the United States Virgin Islands. Ethnic Groups 5:173-198.
1987 Punjabi Immigrants in an American High School. *In* Interpretive Ethnography of Education at Home and Abroad. G.D. Spindler and L.S. Spindler, eds. Hillsdale, NJ: Lawrence Erlbaum. In press.
n.d. Accommodation Without Assimilation: Punjabi Sikh Immigrants in an American High School and Community. In preparation.

Gibson, M.A., and P. Bhachu
1986 Community Forces and School Performance: Punjabi Sikhs in Rural California and Urban Britain. New Community 13:27-39.

Goldfarb, R.
1982 Migrant Farm Workers: A Caste of Despair. Ames: Iowa State University.

Goodenough, W.H.
1963 Cooperation in Change. New York: Russell Sage Foundation.

Goodlad, J.I.
1983 A Study of Schooling: Some Implications for School Improvement. Phi Delta Kappan 64:552-558.

Gottlieb, B., ed.
1981 Social Networks and Social Support. Beverly Hills, CA: Sage.

Grindle, M.S.
1977 Patrons and Clients in the Bureaucracy: Career Networks in Mexico. Latin American Research Review 12:37-66.

Hackenberg, R.A.
1963 Process Formation in Applied Anthropology. Human Organization 21:235-239.
1970 The Social Observatory: Time Series Data for Health and Behavioral Research. Social Science and Medicine 4:343-357.
1971 The Cybernetic Village. Southeast Asian Journal of Sociology 4:5-27.
1973 A Developing City in a Dual Economy: Economic and Demographic Trends in Davao City, Philippines, 1972. Davao City, Philippines: Davao Research and Planning Foundation. Monograph No. 1.
1974 The Poverty Explosion: Population Growth and Income Decline in Davao City: 1972. Philippine Planning Journal 5:15-44.

1977 Exports, Entrepreneurs and Equity: A Solution to the Problems of Population and Poverty in Southeast Asia. *In* Economic Development, Poverty, and Income Distribution. W. Loehr and J. Powelson, eds. Pp. 81-112. Boulder, CO: Westview.
1980 New Patterns of Urbanization in Asia. Population and Development Review 6:391-419.
1981 Housing Demand and Housing Finance. Research Project RP 67-246, Development Economics Department, World Bank, Washington, DC.
1982 The Ecology of Poverty in Davao City, 1972-1979. Report to the Development Economics Department, World Bank, Washington, DC.
1983 The Urban Impact of Agropolitan Development: The Changing Regional Metropolis in the Southern Philippines. Comparative Urban Research 10:69-98.
1985 Bringing Theory Back In: Steps Toward a Policy Science of Applied Anthropology. American Behavioral Scientist 29:205-228.

Hackenberg, R.A., and B.H. Hackenberg
1981 The Field Station as Joint Venture: A New Basis for Applied Anthropology in a Developing Country. Practicing Anthropology 3(3):25-27,44-45.
1984 Developing Intermediate Cities as Agro-Industrial Processing Centers: A Project in Western Panama. Regional Development Dialogue 5:74-109.
1986 The Urban Working Class in the Philippines. *In* The Philippines and U.S. Policy. Carl Lande, ed. Washington, DC: Washington Institute.

Hackenberg, R.A., A.D. Murphy, and H.A. Selby
1984 The Urban Household in Dependent Development. *In* Households: Comparative and Historical Studies of the Domestic Group. R. McC. Netting, R.R. Wilk, and E.J. Arnold, eds. Pp. 187-216. Berkeley: University of California Press.

Hale, K.
1972 Some Questions About Anthropological Linguistics: The Role of Native Knowledge. *In* Reinventing Anthropology. D. Hymes, ed. Pp. 382-397. New York: Vantage Books.

Harper, D., B. Mills, and R. Parris
1974 Exploitation in Migrant Labor Camps. British Journal of Sociology 25:283-295.

Harris, M.
1966 The Cultural Ecology of India's Sacred Cattle. Current Anthropology 7:51-60.

Heighton, R.H., Jr., and C. Heighton
  1978 Applying the Anthropological Perspective to Social
    Policy. In Applied Anthropology in America. E.M. Eddy
    and W.L. Partridge, eds. Pp. 390-411. New York:
    Columbia University Press.
Helm, J., ed.
  1966 Pioneers of American Anthropology. Seattle:
    University of Washington Press.
Hendricks, J., and A.D. Murphy
  1981 From Poverty to Poverty: The Adaptation of Young
    Migrant Households in Oaxaca, Mexico. Urban
    Anthropology 10:53-70.
Herda, E.A., and W.W. Malloy
  1982 An Administrator and an Anthropologist Collaborating
    in Special Education: A Model for Participatory
    Research and Training Programs. Paper presented at the
    annual meeting of the American Anthropological
    Association, Washington, DC.
Hessler, R.M., P.K. New, and J.T. May
  1979 Power, Exchange, and the Research-Development Link.
    Human Organization 38:334-342.
Hewitt de Alcántara, C.
  1976 Modernizing Mexican Agriculture: Socio-Economic
    Implications of Technological Change, 1940-1970.
    Geneva: United Nations Research Institute for Social
    Development.
Hiawatha (KS) Daily World
  1983 Selected articles on the Kickapoo.
Hickman, J.
  1963 The Aymara of Chinchera, Peru: Persistence and
    Change in a Bi-Cultural Context. Ph.D. dissertation,
    Cornell University. Ann Arbor, MI. University
    Microfilms.
Hicks, J.L., and M. Handler
  1978 Ethnicity, Public Policy and Anthropologists. In
    Applied Anthropology in America. E.M. Eddy and W.L.
    Partridge, eds. Pp. 292-325. New York: Columbia
    University Press.
Higgins, M.
  1974 Somos Gente Humilde: An Ethnography of a Poor Urban
    Colonia. Ann Arbor, MI: University Microfilms.
Hill, C.E.
  1985 Patient Care and Public Health: A Commentary. Human
    Organization 44:80.
Himes, J.R.
  1981 The Impact in Peru of the Vicos Project. In Research
    in Economic Anthropology. G.M. Dalton, ed. Pp. 141-
    209. London: Jai Press.

Hinshaw, R., and P. Young
  1979 Action Anthropology in College Administration. *In* Currents in Anthropology: Essays in Honor of Sol Tax. R. Hinshaw, ed. Pp. 513-545. The Hague: Mouton.
Hoben, A.
  1982 Anthropologists and Development. *In* Annual Review of Anthropology. Vol. 2. B.J. Seigel, ed. Pp. 158-166. Palo Alto, CA: Annual Reviews.
Hoffman, C.
  1978 Empowerment Movements and Mental Health: Locus of Control and Committment to the United Farm Workers. Journal of Community Psychology 63:216-221.
Holmberg, A.R.
  1952a Propuesta de la Universidad de Cornell de los EE.UU. Perú Indígena 2(4):87-95.
  1952b Proyecto Perú-Cornell en las Ciéncias Sociales Aplicadas. Perú Indígena 2(5-6):158-166.
  1952c Informe del Doctor Allan R. Holmberg Sobre el Desarrollo del Proyecto Perú-Cornell. Perú Indígena 3(7-8):237-248.
  1955 Participant Intervention in the Field. Human Organization 14:23-26.
  1958 The Research and Development Approach to the Study of Change. Human Organization 17:12-16.
  1960 Changing Community Attitudes and Values in Peru. *In* Social Change in Latin America Today. Council on Foreign Relations. New York: Harper.
  1967 Algunas Relaciones entre la Privación Psico-Biológica y el Cambio Cultural en los Andes. América Indígena 27:3-24.
  1969 Dynamic Functionalism. *In* Politics, Personality, and Social Science in the Twentieth Century. A.A. Rogow, ed. Pp. 159-178. Chicago: University of Chicago Press.
Howe, H., II
  1984 Introduction. Symposium on the Year of the Reports: Responses from the Educational Community. Harvard Educational Review 54:1-5.
Hymes, D.H.
  1972 Introduction. *In* Functions of Language in the Classroom. C.B. Cazden, V. John. and D. Hymes, eds. Pp. xi-lvii. New York: Teachers College Press.
  1980a Educational Ethnology. Anthropology and Education Quarterly 11:3-8.
  1980b Ethnographic Monitoring. *In* Language in Education: Ethnolinguistic Essays. D.H. Hymes, ed. Pp. 104-118. Washington, DC: Center for Applied Linguistics.

IBRD
　1972　Urbanization Sector Working Paper. Washington, DC: World Bank.
　1975　Housing Sector Policy Paper. Washington, DC: World Bank.
　1982　The Philippines: Housing Finance. East Asia and Pacific. Washington, DC: World Bank.
INDECO
　1980　Merida. Mexico City: INDECO.
Indiana Advisory Committee
　1974　Indiana Migrants. Chicago: U.S. Commission on Civil Rights.
Jenkins, J.C.
　1985　The Politics of Insurgency. New York: Columbia University Press.
Johnson, T.M.
　1976　Sociocultural Factors in the Intergroup Perception of Health Problems: A Case of Grower Attitudes Toward Their Migrant Labor. Human Organization 35:79-83.
Keare, D.H., and S. Parris
　1982　Evaluation of Shelter Programs for the Urban Poor. World Bank Staff Working Paper No. 547. Washington, DC: World Bank.
Khush, H.K.
　1965　The Social Participation and Attitudes of the Children of East Indian Immigrants. Master's thesis, Sacramento State College.
Kim, M.
　1982　The Informal Sector in the City of Oaxaca, Mexico. Master's thesis, University of Georgia.
Kimball, S.
　1978　Anthropology as a Policy Science. *In* Applied Anthropology in America. E.M. Eddy and W.L. Partridge, eds. Pp. 277-291. New York: Columbia University Press.
La Brack, B.W.
　1980　The Sikhs of Northern California: A Socio-Historical Study. Ph.D. dissertation, Syracuse University. Ann Arbor, MI: University Microfilms.
Laquian, A.A.
　1971　Rural-Urban Migrants and Metropolitan Development. Toronto: INTERMET.
　1975　Whither Site and Services? Science 192:950-955.
　1983　Basic Housing: Policies for Urban Sites, Services and Shelter in Developing Countries. Ottawa: International Development Research Centre.

Lasswell, H., and A.R. Holmberg
  1966 Toward a General Theory of Directed Value Accumulation and Institutional Development. *In* Comparative Theories of Social Change. H.W. Peter, ed. Pp. 214-235. Ann Arbor, MI: Foundation for Research on Human Behavior.

Leaf, M.J.
  1972 Information and Behavior in a Sikh Village. Berkeley: University of California Press.

de Lepervanche, M.M.
  1984 Indians in a White Australia. Sydney: George Allen and Unwin.

Levy, J.
  1975 Cesar Chavez: Autobiography of La Causa. New York: W.W. Norton.

Lewis, O.
  1954 Group Dynamics in a North Indian Village: A Study of Factions. Programme Evaluation Organization of the Government of India Planning Commission. Delhi: Government of India Press.

Liebow, E.
  1967 Tally's Corner: A Study of Negro Streetcorner Men. Boston: Little, Brown.

Light, L., and N. Kleiber
  1981 Interactive Research in a Feminist Setting: The Vancouver Women's Health Collective. *In* Anthropologists at Home in North America. D.A. Messerschmidt, ed. Pp. 167-182. New York: Cambridge University Press.

Lloyd, P.
  1980 The Young Towns of Lima: Aspects of Urbanization in Peru. New York: Cambridge University Press.

Logan, K.
  1984 Haciendo Pueblo: The Development of a Guadalajaran Suburb. University, AL: University of Alabama Press.

Lomnitz, L.
  1979 Anthropology and Development in Latin America. Human Organization 38:313-17.

London, J., and H. Anderson
  1970 So Shall We Reap. New York: Crowell.

Lorenzen, S.A.
  1986 Employment, Earnings, and Consumption Strategies in Urban Mexico. Ph.D. dissertation, University of Texas, Austin. Ann Arbor, MI: University Microfilms.

Lutes, S.V., and D.D. Stull
  1986 The Kansas Kickapoo Technical Assistance Project: An Experiment in Applied Anthropology. Practicing Anthropology 7(4):16-17.

Lynch, B.D.
  1982 The Vicos Experiment: A Study of the Impact of the Cornell-Peru Project in a Highland Valley. Washington, DC: Agency for International Development (LAC/DP) Contract No. LAC-0044-C-00-1023-00.
McElroy, A., and P.K. Townsend
  1978 Adaptation: A Conceptual Framework. *In* Evolutionary Models and Studies in Human Diversity. R.J. Meier, C.M. Otten, and F. Abdel-Hameed, eds. The Hague: Mouton.
  1979 Medical Anthropology in Ecological Perspective. North Scituate, MA: Duxbury.
McGee, T.G.
  1967 The Southeast Asian City. New York: Praeger.
McWilliams, C.
  1939 Factories in the Field. Boston: Little, Brown.
Majka, L.C., and T.J. Majka
  1982 Farm Workers, Agribusiness, and the State. Philadelphia: Temple University Press.
Mangin, W.P.
  1957 Drinking Among Andean Indians. Quarterly Journal of Studies on Alcohol 18:55-66.
  1979 Thoughts on Twenty-Four Years of Work in Peru: The Vicos Project and Me. *In* Long-Term Field Research in Social Anthropology. G.M. Foster, T. Scudder, E. Colson, and R.V. Kemper, eds. Pp. 65-84. New York: Academic Press.
Mangin, W.P., ed.
  1980 Peasants in Cities: Readings in the Anthropology of Urbanization. Boston: Houghton Mifflin.
Manners, R.A.
  1974 Hualapai Indians II: An Ethnographical Report on the Hualapai (Walapai) Indians of Arizona. New York: Garland.
Marx, K.
  1904 The Critique of Political Economy (orig. 1859). Chicago: International Library.
Maynard, E.
  1974 The Growing Negative Image of the Anthropologist Among American Indians. Human Organization 33:402-404.
Mazess, R.B.
  1975 Biological Adaptation: Aptitudes and Acclimatization. *In* Biosocial Interrelations in Population Adaptation. E.S. Watts, F.E. Johnston, and G.W. Lasker, eds. Pp. 9-18. Chicago: Aldine.
Menninger Foundation
  1978 Comprehensive Health Plan for the Kickapoo of Kansas. Topeka, KS: Menninger Foundation.

Miller, J.G.
  1978 Living Systems. New York: McGraw-Hill.
Montalvo, A.
  1967 Vicos: A Study in Health Culture. Ph.D. dissertation, Cornell University. Ann Arbor, MI: University Microfilms.
Moore, T.E.
  1965 The Slaves We Rent. New York: Random House.
Moran, E.
  1979 Human Adaptability. North Scituate, MA: Duxbury.
Morss, E.R., J.K. Hatch, D.R. Mickelwait, and C.F. Sweet
  1976 Strategies for Small Farmer Development. Boulder, CO: Westview.
Morss, E.R., and V.A. Morss
  1982 U.S. Foreign Aid: An Assessment of New and Traditional Development Strategies. Boulder, CO: Westview.
Munson, L.
  1983 Native/Non-Native Collaborative Efforts: Walking a Socio-political Tightrope. Paper presented at the XIth International Congress of Anthropological and Ethnological Sciences, Vancouver, British Columbia.
Murphy, A.D.
  1973 A Quantitative Model of Goals and Values in Coquito Sector, San Juan, Oaxaca, Mexico. Master's thesis, University of Chicago.
  1979 Urbanization, Development, and Household Adaptive Strategies in Oaxaca, a Secondary City of Mexico. Ann Arbor, MI: University Microfilms.
  1980 Concepts of Community Development among Planners and Participants of Site-and-Service Projects in Southern Mexico. Paper presented at the annual meeting of the Society for Applied Anthropology, Philadelphia, PA.
Murphy, A.D., and H.A. Selby
  1979 Tipologia de Vivienda: Un Estudio Socio-Economico de la Cuidad de Oaxaca. CIDIV (October-November), Mexico City: INDECO.
  1982 The Mexican Urban Household Project. Paper presented at the annual meeting of the Society for Applied Anthropology, Lexington, KY.
Nahmad, S.
  1977 Perspectives on the Future of Mexican Applied Anthropology. Human Organization 36:316-18.
Naylor, L.L.
  1973 Applied Anthropology: Approaches to the Using of Anthropology. Human Organization 32:363-370.

New York Times
  1986 Campbell Soup Accord Ends a Decade of Strife.
     February 24:B7.
Nunez del Prado, O. (with W.F. Whyte)
  1973 Kuyo Chico: Applied Anthropology in an Indian
     Community. Chicago: University of Chicago Press.
Ogbu, J.U.
  1974 The Next Generation. New York: Academic Press.
  1978 Minority Education and Caste. New York: Academic
     Press.
  1982 Cultural Discontinuities and Schooling. Anthropology
     and Education Quarterly 13:290-307.
  1983 Minority Status and Schooling in Plural Societies.
     Comparative Education Review 27:168-190.
  1985 Cultural Boundaries and Minority Youth Orientation
     Toward Work. Paper prepared for the Symposium on
     Adolescents' Orientation Toward Work, Institute of
     Human Development, University of California, Berkeley.
Parades, J.A.
  1976 New Uses for Old Ethnography: A Brief Social History
     of a Research Project with the Eastern Creek Indians,
     or How to be an Applied Anthropologist Without Really
     Trying. Human Organization 35:315-320.
  1985 Any Comments on the Sociology Section, Tony?:
     Committee Work as Applied Anthropology in Fishery
     Management. Human Organization 44:177-182.
Parsons, T.
  1964 A Functional Theory of Change. *In* Social Change. A.
     Etzioni and E. Etzioni, eds. Pp. 83-97. New York: Basic
     Books.
Partridge, W.L., and E.M. Eddy
  1978 The Development of Applied Anthropology in America.
     In Applied Anthropology in America. E.M. Eddy and W.L.
     Partridge, eds. Pp. 3-48. New York: Columbia University
     Press.
Payne, G.K.
  1984 Low-Income Housing in the Developing World: The Role
     of Sites and Services and Settlement Upgrading. New
     York: John Wiley.
Peattie, L.R.
  1968 Reflections on Advocacy Planning. Journal of the
     American Institute of Planners 34:80-88.
Pelto, P.J., and G.H. Pelto
  1978 Anthropological Research. Second Edition. New York:
     Cambridge University Press.
Pelto, P.J., M. Roman, and N. Liriano
  1982 Family Structures in an Urban Puerto Rican
     Community. Urban Anthropology 11:455-474.

Pelto, P.J., and J.J. Schensul
　1986　Toward a Framework for Policy Research in Anthropology. *In* Applied Anthropology in America. Second Edition. E.M. Eddy and W.L. Partridge, eds. New York: Columbia University Press.

Perlmann, J.E.
　1976　The Myth of Marginality: Urban Poverty and Politics in Rio de Janeiro. Berkeley: University of California Press.

Peterson, J.
　1974　The Anthropologist as Advocate. Human Organization 33:311-318.

Philips, S.U.
　1972　Participant Structures and Communicative Competence: Warm Springs Children in Community and Classroom. *In* Functions of Language in the Classroom. C. Cazden, V. John, and D. Hymes, eds. Pp. 370-394. New York: Teachers College Press.

Piddington, R.
　1960　Action Anthropology. Journal of the Polynesian Society 69:199-213.

Ramakrishna, J.
　1979　Health Behavior and Practices of the Sikh Community of the Yuba City Area of California. Ph.D. dissertation, University of California, Berkeley. Ann Arbor, MI: University Microfilms.

Rappaport, R.
　1968　Pigs for the Ancestors. New Haven, CT: Yale University Press.
　1971　The Flow of Energy in an Agricultural Society. Scientific American 224(3):116-132.

Rider, C.D.
　1976　Preparing For Teacher Training in the Alaskan "Bush." *In* What We Can Do For Each Other. G. Cochrane, ed. Pp. 67-74. Amsterdam: B.R. Gruner.

Roupp, P., ed.
　1953　Approaches to Community Development. The Hague: Van Hoeve.

Royce, A.P.
　1982　Ethnic Identity: Strategies of Diversity. Bloomington: Indiana University Press.

Rubel, A.
　1966　Across the Tracks: Mexican Americans in a Texas City. Austin: University of Texas Press.

Rudd, P.
　1975　The United Farm Workers Clinic in Delano, California: A Study of the Rural Poor. Public Health Reports 90:331-339.

Sarason, S.B.
  1983 The Culture of the School and the Problem of Change. Boston: Allyn and Bacon.
Schensul, J.J.
  1985a Applying Ethnography in Educational Change. Anthropology and Education Quarterly 16:149-164.
  1985b Systems Consistency in Field Research, Dissemination, and Social Change. American Behavioral Scientist 29:186-204.
  1985c Cultural Transmission, Cultural Reinterpretation and Cultural Transformation in a Puerto Rican Community. Paper presented at the annual meeting of the American Anthropological Association, Washington, DC.
Schensul, J.J., I. Nieves, and M. Martinez
  1982 The Crisis Event in the Puerto Rican Community. Urban Anthropology 11:534-568.
Schensul, J.J., and G. Stern
  1985 Introduction: Collaborative Research and Social Action. American Behavioral Scientist 29:133-138.
Schensul, S.L.
  1974 Skills Needed in Action Anthropology: Lessons from El Centro de la Causa. Human Organization 33:203-209.
  1985 Science, Theory and Application in Anthropology. American Behavioral Scientist 29:164-185.
Schensul, S.L., and M.G. Borrero
  1982 Introduction: The Hispanic Health Council. Urban Anthropology 11:1-8.
Schensul, S.L., and J.J. Schensul
  1978 Advocacy and Applied Anthropology. In Social Scientists as Advocates: Views from the Applied Disciplines. G. Weber and G. McCall, eds. Pp. 121-164. Beverly Hills, CA: Sage.
  1982 Helping Resource Use in a Puerto Rican Community. Urban Anthropology 11:59-80.
Schlesier, K.H.
  1974 Action Anthropology and the Southern Cheyenne. Current Anthropology 15:277-283.
Schultz, J.A., and D.M. Kendall
  1985 Kickapoo Traditional Culture Series (The Flute Maker, The Herbalist, The Bustle Maker, The Dinner Dance). 3/4" videotape cassettes, color. Lawrence, KS: Summit Street Productions.
Selby, H.A., and G.G. Hendrix
  1976 Policy Planning and Poverty: Notes on a Mexican Case. In Anthropology and the Public Interest. Peggy R. Sanday, ed. Pp. 219-244. New York: Academic Press.

Selby, H.A., and A. D. Murphy
 1982 The Mexican Urban Household and the Decision to Migrate to the United States. Philadelphia: Institute for the Study of Human Issues.
Selby, H.A., A. Murphy, I. Cabrera, and A. Castaneda
 1987 Battling Urban Poverty from Below: A Profile of the Poor in Two Mexican Cities. American Anthropologist. In Press.
Shankar, R.A.
 1971 Integration Goal Definition of the East Indian Students in the Sutter County Area. Master's thesis, Chico State University.
Siegel, B., and A.R. Beals
 1960 Pervasive Factionalism. American Anthropologist 62:394-417.
Snyder, J.
 1960 Group Relations and Social Change in an Andean Village. Ph.D. dissertation, Cornell University. Ann Arbor, MI: University Microfilms.
Sosnick, S.H.
 1978 Hired Hands. Santa Barbara, CA: McNally and Loftin, West.
Spicer, E.H.
 1952 Human Problems and Technological Change. New York: Russell Sage.
 1962 Cycles of Conquest: The Impact of Spain, Mexico, and the United States on the Indians of the Southwest, 1533-1960. Tucson: University of Arizona Press.
Stein, W.W.
 1961 Hualcan: Life in the Highlands of Peru. Ithaca, NY: Cornell University Press.
 1971 Nuevas Semillas de Papa para Vicos: Cambio Agrícola en los Andes. América Indígena 31:51-83.
 1972 Changing Vicos Agriculture. State University of New York, Buffalo: Council on International Studies. Special Studies No. 15.
 1985a Townspeople and Countrypeople in the Callejón de Huaylas. In Peruvian Context of Change. W. W. Stein, ed. Pp. 211-231. New Brunswick, NJ: Transaction Books.
 1985b To Let Those We Study Come First: Critical Reflections on the Peru-Cornell Project. Paper presented at the annual meeting of the American Anthropological Association, Washington, DC.
Stepick, A.
 1974 The Rationality of the Urban Poor. Ann Arbor, MI. University Microfilms.

Stepick, A., and A.D. Murphy
   1980   Comparing Squatter Settlements and Government Self-Help Projects as Housing Solutions in Oaxaca, Mexico. Human Organization 39:339-43.
Stern, G.
   1985   Research, Action, and Social Betterment. American Behavioral Scientist 29:229-248.
Stern, J.J.
   1970   The Meaning of "Adaptation" and Its Relation to the Phenomenon of Natural Selection. *In* Evolutionary Biology, Vol. 4. T. Dobzhansky, ed. New York: Appleton-Century-Crofts.
Steward J.H.
   1955   Theory of Culture Change. Urbana: University of Illinois Press.
Stini, W.A.
   1975   Ecology and Human Adaptation. Dubuque: Brown.
Stucki, L.R.
   1967   Anthropologists and Indians: A New Look at the Fox Project. Plains Anthropologist 12:300-317.
Stull, D.D.
   1984a Kiikaapoa: The Kansas Kickapoo. Horton, KS: Kickapoo Tribal Press.
   1984b On the Banks of the Grasshopper: Oral Traditions of the Kansas Kickapoo. Powhattan, KS: Kickapoo Tribal Press.
   n.d.   Kiikaapoa: The Kansas Kickapoo. Middle School Edition. Powhattan, KS: Kickapoo Tribal Press. Camera-ready copy awaiting publication.
Stull, D.D., G. Bernofsky, and B. Hirsch
   1979   Neshnabek: The People. 16mm film, black and white, optical sound, 30 minutes. Berkeley: University of California Extension Media Center.
Stull, D.D., L.S. Grell, and T. Weston
   1985   Kickapoo Nation: The Ways of Our People. Powhattan, KS: Kickapoo Tribal Press.
Stull, D.D., and D.M. Kendall
   1982   Return to Sovereignty: Self-Determination and the Kansas Kickapoo. 3/4" videotape cassette, color, 46 minutes. Lawrence: Institute for Public Policy and Business Research, University of Kansas.
Stull, D.D., and F. Moos
   1981   A Brief Overview of the Role of Anthropology in Public Policy. Policy Studies Review 1:19-27.
Stull, D.D., J.A. Schultz, and K. Cadue, Sr.
   1986   Rights Without Resources: The Rise and Fall of the Kansas Kickapoo. Policy Studies Journal. In Press.

Stull, D.D., J.A. Schultz, and D.M. Kendall
  1985 Another Wind is Moving: The Off-Reservation Indian Boarding School. 3/4" videotape cassette, color, 59 minutes. Berkeley: University of California Extension Media Center.
Tax, S.
  1958 The Fox Project. Human Organization 17:17-19.
Tendler, J.
  1975 Inside Foreign Aid. Baltimore, MD: Johns Hopkins University Press.
  1982 Turning Private Voluntary Organizations into Development Agencies: Questions for Evaluation. AID Program Discussion Paper No. 12. Washington, DC: Agency for International Development.
Thompson, L.
  1965 Is Applied Anthropology Helping to Develop a Science of Man? Human Organization 24:277-287.
Toledo Blade
  1986 FLOC Signs Contract with Campbell, Growers on Rights of Farm Workers. February 20:1.
Turner, J.C.
  1967 Barriers and Channels for Housing Development in Modernizing Countries. Journal of the American Institute for Planners 34:254-263.
United Indian Tribes of Western Oklahoma and Kansas
  1975 Land Use Plan for Kickapoo Reservation. Mimeographed.
U.S. Senate Subcommittee on Migratory Labor
  1970 Migrant and Seasonal Farmwork Powerlessness. Washington, DC: U.S. Government Printing Office.
Valdes, D.N.
  1984 From Following the Corps to Chasing the Corporation: The Farm Labor Organizing Committee, 1967-1983. *In* The Chicano Struggle. National Association for Chicano Studies. Binghamton, NY: Bilingual Press.
Vantine, L.
  1984 Native American Language Instruction at the Kickapoo Nation School: A Feasibility Study. Report submitted to the Administration and Board of the Kickapoo Nation School, Powhattan, KS, August 1.
van Willigen, J.
  1981 Applied Anthropology and Cultural Persistence. *In* Persistent Peoples: Cultural Enclaves in Perspective. G.P. Castile and G. Kushner, eds. Pp. 153-167. Tucson: University of Arizona Press.
Vazquez Varela, M.C.
  1952 La Antropologia Cultural y Nuestro Problema del Indio. Perú Indígena 2(5-6):7-157.

1963 Proceso de Migracion en la Comunidad de Vicos, Ancash. *In* Migracion e Integracion en el Peru. H.F. Dobyns and M.C. Vazquez, eds. Pp. 93-102. Lima: Editorial Estudios Andinos.
1965 Educacion Rural en el Callejon de Huaylas. Lima: Editorial Estudios Andinos.
1967 Un Caso de Descriminacion en las Elecciones Municipales de 1966. WAMANI 2(1):30-44.

Vazquez Varela, M.C., and A.R. Holmberg
1966 The Castas: Unilineal Kin Groups in Vicos, Peru. Ethnology 5:283-303.

Voegelin, C.F., and F.M. Voegelin
1972 Linguistics-at-a-distance and Ethnography-on-the-spot. Unpublished manuscript.

Wallace, A.F.C.
1956 Revitalization Movements. American Anthropologist 58:264-281.

Watahomigie, L.J., J. Bender, and A.Y. Yamamoto
1981 Possession Expressions and Semantic Classification of Nouns. *In* Occasional Papers on Linguistics No. 9. James E. Redden, ed. Pp. 100-111. Carbondale, IL: Department of Linguistics, Southern Illinois University.

Watahomigie, L.J., J. Bender, and A.Y. Yamamoto (with E. Mapatis, J. Manakaja, and M. Powskey)
1982 Hualapai Reference Grammar. Los Angeles: American Indian Studies Center, University of California, Los Angeles.

Wax, R.H.
1971 Doing Fieldwork: Warnings and Advice. Chicago: University of Chicago Press.

Weaver, T.
1985 Anthropology as a Policy Science: Part I, A Critique. Human Organization 44:97-105.

Weaver, T., ed.
1974 Indians of Arizona: A Contemporary Perspective. Tucson: University of Arizona Press.

Wenzel, L.
1966 The Identification and Analysis of Certain Value Orientations of Two Generations of East Indians in California. Ph.D. dissertation, University of the Pacific. Ann Arbor, MI: University Microfilms.

Willard, W.
1977 The Agency Camp Project. Human Organization 36:352-362.

Williams, G.C.
    1966   Adaptation and Natural Selection: A Critique of Some Evolutionary Thought. Princeton, NJ: Princeton University Press.
Yeh, S.H.K., and A.A. Laquian
    1979   Housing Asia's Millions: Problems, Policies and Prospects for Housing in Southeast Asia. Ottawa: International Development Research Centre.
Yeung, Y.M., ed.
    1983   A Place to Live: More Effective Low Cost Housing in Asia. Ottawa: International Development Research Centre.

Contributors

W.K. ("KEN") BARGER is associate professor of anthropology at Indiana University at Indianapolis. He has worked with migrant farmworkers in health and education projects and with the farm labor movement in the Midwest and California in a number of advocacy and applied research projects.

MA PREM BHAVATI is a community health researcher and educator with the Hispanic Health Council. She has extensive experience in the areas of nutrition, maternal and child health, and adolescent substance abuse. She was one of the original members of the Comadrona Program team and is currently coordinating a regional survey of adolescent smoking behavior.

MARIA GONZALEZ BORRERO is executive director of the Hispanic Health Council, a community-based action research institute in Hartford, Connecticut which addresses health and educational issues facing Puerto Ricans and other Hispanics locally and nationally. She is well known for her work in maternal and child health, child abuse, and education. She holds a faculty appointment in the Department of Community Medicine, University of Connecticut.

IGNACIO CABRERA FERNÁNDEZ is the *Delegado Estatal de la Secretaría de Desarrollo Urbano y Ecologia* for the State of Sonora, Mexico, a position he assumed after completing a master's degree in anthropology at the University of Georgia. An architect by training, his publications include *Merida: Diagnostico de Vivienda* (INDECO 1979) and several articles dealing with the problems of urbanization and development in Sonora.

KEN CADUE, SR. is a member of the Kickapoo Tribe in Kansas; he was born on the reservation and has spent most of his life there. He helped found the Topeka (Kansas) Indian Center and served as its executive director. A past secretary of the Kickapoo Tribal Council, he has also directed several tribal programs including the Administration for Native Americans and the Kickapoo Housing Authority. In 1981 he helped found the Kickapoo Nation School and served on its school board from 1983 to 1985. Presently, he attends Haskell Indian Junior College in Lawrence, Kansas.

PAUL L. DOUGHTY is professor of anthropology and Latin American studies at the University of Florida. He has worked as a community development specialist in Mexico, El Salvador, and Guatemala; conducted extensive applied research in Peru on rural-urban relations, migration, development, and social change, and studied the social effects of chronic cannabis use in Costa Rica. He served as a consultant on post-earthquake development in Peru and Guatemala and has conducted program evaluations of the Peace Corps and U.S. food assistance programs in Peru. He received his Ph.D. from Cornell University in 1963 and later taught anthropology at Indiana University where he was also director of the Latin American Studies Program. From 1971 to 1977 he was chair of the Department of Anthropology, University of Florida and is a past president of the Latin American Studies Association.

MARGARET A. GIBSON, an educational anthropologist, is a research associate of the Survey Research Center, University of California, Berkeley (1986-87) and adjunct professor of anthropology, California State University, Sacramento. She is currently completing two books related to her interest in the school adaptation patterns of immigrant minorities; the first a case study of the Punjabi Sikhs and the second a comparative work (coedited with John Ogbu) on immigrant and nonimmigrant minorities in the U.S. and abroad. Her previous publications deal with community forces and schooling, multicultural education, and the interplay between ethnicity and gender in the multiethnic schools of St. Croix.

ROBERT A. AND BEVERLY H. HACKENBERG are research associates of the Institute of Behavioral Science, University of Colorado. Robert Hackenberg is also professor of anthropology at that institution. They serve as codirectors of Davao Research and Planning Foundation, Inc., Davao City, Philippines, through which the data presented in their paper were obtained. Much of that material was prepared while both served as senior research fellows of the East West Population Institute, East West Center, Honolulu.

DONNA DENELLI-HESS is a medical anthropologist with expertise in adolescent and maternal and child health research and intervention. She currently coordinates maternal and child health programs at the Hispanic Health Council and is affiliated with the medical anthropology program of the University of Connecticut.

ARTHUR D. MURPHY is assistant professor of anthropology at Baylor University. Raised in Latin America, he began working in Oaxaca, Mexico in the early 1970s. His publications dealing with housing and household-level adaptation to the Mexican urban system include: "A Comparison of Household Resource Utilization Patterns in Four Mexican Cities" (*Urban Anthropology* 10:3, 1981) with Henry A. Selby and "3500 Years of Housing in Oaxaca" (*Ekistics* 307, 1984) with Steve Kowalewski and Ignacio Cabrera. Currently he is finishing books on the city of Oaxaca with Alex Stepick and on survival strategies for ordinary Mexican urban households with Henry A. Selby and Stephen A. Lorenzen. Both manuscripts grew out of the project discussed here.

ERNESTO REZA is a doctoral candidate in organizational psychology at the University of Michigan and has served on the staff of the Farm Labor Organizing Committee (FLOC). He has also been involved in advocacy and applied research with the farm labor movement in the Midwest and California.

IGNACIO RUIZ LOVE teaches sociology and development at the University of Navajoa, Mexico. He has published several short stories in addition to serving as a consultant for various government agencies and agricultural developers in Sonora and Sinaloa.

JEAN J. SCHENSUL is executive director of the Community Council of the Capitol Region, Hartford, Connecticut, an urban policy research institute. She also holds faculty appointments in anthropology and community medicine at the University of Connecticut. Formerly associate director of the Hispanic Health Council, she has been involved in action research in Hartford's Puerto Rican community and in Sri Lanka and Peru since 1978.

STEPHEN L. SCHENSUL is associate professor of community medicine and director of the University of Connecticut

Center for International Community Health Studies. An anthropologist, his work has concentrated on applied health and mental health research and institution building in urban areas of the United States, Latin America, and Sri Lanka. He has published extensively on applied research methods and on social support systems and health, health care utilization, and reproductive health among Hispanic women.

JERRY A. SCHULTZ is a doctoral student in anthropology and a program assistant in the Center for East Asian Studies at the University of Kansas. He has served as a graduate research assistant in the Department of Anthropology and the Center for Public Affairs at the University of Kansas and as a tribal planner for the Kickapoo Tribe in Kansas. From 1983 to 1985 he was superintendent of the Kickapoo Nation School. Currently, he is working on a dissertation on Indian contract schools.

HENRY A. SELBY is professor of anthropology at the University of Texas at Austin. He has worked in Mexico since the mid-1960s, when he went to Oaxaca to study deviance in a Zapotec community. His publications include *Kinship and Social Organization* (Macmillan 1968) with Ira Buchler; *Zapotec Deviance* (University of Texas Press 1974); "Policy Planning and Poverty, Notes on a Mexican Case" with Gary G. Hendrix, in Peggy R. Sanday, ed., *Anthropology and the Public Interest* (Academic Press 1976); and *The Mexican Urban Household and the Decision to Migrate to the United States* (ISHI 1982) with Arthur D. Murphy.

DONALD D. STULL is associate professor of anthropology and research associate of the Institute for Public Policy and Business Research at the University of Kansas. His major fieldwork has been among urban Papago Indians in Arizona, reservation Potawatomi and Kickapoo Indians in Kansas, and in a public bureaucracy. His publications and documentaries focus on contemporary Indian affairs and policy.

LUCILLE J. WATAHOMIGIE is a member of the Hualapai Tribe of Arizona. She was raised on the reservation, where she received a traditional upbringing. After earning her master's in education from the University of Arizona in 1973, she became associate director of the Teacher Education Program for Indian Students at that institution. Currently she is assistant principal and director of the Bilingual Education Program at Peach Springs (Arizona) Public School. Under her direction, this program has become one of the most successful in the country, receiving a Demonstration Program Award for 1983-1985.

AKIRA Y. YAMAMOTO is professor of anthropology and linguistics at the University of Kansas. He has spent many years studying Yuman languages and since 1976 has worked closely with the Hualapai Bilingual/Bicultural Education Program. He has coauthored numerous papers and presentations with other members of the Haulapai Bilingual staff. Born in Japan, Yamamoto studied at Indiana University, where he received an M.A. in linguistics and a Ph.D. in anthropology.

Index

Aboriginal Protection Society, 1
Acculturation, 55
ACT. *See* Action Coordinating Team
Action anthropologists, 7, 8, 10, 33, 37, 53, 94-98, 128, 212. *See also* Applied research; Collaborative research
Action Coordinating Team (ACT) (Davao City), 191, 192
Adaptation, 57-59, 63, 65, 70-72, 181, 184, 196
Advocacy anthropologists. *See* Action Anthropologists
Aerial photographs, 168, 169
AFL-CIO. *See* Indiana AFL-CIO
Agar, M.H., 38, 48
Agency for International Development, U.S. (USAID), 141, 150, 151, 152, 198
Agrarian reform, 129, 144
Agrarian University (Peru), 142
Agribusiness, 61, 62, 63, 64, 65, 69, 70, 71, 181
Agricultural Labor Relations Act (Calif.), 61
AILDI. *See* American Indian Languages Development Institute
Alcoholism, 150
American Anthropological Association, 4
American Behavioral Scientist, 4
American Indian Languages Development Institute (AILDI), 87-88, 91
American Indians, 33-34. *See also* Fox Project; Hualapai; Iowa Indians; Kickapoo; Prairie Band Potawatomi
Americanization, 106-107
American Philosophical Society Phillips Fund, 86
Ancash Department (Peru), 135
Ancash Program (Peru), 141, 142, 143, 144, 145
Androcentric culture, 149
"Anthropological Theory and Collaborative Research" session (1982), 4
Anthropology, 1, 3, 10, 79, 211-212, 217

Applied research, 1, 3-4, 10, 34, 78, 207, 211-212, 213, 218
Aquino, C., 203
Arensberg, C.M., 160
Arizona, 80, 82
Arizona State Department of Education, 88, 93
Arthur, Chester A., 80
Asian Development Bank, 190
Asian Indians. *See* Punjabis
Ateneo de Davao University, 194
Aymara Indians, 132

Babb, F.E., 149
Bagong Lipunan. *See* New Society
Barger, W.K., 8, 64, 65, 69, 214
Barnett, Homer, 133, 150
Basin-plateau type, 80
Beltrán, Pedro, 141
Bender, Jorigine, 88
BIA. *See* Bureau of Indian Affairs
Bilingual/bicultural resource materials, 18. *See also* Hualapai Bilingual/Bicultural Education Program
Bilingual Education Service Center, 101-102, 111
Billingshurst, Guillermo, 139
Birth attendant. *See* Comadrona Program
Birth weight, 20, 21, 26
Bolivia, 141
Borrero, M.G., 120
Boycotts, 61, 62, 64, 65, 66, 67, 68, 71
Brazil, 185
Breastfeeding, 17, 18, 20, 21, 27
Breese, G., 179
Broker role, 216
Bureau of Community Health Services (Boston Regional Office), 20
Bureau of Indian Affairs (BIA), 39, 40, 43, 45, 81, 217
Burnout, 48

Cadue, Ken, Sr., 8, 36, 37
Cagayan de Oro (Philippines), 196
California, 61, 99, 100
California Achievement Test, 93
Callejón de Huaylas (Peru) 135, 136(fig.), 138, 144, 151
Campbell Soup Company, 62-63, 64, 65, 66, 67, 68, 69, 70, 71
Carmona (Manila), 191
Carnegie Corporation, 139, 153
Carter, Jimmy, 39
Cazden, Courtney B., 119
CCOD. *See* Coordinating Council of Davao
Cebu (Philippines), 196
Center for Applied Linguistics, 37
Center for Public Affairs. *See* Institute for Public Policy and Business Research
Central Algonquian language family, 35
Chancos thermal springs (Peru), 143, 144, 145, 146, 147, 152
CHD. *See* Community Health Division
Child advocacy committee, 22
Child labor, 60, 61, 66
Christian Family Movement, 185
Claver, Francisco, 183
Cochrane, G., 131

Collaborative research,
    1-2, 3, 8, 72, 122-
    123, 160, 212-213
  approaches, 214-217
  case studies, 4-5, 28,
    29-31, 41, 47, 48-50,
    53-54, 97-98, 153,
    172-174, 206-208,
    218-219
  and decision making,
    53, 130, 131
  defined, 9, 31
  principles, 7, 10,
    171-172
  process, 11-12, 99, 107-
    108
  publications, 4
  and Third World, 127-
    128, 130
  types, 120-121
  See also Intervention;
    Knowledge utilization;
    Policy clusters
"Collaborative Research and
    Scientific Method"
    session (1981), 4
Colonias, 162, 163
Colorado River Indian Reservation, 80
Comadrona Program, 13, 15-20,
    23, 24, 29
  administration, 18-19
  client profile, 24-27
  concepts, 23-24
  evaluation, 20-23
  research, 19, 20, 28
  results, 20
  staff, 18-19, 21-22, 23
Committee for the Protection
    of Standard Education,
    102, 110
Community action project
    (1981-1982), 56, 64,
    65-69, 70, 71-72
Community development, 5, 7,
    8, 11, 33, 132
  Indian, 33, 34, 36, 90-91
  urban, 165-166, 180

Community Health Division
    (CHD) (Conn. State
    Dept. of Health), 15
Community/institutional
    participants, 213-217
Compadrazco, 16
Competency tests, 100, 101
Comprehensive Test of
    Basic Skills (CTBS),
    92
Conflict model, 56
Connecticut Department of
    Health Services
    (DHS), 15
Connecticut State Health
    Department, 12, 15,
    213
Contracts, 60, 62, 71
Cooperación Popular program (Peru), 143
Coordinating Council of
    Davao (CCOD), 191
    192, 194
CORDEANCASH (Peruvian
    regional development
    authority), 152
Cordillera Blanca (Peru),
    135, 136(fig.)
Cornell-Peru Project (CPP)
    (1952-1966), 127, 129
    131, 132, 139, 140-
    143, 145, 154, 212,
    214
  activities, 140, 141-
    142, 143, 151
  and corn, 143
  cost of, 153
  critics, 150
  films, 141, 142
  funding, 134, 139, 153
  goals, 132-134, 137,
    148, 151
  and government, 134
    137, 140, 143, 151,
    153
  location, 135-137
  multidisciplinary
    studies, 137

periods, 148
and potatoes, 141, 142, 144, 149
school, 142, 148-149, 151
and travel and migration, 150
and women, 149
Cornell University, 129, 134, 139, 153
CPP. *See* Cornell-Peru Project
Crewleaders, 60
CTBS. *See* Comprehensive Test of Basic Skills
Cuarentena, 15, 16, 17
Cultural change, 52, 53, 128. *See also* Sociocultural change
Cultural continuities/discontinuities, 104
Cultural ecology, 56
Cultural maintenance, 78-79
Culture of the School and the Problem of Change, The (Sarason), 119

Dakar (Senegal), 200
DAP. *See* Development Academy of the Philippines
Davao City (Philippines), 128, 181-183, 184, 185, 187, 190, 191, 193, 194, 195, 196, 198, 199, 200, 201, 203, 204, 206, 208, 214. *See also* Squatter settlements
Davao del Sur (Philippines), 185
Davao Development Foundation (DDF), 185, 186, 187, 188, 189, 190, 191, 192, 213-214
Davao Light and Power Company, 190
Davao Research and Planning Foundation, Inc., (DRPF), 186-187, 188, 189, 190, 191, 192, 193, 194, 195, 196, 198-199, 200, 201, 202, 203, 206, 207, 208, 214
funding, 198, 200, 202, 206, 208
DDF. *See* Davao Development Foundation
DED. *See* World Bank, Development Economics Department
De Groot, Barbara, 200
De Groot, David, 199, 200
Dependent variables, 13, 14(fig.)
Developing City in a Dual Economy, A: Economic and Demographic Trends in Davao City, 1972 (Hackenberg), 188
Development Academy of the Philippines (DAP), 194, 195, 198
Developmental agencies approach, 214, 215-216
Development programs, 129 130-132, 151-153, 159, 162, 179-180
DHS. *See* Connecticut Department of Health Services
Dialectical systems concept, 55, 56
Doaba area (Punjab), 111
"Doing Fieldwork: Warnings and Advice" (Wax), 99
Doughty, Paul L., 127, 212
DRPF. *See* Davao Research and Planning Foundation, Inc.
Dunlop Commission, 62
DuPuis, Lindreth ("Bud"), 45

Earthquake (Peru, 1970), 144, 145

Earthquake redevelopment commission (ORDEZA), 145, 146, 151, 152
East-West Center, 198
Echeverría, Luis, 160
Economic Development Administration (EDA), 36
Economists, 207
EDA. *See* Economic Development Administration
Education, Department of, 45, 46
Educational anthropologist, 99, 107
Education projects. *See* Hualapai Bilingual/Bicultural Education Program; Kansas Kickapoo Technical Assistance Project; Punjabi Education Project
El Salvador, 200, 202
Encomienda, 138
English as a Second Language (ESL), 84, 88, 102, 105, 106, 119
Environment, 57, 58, 59, 61, 63, 70, 135-137, 215-217
Erasmus, C.J., 150
ESL. *See* English as a Second Language
Ethnic minority communities, 7, 8, 10. *See also* Puerto Rican community; Punjabis
Ethnographic film, 37, 46
Exchange model, 108
Exchange network, 167

Factionalism, 115, 116-117, 121, 125(n12)
Family planning, 17
Farm labor
living and working conditions, 59-61, 62, 66
movement, 56, 59, 61-64, 68, 70, 71, 214. *See also* Boycotts; Community action project
number, 60
recruitment, 60
strike (1978), 62
Farm Labor Organizing Committee (FLOC), 61-63, 64, 65, 66, 67, 68, 69, 70-71
Federal funding. *See* Davao Research and Planning Foundation, Inc., funding; Punjabi Education Project, funding; Title V grant; Title VII funding; *under* Kickapoo
Feldman, Kerry D., 192
Fictive kinship relationships, 166-167
Field notes, 113
Films, 37, 43, 46, 47, 141, 142
FLOC. *See* Farm Labor Organizing Committee
Florida, 60
Food for Peace programs, 153
Ford Foundation, 198
Foreign aid, 130, 132, 162, 190
Forestry Service (Peru), 143, 145
Foster, George, 10
FOVI (Mexican housing fund), 177(n3)
Fox Project, 7, 33, 53, 127, 212
Fraccionamiento, 164

Garcia, R., 120
Garcilaso de la Vega University (Lima), 146

Garden-city development, 191
Geertz, C., 183
Gentrification, 25
Gibson, Margaret A., 8
Gleaning, 149
Godparents. See *Compadrazco*
Goodlad, John I., 118
Green Revolution, 183
Grell, Lindy, 40, 44, 47
Group internal resources, 57-58, 59, 61, 63, 69, 70, 78, 214-215, 216
Gurdwaras, 108, 115

Hacienda, 129, 133, 135, 138, 139, 152, 154(n3)
Hacienda Huaypán (Peru), 141, 152
Hackenberg, Beverly H., 128, 185, 213
Hackenberg, Robert A., 128 188, 194, 213
Hale, Kenneth, 79
Hartford (Conn.). See Puerto Rican community
Hartford City Health Department, 12, 13
Havasupai, 80
Havatone, Earl, 83, 84, 85
HBBEP. See Hualapai Bilingual/Bicultural Education Program
Health programs. See Kansas Kickapoo Technical Assistance Project; Maternal and child health
Hegel, Georg, 56
Hessler, R.M., 108
HHC. See Hispanic Health Council
High-risk pregnancies, 20, 26, 27
Hinton, Leanne, 85, 87, 88
Hispanic Health Council (HHC), 8, 12, 13, 15, 22, 213
Hispanic Maternal and Child Preventive Health Network, 15
Hispano elite (Philippines), 185, 189
Holmberg, Allan R., 127, 128, 132, 133, 139, 148, 153
HOLT. See Hualapai Oral Language Test
Home enterprises. See *Tiendas/tienditas*
Honga, Jane, 82, 83, 85, 86, 89
Hopi, 80
Housing and Urban Development, Department of (HUD), 36, 81
"Housing Demand and Housing Finance" (DED), 201, 202
Housing Finance (World Bank), 202
Housing projects, 185. See also Mexican Urban Housing Project; Squatter settlements
Hualapai, 8, 80-81, 82-84, 214
Hualapai Bilingual/Bicultural Education Program (HBBEP)(1975), 8, 36, 77-78, 79, 81, 83, 88-89
  activities, 84, 91
  and community, 89-91, 93, 94, 95, 97-98
  director, 84, 89
  funding, 86, 87, 90
  goals, 85-86
  and linguistic research, 85, 86
  parent advisory committee (1975), 84, 89, 90
  publications, 87, 91
  staff, 84, 86, 87, 88, 89, 91, 97

success factors, 89-94
testing, 92-93, 94
training, 87-88, 89,
   90, 94
writing system, 85
Hualapai Early Learning
   Program, 81
Hualapai Headstart,
   81
Hualapai Oral Language
   Test (HOLT), 92
*Hualapai Reference
   Grammar*, 87
Huapra estate massacre
   (1960, Peru), 141
Huaraz Beneficent Society, 141, 142,
   144
HUD. See Housing and
   Urban Development,
   Department of
Human rights, 135, 137,
   148, 155(n5)

IBRD (International Bank
   for Reconstruction
   and Development).
   See World Bank
IDB. *See* Interamerican
   Development Bank
IDRC. *See* International
   Development Research
   Centre
Inca Empire, 138
INDECO. *See Instituto
   Nacional para el
   Desarrollo de la
   Comunidad y de la
   Vivienda Popular*
Independent variables,
   13, 14(fig.)
Indiana, 60
Indiana AFL-CIO (American Federation of
   Labor-Congress of
   Industrial Organizations), 63

Indiana Council of
   Churches, 63
Indianapolis Farm Worker
   Support Committee,
   63, 64, 71
Indianapolis (Ind.)
   schools, 65-69
Indiana University Summer
   Field Station (Flagstaff, Ariz.), 82
Indian Bilingual National Demonstration
   Program, 77
Indian boarding schools
   videotape, 46
Indian Institute (Peru),
   134
Indian Reorganization Act,
   (1934), 35, 80
Indian self-determination,
   33, 34, 36, 39, 42,
   50, 90-91
   videotape documentary,
   43
Indo-American Education
   Association, 110,
   115-117, 120
Infant mortality, 20, 22
Inflation, 194
Informal ethnography, 38
Informal sector, 186, 187,
   188, 194. *See also
   Tiendas/tienditas*
Innovation, 56, 133
Institute for Public
   Policy and Business
   Research (Univ. of
   Kansas), 41, 43
*Instituto Nacional para el
   Desarrollo de la Comunidad y de la
   Vivienda Popular*
   (INDECO) (Mexico),
   159, 160-161, 162,
   163-164, 165, 172,
   175, 213
   —MEXICO, 162

-OAXACA, 161-162, 163, 166, 169, 172
  See also Mexican Urban Housing Project
Interamerican Development Bank (IDB), 143, 144
International Bank for Reconstruction and Development (IBRD). *See* World Bank
International Development Research Centre (IDRC) (Canada), 200, 202
Intersectoral approach, 214, 216-217
Intervening variables, 13, 14(fig.)
Intervention, 2, 10, 11, 12, 13, 119, 148, 180, 208
  institutionalization of, 196-197, 215-216
  phases, 181, 184, 189, 196, 201
Iowa Indians, 36

Jat Sikhs, 100
Java, 183
Jesuits, 185
Johnson, Lyndon B., 33
Joint ventures, 189-190

Kansas Committee for the Humanities, 37
Kansas Kickapoo Technical Assistance Project (KKTAP) (1981-1985), 34, 52, 54
  disbanded, 47
  funding, 42, 43, 46
  goals, 41-42, 46, 47, 49
  initial period, 35-38
  interim period, 38-40
  management and planning, 42, 49
  programs, 43, 45-47, 50
  staff, 40, 41, 43, 44, 47-48
  staff-tribe relations, 48-50, 53-54
  training program, 42, 48
Kassebaum, Nancy, 45
Keare, Douglas, 193
Kenekuk (prophet), 35
Kennedy, Edward, 141
Keo, Keith, 39
Kesadhari, 111
Kickapoo, 8, 34, 35, 39, 40, 45-46, 214
  and federal funding, 36, 39, 40, 41, 42, 43-44, 45, 50, 51, 52
  Nation School, 38-39, 43, 44-45, 46-47
  organization, 42
  reservation, 35, 36
  and self-determination, 42, 43, 51-52
  self-sufficiency, 34, 36, 38, 39, 51
  traditional language and culture projects, 34, 36, 37, 38, 46
  See also Kansas Kickapoo Technical Assistance Project
Kimball, S., 31
Kiwanis Club, 188
KKTAP. *See* Kansas Kickapoo Technical Assistance Project
Knowledge utilization, 9, 12, 30

Labels program (Campbell Soup Company), 65-66, 67, 68, 69, 70, 71, 72
Labor contractors. *See* Crewleaders
Labor room accompaniment, 17
Lamaze training, 17, 21
Lanang District (Philippines), 185, 186, 190

Lanang Homeseekers Association, 190
Land reform, 144, 190, 198
Langdon, Margaret, 85, 88
Language Assessment Scale (LAS), 92
Laquian, Aprodicio A., 179, 192
LAS. *See* Language Assessment Scale
Latin American Indians. *See* Aymara Indians; Quechua Indians
LDCs (less-developed countries). *See* Third World
Leguia, Augusto B., 139
Less-developed countries (LDCs). *See* Third World
Letters of Instruction (LOIs) (Philippines), 190, 198, 199, 206
Liberal party (Philippines), 188
Lima (Peru), 193
Linguistics research, 37, 47, 79, 85, 95-97
  applied, 78
  See also Hualapai Bilingual/Bicultural Education Program
Lions Club, 188
Loeb, James, 141
LOIs. *See* Letters of Instruction
Lopez, Elias B., 203
Lusaka, (Zambia), 200
Lutes, Steven V., 38, 39, 40, 41, 43, 44, 45, 47, 48
Luzon (Philippines), 194

McCarty, Teresa, 88
McGee, T.G., 179
Maintenance of continuity, 201, 205
Mandug (Philippines), 185, 186, 188, 192
Mangin, William P., 192
Manila (Philippines), 181, 182, 190, 191, 193, 194, 195, 197, 200, 203
Marcará District (Peru), 135, 137, 151-152, 153
Marcos, Ferdinand, 184, 188, 189, 191, 203, 205, 206
Marcos, Imelda Romualdez, 190, 194, 195, 197, 198
Marx, Karl, 56
Massachusetts Institute of Technology (MIT) Center for Urban Planning, 168
Maternal and child health (MCH), 12, 18, 22, 28
  funds, 15
  medical/epidemiological model, 13, 14(fig.), 19, 20, 21
  multiethnic emphasis, 23
  sociological model, 13, 14(fig.), 19, 20, 23
  See also Comadrona Program; Puerto Rican community
Maternal and Child Health Section (Conn. State Dept. of Health), 15
May, J.T., 108
Mazeway reformulation, 56
MCH. *See* Maternal and child health
MDC. *See* Mindinao Development Center
Medical anthropologists, 13, 19-20, 23
Medical insurance, 60, 61, 62
Mestizos, 132, 135

Mexican Americans, 60, 100, 103
Mexican Urban Housing Project, 128, 165-174
 and community, 166
 phases, 165, 171
 and *técnicos*, 170, 175
Mexico, 159, 169, 174, 217
Mexico City, 193
Michigan, 60, 62
Midwives, 18
Migrant Education staff, 109, 118
Migrant workers. See Farm labor
Mindanao (Philippines), 181, 183-184, 189
Mindanao Development Authority, 189
Mindanao Development Center (MDC), 185
Mines, 80
Ministry of Agriculture (Peru), 144, 145, 151
 extension program (SCIPA), 141
Ministry of Education, (Peru), 145, 146
Ministry of Energy and Mining (Peru), 145
Ministry of Health (Peru), 145, 146
Ministry of Human Settlements (Philippines), 195, 197
Ministry of Labor and Indian Affairs (Peru), 134, 137, 141, 143
Minorities, 58, 106. See also Ethnic minority communities
Minority Language Affairs, 87
Mintal (Philippines), 191
MIT. See Massachusetts Institute of Technology
Mita Peasant Community (Peru), 151, 153
Mojave, 80
Monge Medrano, Carlos, 132, 142
Multilinear evolutionary model, 56
Multinational corporations, 60, 189. See also Agribusiness
Munro, Pamela, 88
Munson, L., 90
Murphy, Arthur D., 128, 213

Nacionalista party (Philippines), 189
National Endowment for the Humanities (NEH), 86, 87
National Housing Authority (NHA) (Philippines), 195, 196, 197, 199, 200, 202-203, 205, 206, 207
 Research and Analysis Division (RAD), 199, 200, 203
National Institute for Community Development. See *Instituto Nacional para el Desarrollo de la Comunidad y de la Vivienda Popular*
National Institute of Education (NIE), 103, 114, 115, 116
National Institutes of Health, 184, 187, 198
National Labor Relations Act (1935), 60
National Multifunctional Bilingual Centers, 95
National Science Foundation (NSF), 161
NEH. See National Endowment for the Humanities

New, P.K., 108
New Matina project (Davao City), 199, 200, 201, 202, 205
New Society (Philippines), 194, 197
NHA. See National Housing Authority
NIE. See National Institute of Education
Nixon, Richard M., 33
Northern Arizona University, 88
NSF. See National Science Foundation
Nuclear households, 25

Oaxaca (Mexico), 159, 161, 162, 163, 164, 213, 214. See also Mexican Urban Housing Project
OCR. See Office for Civil Rights
Office for Civil Rights (OCR), 102
Office of Bilingual Education, 87
Office of Indian Affairs, 80. See also Bureau of Indian Affairs
Ohio, 60, 62
Oil crisis (1973), 194
ORDENOR (Peruvian agency), 146
ORDEZA. See Earthquake redevelopment commission

Pai branch (Yuman language), 80
Pararín Peasant Community (Peru), 143
Participant observation, 52-53, 213
Participatory rights, 60, 61, 62, 130
Patrilineal society, 149
Patronage, 183

Patron-client systems, 186
PBSP. See Philippine Business for Social Progress
PDs. See Presidential Decrees
Peace Corps, 142, 143, 144, 145, 151
Peach Springs settlement (Hualapai), 80-81
  School, 81, 83, 84, 86, 88
Peasant Affairs Bureau (Peru), 144
Peasant Communities (Peru), 135, 143, 144, 151-152, 154(n3)
Peonage, 135, 138, 140, 144
Peru, 127, 129, 132, 144, 151, 217. See also Cornell-Peru Project
Pesticides, 60, 61
Peterson, J., 10
Philippine Business for Social Progress (PBSP), 193, 198
Philippines, 128, 189-190, 203, 205, 206, 208
  martial law (1972), 188, 191, 195
  See also Davao City
Phonemic-based system, 85
Piapi (Davao City), 187-188, 190, 195, 199, 200, 201, 202, 204-205, 207
Pizarro, Francisco, 138
Plan Nacional de Integración de la Población Aborigen (PNIPA) (Peru), 141, 143
PNIPA. See *Plan Nacional de Integración de la Población Aborigen*
Policy clusters, 11, 29

in Comadrona Program,
13, 15, 19, 21, 22,
23, 28
and theories of action,
11-12, 27, 31
Policy research clusters,
11
Political economy, 180
Political intervention, 2,
184, 188, 189, 194,
195, 198, 206
Population Center Foundation (Philippines),
198
Population Commission
(Philippines), 198
Potawatomi, *See* Prairie
Band Potawatomi
Powskey, Malinda, 88
Prado, Manuel, 141
Prairie Band Potawatomi,
35, 36, 37
Prenatal care, 13, 17, 18,
21, 23, 26-27
Presidential Decrees (PDs)
(Philippines), 190,
198, 206
Presidential Regional
Office for Development (PROD), 189
"Principles of English Linguistics" course, 88
"Principles of Indian
Curriculum Development" course, 88
Private donor organizations, 22, 23
Private sector (Philippines), 185, 188, 190,
204. *See also* Davao
Development Foundation
PROD. *See* Presidential
Regional Office for
Development
Program plan, 218
Program Quality Review
Inventory, 93
Progressive project re-
design, 207-208
"Projects view," 197, 201,
202
Public Beneficent Society,
139, 140, 141
Public Law 480. *See* Food
for Peace programs
Puerto Rican community
(Hartford, Conn.), 9-
10, 12-13, 15, 22,
24, 214
activists, 13
housing, 24, 25
perspectives, 13,
14(fig.)
and research on pregnancy, 19
service access, 13, 16,
17, 18, 20, 21, 26-27
support networks, 15-
16, 17, 19, 20, 21,
22, 23, 24, 26-27
See also Comadrona Program
Punjabi Education Project
(1980), 99
analysis and reports,
114, 118, 123, 124
(n6)
and change, 119-120,
121
and community, 108-110,
114, 120, 121, 122
difficulties, 112-113,
114, 115, 120, 122.
See also Factionalism
director, 112
funding, 103, 115, 116
and mainstream students, 107, 108-109,
110
research team, 103-104,
108, 111-114, 122
and school district,
108, 114, 117-119,
120
survey results, 104-107

Punjabi-English bilingual
    education program,
    101, 102
Punjabis, 8, 99, 100-103,
    105-107, 124(n3), 214
Purchase-of-services
    agreement, 43

Quechua Indians, 129, 132

RAD. *See* National Housing
    Authority, Research
    and Analysis Division
Reagan, Ronald, 39, 40
Recuayhuanca (Peru), 135
Reforestation (Vicos), 143,
    146
Regional Program for Indian
    Area Development
    (Peru), 143
Retirement pensions, 61
Reza, Ernesto, 8, 64, 65,
    66, 67, 69, 214
Rider, C.D., 96
Rockefeller Foundation, 198
Rouillard, John, 87
Rural development, 129, 130
Rural-to-urban migration,
    150, 179, 184. *See
    also* Squatter
    settlements

SAHOP. *See Secretaría de
    Asentimientos Humanos
    y Obras Públicas*
San Antonio del Atoyac
    (Oaxaca *colonia*), 163,
    164-165
San Diego State University,
    87
San Marcos University, 139
San Salvador (El Salvador),
    200
Santa River, 135, 136
    (fig.), 152
Santos, Luis T., 200, 204
Sapang Palay (Manila), 191
Sarason, Seymour B., 119

Satellite communities,
    188, 194
Schensul, Jean J., 4, 8,
    10, 120, 213
Schensul, Stephen L., 10
School health task force,
    22
Schultz, Jerry A., 8, 40,
    44, 45, 47
SCIPA. *See* Ministry of
    Agriculture, exten-
    sion program
SEARCH (language dominance
    test), 84
*Secretaría de Asenti-
    mientos Humanos y
    Obras Públicas*
    (SAHOP)(Mexico), 167
Sector, 1-2, 11. *See also*
    Intersectoral
    approach
"Sectoral view," 197, 201
Self-determination, 212.
    See also Indian self-
    determination
Sendero Luminosa movement
    (Peru), 147
Senegal, 200, 202
Shops. *See Tiendas/
    tienditas*
Shumáy (Peru), 135,
    136(fig.), 151, 153
Sikhs. *See* Punjabis
Sikh temple, 108
SINAMOS (Peruvian organi-
    zation), 145
Sinyella, Maude, 82
SIR. *See* Slum Improvement
    and Resettlement
Site-and-services com-
    munity studies, 162,
    163, 169, 179, 180,
    186, 193, 195-196,
    197, 200, 202, 203,
    204, 205, 207
    evaluation and monitor-
    ing, 199, 200, 201,
    207-208

Slum Improvement and Resettlement (SIR) (Philippines), 199, 203, 204, 205, 207
Social change, 1, 2, 3, 7, 8, 9, 121, 127, 128
  applied, 59, 69, 70, 72
  and development programs, 131, 132, 133, 148-151
  educational, 100
  impact, 55
  microevolution, 201
  models, 55, 56-59, 70, 218
  process, 10-12, 55-56, 57, 58, 69, 198
  and redefined traditional cultural elements, 24
Social issues coalitions. See Policy clusters
Society for Applied Anthropology, 4
Sociocultural adaptation, 57-59. See also Adaptation
Sociocultural change, 55, 56, 69-72
Socioeconomic development, 127, 206-207
South Asian immigrant community. See Punjabis
Spanish colonial regime, 138
Squatter settlements, 179, 180, 182-183, 184, 185, 198, 206
  associations, 183, 186, 190, 196, 204
  development, 190, 193, 194, 195, 196, 197, 204-205, 207
  and location, 186, 187-188, 192
  population, 191-192, 205
Squatter's rights, 183

Stein, W.W., 150
Stern, Gwen, 4
Steward, J.H., 56
Stress, 150
Stull, Donald D., 4, 8, 35-36, 37, 38, 39, 40, 41, 42, 45, 46, 47, 48, 213
Subdivision. See Fraccionamiento
Support groups, 61, 62-63, 64, 70-71. See also Community action project
Syncretism, 56
Synthesis, 58
  re-, 71
Systems models, 55, 56-59, 70

Talomo Beach (Davao City), 185
Target community approach, 214-215
Tax, Sol, 7, 10, 127
Técnicos, 168, 169, 170, 171, 173, 175
Teenage pregnancy, 20, 22, 25, 27
Texas, 60
Third World, 127, 130, 179, 182
Thompson, L., 70
Tiendas/tienditas, 163, 164-165
Time frames, 59
Tipología de Vivienda, 169
Title V grant, 12, 15
Title VII funding, 83, 87
Tobias, Gaudencio, 195, 203
Tomato industry, 60. See also Campbell Soup Company
Tondo/Dagat-dagatan settlement (Manila), 193, 195, 197

Trait-replacement model, 55
Turner, John C., 192, 193
Typhoons, 194

UFW. *See* United Farm Workers of America
UNDP. *See* United Nations Development Program
United Farm Workers of America (UFW), 61, 62, 63, 64
United Nations Development Program (UNDP), 190, 192
"Universities, Professionals, and Communities: Developing Linkages for Effective Social Action" session (1982), 4
University of Ancash (Peru), 146
University of Arizona, 83, 88
University of Colorado, 183
University of Kansas, 37, 41, 42, 43
   General Research Fund, 87
Upland language group, 80, 82
Uqualla, Josie, 88
Urbanization, 179, 181-182
   nonindustrialized, 184
Urban poor, 11, 24, 179, 193, 202
Urban poverty study, 168. *See also* Squatter settlements
USAID. *See* Agency for International Development, U.S.

Valley County Employment and Training Office, 118
Valleyside (Calif.), 8, 123(n1)

school district, 100, 101, 102, 103
See also Punjabi Education Project
Varayoc, 140
Vazquez Varela, Mario C., 132, 133, 139, 142
Velasquez, Baldemar, 61, 62, 64
Venezuela, 185
Vicos
   chronology (1470-1986), 138-147
   post-1966, 144-147, 152
   See also Cornell-Peru Project
Vlasic pickle products, 62
Voegelin, C.F., 82

Watahomigie, Lucille J., 8, 83, 84, 85, 86, 87, 88, 89, 90, 213
Wax, Rosalie H., 99, 113
Women's Anthropological Society, 1
Workers' compensation, 61
World Bank (IBRD), 179, 180, 190, 195, 196, 198, 199, 200, 202, 203, 206, 207, 214
   Development Economics Department (DED), 193, 195, 197, 200, 201
World market commodities, 182, 203

Yamamoto, Akira Y., 8, 82-83, 85-86, 87, 88, 94, 213
Yavapai, 80
Yo Trabajo en Vicos (film), 141
Yuman language family, 80, 85

Zambia, 200, 202
Zepeda, Ofelia, 88

LIBRARY OF DAVIDSON COLLEGE

Books on regular loan may be checked out for **two weeks**. Books must be presented at the Circulation Desk in order to be renewed.

A fine is charged after date due.

Special books are subject to special regulations at the discretion of the library staff.